Essential Pleasures

Essential Pleasures

A NEW ANTHOLOGY OF
Poems to Read Aloud

EDITED BY
Robert Pinsky

W. W. Norton & Company
NEW YORK   LONDON

For information about special discounts for bulk
purchases, please contact W. W. Norton Special Sales at
specialsales@wwnorton.com or 800-233-4830

Manufacturing by Courier Westford
Book design by Brooke Koven
Production manager: Julia Druskin

Essential pleasures : a new anthology of poems
to read aloud / edited by Robert Pinsky.— 1st ed.
p. cm.
Includes index.
ISBN 978-0-393-06608-1
1. Poetry—Collections. I. Pinsky, Robert.
PN6101.E87 2009
808.81—dc22

2008055985

W. W. Norton & Company, Inc.
500 Fifth Avenue, New York, N.Y. 10110
www.wwnorton.com

W. W. Norton & Company Ltd.
Castle House, 75/76 Wells Street, London W1T 3QT

1 2 3 4 5 6 7 8 9 0

CONTENTS

Part III〜

BALLADS, REPETITIONS, REFRAINS

Part VII   429
PARODIES, RIPOSTES, JOKES, AND INSULTS

INTRODUCTION

* *

PLEASURE IN POETRY, like speech itself, is both intellectual and bodily. Spoken language, an elaborate code of articulated grunts, provides a satisfaction central to life, with all the immediacy of our senses. Though complex, the pleasure is not arcane. We learn it as we learn to speak: informally and avidly. A small child who enjoys the anonymous, traditional sentence,

> Moses supposes his toeses are roses,
> But Moses supposes erroneously

feels a tickle of gratification, conceptual and sensory, as the sounds perform their combat dance with the meanings, joining and parting. In this example, that intricate choreography involves teasing forms of the plural. The sounds are similar and the meanings vary: body and mind, in an experience that is essential to the art of poetry.

Poetry in American Sign Language, a language that intricately formalizes bodily gestures, also demonstrates this fundamental principle, coordinating body and mind in the creation of meaning. The appetite for that dual action is tremendous; poetry is its concentrated form.

A few examples can begin to demonstrate variety. The interplay of physical sounds and forms of meaning, a fancy-work of pleasure and aggression, animates the final line of the following passage, from "Corinna's Going A-Maying" (p. 365) by Robert Herrick. In a custom older than Christianity, people are celebrating the season of rebirth by hanging branches in blossom all over town. This playful May-ing tradition is giddy—as is the poet, and so are the sounds of the words. Note the third-from-last line of this quotation:

> Come, my Corinna, come; and, coming mark
> How each field turns a street, each street a park
>   Made green and trimmed with trees; see how
>   Devotion gives each house a bough
>   Or branch: each porch, each door ere this,
>   An Ark, a tabernacle is,
> Made up of whitethorn neatly enterwove,
> As if here were those cooler shades of love.
>   Can such delights be in the street
>   And open fields, and we not see 't?
>   Come, we'll abroad; and let's obey
>   The proclamation made for May,
> And sin no more, as we have done, by staying;
> But, my Corinna, come, let's go a-Maying.

"The proclamation made for May": the line has an immediately attractive lilt, an artful effect perceptible before analysis. On reflection, a reader may (or may not) note that the single sound *may* recurs three times with three different meanings, and in three different forms.

Hearing that kind of vocal gesture, we respond to it almost as intuitively as we respond to a lifted hand or a raised voice. Wallace Stevens in "The Snow Man" (p. 415) writes about the likelihood of hearing misery

>   in the sound of the wind,
> In the sound of a few leaves,
>
> Which is the sound of the land
> Full of the same wind
> That is blowing in the same bare place

The three repetitions of "sound" and the two repetitions of "wind" communicate their emotional effect, felt before any reader counts the repetitions or notes the same consonant sound at the end of both "sound" and "wind," with that same sound repeated at the end of "land." Analysis can refine and enrich understanding of the feeling and the ideas, but the fact of the actual words is primary and essential: you can hear it. The words create something like an actual voice. In an interesting psychological process, that voice is in a way the reader's and in a way the poet's. Maybe it should be thought of as many voices, since it speaks each time anyone reads the poem—even if the reading is silent, even if the sounds are imagined only faintly. In any case, the sounds of the words and sentences and lines of "The Snow Man" make their audible gesture to anyone thinking about the possibility of hearing such a January wind without hearing misery in it, as if that wind too were a voice.

Here is another example, by Gwendolyn Brooks (p. 12):

WE REAL COOL

THE POOL PLAYERS.
SEVEN AT THE GOLDEN SHOVEL.

We real cool. We
Left school. We

Lurk late. We
Strike straight. We

Sing sin. We
Thin gin. We

Jazz June. We
Die soon.

There is a lot to be said about "We Real Cool": its experience, its voices and the implicit voice that quotes them, the significance of the word that ends every line but one and begins only one line. But before such useful analysis or information is formulated, something primary and significant has been heard and felt.

Analysis and understanding heighten appreciation. Sometimes, however, they obtrude: trying to force knowledge before pleasure has a chance. Pointing this out is not sentimental or anti-intellectual; on the contrary, the goal should be to encourage intellectual precision by putting it in a stringent, fitting relation to the actual experience of the poem. Well-meaning teaching can muddle that process by leaving out the experience.

The audible, vocal element in "The Snow Man" and in "Corinna's Going A-Maying" calls on something more ancient, involuntary, and profound even than a "tradition." The child's response to the interplay of mind and sound in the anonymous rhyme about Moses and his toes, or in nursery rhymes, or in Dr. Seuss's "Green Eggs and Ham," reaches back thousands of years, through Seuss's predecessors (and models) Edward Lear and Robert Louis Stevenson, and back through the poets they read, Wordsworth and Horace and Homer, and further back to the origins of humankind. The same relation to an all-but-infinite past characterizes poems by Robert Herrick and Wallace Stevens and Gwendolyn Brooks.

LIKE THE arts of dancing, singing, miming, drawing, the art of poetry involves an essential appetite. The sounds of words in an infinitely varying relation to their meanings—an organism of vowels and consonants and cadences flirting with an organism of meanings, playing with it, agreeing with it, arguing with it, converging, departing, twisting, energizing, goofing, weeping, punctuating, ironizing—embody an essential, pleasurable action.

I have chosen and organized the poems in this anthology by trying to make that essential action—the course of pleasure in hearing a poem—as clear as possible. Guided by tradition as well as my own taste, I have tried to present enticing examples, arranged to demonstrate principles. The first two sections concentrate on the nature of the poetic line, starting with short lines because the shorter the lines are, the more often you can hear the ways different lines begin and end. "We Real Cool" is an example. For another, here are the opening stanzas of Robert Frost's "To Earthward" (p. 24):

> Love at the lips was touch
> As sweet as I could bear;
> And once that seemed too much;
> I lived on air

That crossed me from sweet things
The flow of—was it musk
From hidden grapevine springs
Down hill at dusk?

To my hearing, the energy of the sentence reaches hard across the rhyme of "I lived on air" in a gesture of yearning. In contrast, the sentence and line agree on a pause after "I could bear." The full stop after "dusk" on a question makes an interesting counterpoint to the questioning hesitation where the sentence spills past "was it musk." It is nearly impossible to describe these nuances of movement and pause, tracing the dance between meaning and form—but reading Frost's sentence aloud, listening to the rhymes as they mark hesitation or eagerness: that is the idea.

The second section of the anthology presents examples of a quite different kind of line, the extended, compendious or fountain energy of a line like that of Walt Whitman or Christopher Smart, or Allen Ginsberg's "A Supermarket in California" (p. 70):

What thoughts I have of you tonight, Walt Whitman, for I
walked down the streets under the trees with a headache
self-conscious looking at the full moon.

The moon, the self-consciousness, the streets and trees charge through the capacious, unifying rhythm of the line with a hard-driving purpose as well as abundance. These extremes in kind of line demonstrate the varying nature of lines—that each one is different—and the fluent nature of poetry itself.

Because the term "ballad" suggests both a kind of line and a kind of subject matter or tone, the third section makes a transition from formal ways of thinking and hearing to a more thematic approach. The ballad stanza is associated with actual musical patterns and with certain kinds of material: sensational narratives, elliptically presented, often with dialogue and rapid shifts of scene. Because ballads are songs or songlike, and often involve refrains, this section includes regular, audible repetition: sometimes abbreviated with an "etc." in printed books, but vital in the hearing of the poem.

The subsequent, more thematic sections—love poems, stories, and such—I intend to be casual and loose groupings. Most poems could fit into more than one of the headings, which are meant to be interesting, not absolute. For example, William Cowper's "Epitaph on a Hare" (p. 130) is a ballad and a love poem and a celebration that tells a story. It is also funny. The organization into parts tries to celebrate the variety and depth of poetry, with a structure that is informal but thoughtful.

I have worked to make a collection of poems attractive for the reader to say aloud, or to imagine saying aloud. The book is not a selection of my favorite poems, and certainly not an attempt to construct and fortify a "canon." Time punishes rigid, would-be-authoritative lists of that kind—not that all anthologies do not, sooner or later, become dated. Humbled by that fact, an anthologist (the root of the word has to do with gathering flowers) can gladly include familiar perennials such as "The Midnight Ride of Paul Revere." I have also worked hard to come up with good poems that will be new to most readers. My one strict rule is that everything here—even if it is also a visually shaped poem, or a prose poem—conveys the vocal feeling of poetry: an art as urgent and various as the human voice itself, encompassing all that a voice can express.

I

SHORT LINES, FREQUENT RHYMES

❖ ❖

To ILLUSTRATE WHAT a line of poetry is, and why writing in lines is worth the effort, I might choose these lines by Thomas Campion from the poem on page 15:

> Now winter nights enlarge
>   The number of their hours;
> And clouds their storms discharge
>   Upon the airy towers.
> Let now the chimneys blaze
>   And cups o'erflow with wine,
> Let well-tuned words amaze
>   With harmony divine.
> Now yellow waxen lights
>   Shall wait on honey love
> While youthful revels, masques, and courtly sights
>   Sleep's leaden spells remove.

I like this example not just because the rhymes sound good, and not just because the short lines make the rhymes more frequent and prominent. It's the way Campion's verbs, in this example, often reach across the rhymes, while his nouns often clinch the rhyme with a full stop or a pause.

In the first four lines, "enlarge" sort of hurries or expands toward "The number"; and in a similar way the energy of "discharge" moves along toward "Upon." The first and third lines keep the energy of the sentence pressing past the rhyme, while the second and fourth lines culminate the energy on the stopping-places of "hours" and "towers." The pressing ahead and the coming to a pause embody, in the movement of a spoken sentence, two kinds of emphasis, clarified and strengthened by the rhyming lines. The way the grammatical energy of the sentence rushes past the end-rhyme probably helps the connotations of the word "enlarge" spill over: so that the feeling of enlarging applies to the towers as well as to its actual object, the number of hours. In a similar way, I think, the movement of the lines enhances the energy of the verb "discharge."

Campion deploys his verbs and nouns in a very similar way in the next four lines, alternating verb and noun. But this time, on the first verb, "blaze," the sentence comes to more of a rest, while "amaze" reaches forward, more in the way of "enlarge" and "discharge":

> Let now the chimneys blaze
>   And cups o'erflow with wine,
> Let well-tuned words amaze
>   With harmony divine.

After that, the relation between sentence and line keeps varying, in ways full of movement. Campion is an expert: he doesn't need to manage that movement consciously at every point. It is part of how he goes about evoking a wonderful party, with a winter storm blowing outside the happy beehive-castle, with its honey and waxen lights. There is so much movement between line and sentence, that when Campion makes a one-line sentence—"All do not all things well"—the perfectly contained match of line and sentence creates another kind of emphasis, as when a dancer pauses unexpectedly between leaps.

Because the lines are short, there are many opportunities to hear the kind of movement I have described, the interplay between the sentences and the lines. Sometimes the pleasure and significance reside in how different the line and the sentence are, in their stops and starts—as in this example from the poem by Thom Gunn on page 26:

> I thought I was so tough,
> But gentled at your hands,
> Cannot be quick enough
> To fly for you and show
> That when I go I go
> At your commands.

Between the two repetitions of "I go" the grammar pauses while the energy of the line does not. Analysis of this one small moment and its effect could go on and on—but at some point one has to acknowledge that the arrangement of words has the subtle effect of art, distinct though beyond description.

Also distinct, and also subtle beyond analysis, is the artful arrangement by William Carlos Williams of the consonant sounds, vowel sounds, lines, and sentences in his "Fine Work with Pitch and Copper" on page 50. Here is the first sentence:

> Now they are resting
> in the fleckless light
> separately in unison
>
> like the sacks
> of sifted stone stacked
> regularly by twos
>
> about the flat roof
> ready after lunch
> to be opened and strewn

The point is not to analyze the lines, but to listen as one reads them aloud, letting yourself hear different sets of similar sounds (for instance the vowel in "resting," "fleckless" and "separately" and the contrasting vowel in "unison," "twos," "roof" and "strewn"—or maybe the consonants in "regularly," "ready" and "roof" contrasted with all of those "s" words in the second stanza).

These matters of how lines work are in a way small, fine, minute matters: little pauses and variations. But in another way, they are tremendous: a pause can be heartbreaking; the variations in how a sentence moves across rhymes can be like the most penetrating music, as in the last stanzas of Emily Dickinson's poem on pages 18–19. The emotion created by the pauses and motion forward is large:

> If certain, when this life was out—
> That yours and mine, should be
> I'd toss it yonder, like a Rind,
> And take Eternity—
>
> But, now, uncertain of the length
> Of this, that is between,
> It goads me, like the Goblin Bee—
> That will not state—its sting.

William Blake

(1757–1827)

INFANT JOY

"I have no name,
I am but two days old."
What shall I call thee?
"I happy am,
Joy is my name."
Sweet joy befall thee!

Pretty joy!
Sweet joy but two days old,
Sweet joy I call thee;
Thou dost smile,
I sing the while—
Sweet joy befall thee.

THE SICK ROSE

O rose, thou art sick;
The invisible worm
That flies in the night,
In the howling storm,

Has found out thy bed
Of crimson joy,
And his dark secret love
Does thy life destroy.

Gwendolyn Brooks

(1917–2000)

WE REAL COOL

THE POOL PLAYERS.
SEVEN AT THE GOLDEN SHOVEL.

We real cool. We
Left school. We

Lurk late. We
Strike straight. We

Sing sin. We
Thin gin. We

Jazz June. We
Die soon.

George Gordon, Lord Byron

(1788–1824)

WHEN WE TWO PARTED

When we two parted
   In silence and tears,
Half broken-hearted
   To sever for years,
Pale grew thy cheek and cold,
   Colder thy kiss;
Truly that hour foretold
   Sorrow to this.

The dew of the morning
   Sunk chill on my brow—
It felt like the warning
   Of what I feel now.
Thy vows are all broken,
   And light is thy fame;
I hear thy name spoken,
   And share in its shame.

They name thee before me,
   A knell to mine ear;
A shudder comes o'er me—
   Why wert thou so dear?
They know not I knew thee,
   Who knew thee too well—
Long, long shall I rue thee,
   Too deeply to tell.

In secret we met—
   In silence I grieve,
That thy heart could forget,
   Thy spirit deceive.
If I should meet thee
   After long years,
How should I greet thee?—
   With silence and tears.

Thomas Campion

(1567–1620)

Now Winter Nights Enlarge

Now winter nights enlarge
    The number of their hours;
And clouds their storms discharge
    Upon the airy towers.
Let now the chimneys blaze
    And cups o'erflow with wine,
Let well-tuned words amaze
    With harmony divine.
Now yellow waxen lights
    Shall wait on honey love
While youthful revels, masques, and courtly sights
    Sleep's leaden spells remove.

This time doth well dispense
    With lovers' long discourse;
Much speech hath some defense,
    Though beauty no remorse.
All do not all things well;
    Some measures comely tread,
Some knotted riddles tell,
    Some poems smoothly read.
The summer hath his joys,
    And winter his delights;
Though love and all his pleasures are but toys,
    They shorten tedious nights.

J. V. Cunningham

(1911–1985)

FOR MY CONTEMPORARIES

How time reverses
The proud in heart!
I now make verses
Who aimed at art.

But I sleep well.
Ambitious boys
Whose big lines swell
With spiritual noise,

Despise me not!
And be not queasy
To praise somewhat:
Verse is not easy.

But rage who will.
Time that procured me
Good sense and skill
Of madness cured me.

Emily Dickinson

(1830–1886)

WILD NIGHTS—WILD NIGHTS! (249)

Wild Nights—Wild Nights!
Were I with thee
Wild Nights should be
Our luxury!

Futile—the Winds—
To a Heart in port—
Done with the Compass—
Done with the Chart!

Rowing in Eden—
Ah, the Sea!
Might I but moor—Tonight—
In Thee!

"HOPE" IS THE THING WITH FEATHERS— (254)

"Hope" is the thing with feathers—
That perches in the soul—
And sings the tune without the words—
And never stops—at all—

And sweetest—in the Gale—is heard—
And sore must be the storm—
That could abash the little Bird
That kept so many warm—

I've heard it in the chillest land—
And on the strangest Sea—
Yet, never, in Extremity,
It asked a crumb—of Me.

THE SOUL SELECTS HER OWN SOCIETY (303)

The Soul selects her own Society—
Then—shuts the Door—
To her divine Majority—
Present no more—

Unmoved—she notes the Chariots—pausing—
At her low Gate—
Unmoved—an Emperor be kneeling
Upon her Mat—

I've known her—from an ample nation—
Choose One—
Then—close the Valves of her attention—
Like Stone—

IF YOU WERE COMING IN THE FALL (511)

If you were coming in the Fall,
I'd brush the Summer by
With half a smile, and half a spurn,
As Housewives do, a Fly.

If I could see you in a year,
I'd wind the months in balls—
And put them each in separate Drawers,
For fear the numbers fuse—

If only Centuries, delayed,
I'd count them on my Hand,
Subtracting, till my fingers dropped
Into Van Dieman's Land.

If certain, when this life was out—
That yours and mine, should be
I'd toss it yonder, like a Rind,
And take Eternity—

But, now, uncertain of the length
Of this, that is between,
It goads me, like the Goblin Bee—
That will not state—its sting.

THE POETS LIGHT BUT LAMPS— (883)

The Poets light but Lamps—
Themselves—go out—
The Wicks they stimulate—
If vital Light

Inhere as do the Suns—
Each Age a Lens
Disseminating their
Circumference—

John Donne

(1572–1631)

SONG

Sweetest love, I do not go,
   For weariness of thee,
Nor in hope the world can show
   A fitter love for me;
     But since that I
Must die at last, 'tis best
To use myself in jest
   Thus by feigned deaths to die.

Yesternight the sun went hence,
   And yet is here to-day;
He hath no desire nor sense,
   Nor half so short a way;
     Then fear not me,
But believe that I shall make
Speedier journeys, since I take
   More wings and spurs than he.

O how feeble is man's power,
   That if good fortune fall,
Cannot add another hour
   Nor a lost hour recall!
     But come bad chance,
And we join to it our strength,
And we teach it art and length,
   Itself o'er us to advance.

When thou sigh'st, thou sigh'st not wind,
    But sigh'st my soul away;
When thou weep'st, unkindly kind,
    My life's blood doth decay.
        It cannot be
That thou lov'st me, as thou say'st,
If in thine my life thou waste,
    That art the best of me.

Let not thy divining heart
    Forethink me any ill,
Destiny may take thy part,
    And may thy fears fulfil;
        But think that we
Are but turned aside to sleep;
They who one another keep
    Alive, ne'er parted be.

Rita Dove

(b. 1952)

GOSPEL

Swing low so I
can step inside—
a humming ship of voices
big with all

the wrongs done
done them.
No sound this generous
could fail:

ride joy until
it cracks like an egg,
make sorrow
seethe and whisper.

From a fortress
of animal misery
soars the chill voice
of the tenor, enraptured

with sacrifice.
What do I see,
he complains, notes
brightly rising

towards a sky
blank with promise.

Yet how healthy
the single contralto

settling deeper
into her watery furs!
Carry me home,
she cajoles, bearing

down. Candelabras
brim. But he slips
through God's net and swims
heavenward, warbling.

Robert Frost

(1874–1963)

DUST OF SNOW

The way a crow
Shook down on me
The dust of snow
From a hemlock tree

Has given my heart
A change of mood
And saved some part
Of a day I had rued.

TO EARTHWARD

Love at the lips was touch
As sweet as I could bear;
And once that seemed too much;
I lived on air

That crossed me from sweet things
The flow of—was it musk
From hidden grapevine springs
Down hill at dusk?

I had the swirl and ache
From sprays of honeysuckle

That when they're gathered shake
Dew on the knuckle.

I craved strong sweets, but those
Seemed strong when I was young;
The petal of the rose
It was that stung.

Now no joy but lacks salt
That is not dashed with pain
And weariness and fault;
I crave the stain

Of tears, the aftermark
Of almost too much love,
The sweet of bitter bark
And burning clove.

When stiff and sore and scarred
I take away my hand
From leaning on it hard
In grass and sand,

The hurt is not enough:
I long for weight and strength
To feel the earth as rough
To all my length.

Thom Gunn

(1929–2004)

—◦—

TAMER AND HAWK

I thought I was so tough,
But gentled at your hands,
Cannot be quick enough
To fly for you and show
That when I go I go
At your commands.

Even in flight above
I am no longer free:
You seeled me with your love,
I am blind to other birds—
The habit of your words
Has hooded me.

As formerly, I wheel
I hover and I twist,
But only want the feel,
In my possessive thought,
Of catcher and of caught
Upon your wrist.

You but half civilize,
Taming me in this way.
Through having only eyes
For you I fear to lose,
I lose to keep, and choose
Tamer as prey.

Thomas Hardy

(1840–1928)

THE SELF-UNSEEING

Here is the ancient floor,
Footworn and hollowed and thin,
Here was the former door
Where the dead feet walked in.

She sat here in her chair,
Smiling into the fire;
He who played stood there,
Bowing it higher and higher.

Childlike, I danced in a dream;
Blessings emblazoned that day;
Everything glowed with a gleam;
Yet we were looking away!

Robert Herrick

(1591–1674)

A Ring presented to Julia

Julia, I bring
    To thee this Ring,
Made for thy finger fit;
    To shew by this,
    That our love is
(Or sho'd be) like to it.

    Close though it be,
    The joint is free:
So when Love's yoke is on,
    It must not gall,
    Or fret at all
With hard oppression.

    But it must play
    Still either way;
And be, too, such a yoke,
    As not too wide,
    To over-slide;
Or be so strait to choak.

    So we, who beare,
    This beame, must reare
Our selves to such a height:
    As that the stay
    Of either may
Create the burden light.

And as this round
Is no where found
To flaw, or else to sever:
So let our love
As endless prove;
And pure as Gold for ever.

Gerard Manley Hopkins
(1844–1889)

Spring and Fall
to a Young Child

Margaret, are you grieving
Over Goldengrove unleaving?
Leaves, like the things of man, you
With your fresh thoughts care for, can you?
Ah! as the heart grows older
It will come to such sights colder
By and by, nor spare a sigh
Though worlds of wanwood leafmeal lie;
And yet you *will* weep and know why.
Now no matter, child, the name:
Sorrow's springs are the same.
Nor mouth had, no nor mind, expressed
What héart héard of, ghóst guéssed:
It is the blight man was born for,
It is Margaret you mourn for.

Jane Kenyon
(1947–1995)

OTHERWISE

I got out of bed
on two strong legs.
It might have been
otherwise. I ate
cereal, sweet
milk, ripe, flawless
peach. It might
have been otherwise.
I took the dog uphill
to the birch wood.
All morning I did
the work I love.

At noon I lay down
with my mate. It might
have been otherwise.
We ate dinner together
at a table with silver
candlesticks. It might
have been otherwise.
I slept in a bed
in a room with paintings
on the walls, and
planned another day
just like this day.
But one day, I know,
it will be otherwise.

Yusef Komunyakaa

(b. 1947)

FACING IT

My black face fades,
hiding inside the black granite.
I said I wouldn't,
dammit: No tears.
I'm stone. I'm flesh.
My clouded reflection eyes me
like a bird of prey, the profile of night
slanted against morning. I turn
this way—the stone lets me go.
I turn that way—I'm inside
the Vietnam Veterans Memorial
again, depending on the light
to make a difference.
I go down the 58,022 names,
half-expecting to find
my own in letters like smoke.
I touch the name Andrew Johnson;
I see the booby trap's white flash.
Names shimmer on a woman's blouse
but when she walks away
the names stay on the wall.
Brushstrokes flash, a red bird's
wings cutting across my stare.
The sky. A plane in the sky.
A white vet's image floats
closer to me, then his pale eyes

look through mine. I'm a window.
He's lost his right arm
inside the stone. In the black mirror
a woman's trying to erase names:
No, she's brushing a boy's hair.

Czeslaw Milosz

translated by Robert Pinsky

(1911–2004)

SONG ON PORCELAIN

Rose colored cup and saucer,
Flowery demitasses:
They lie beside the river
Where an armored column passes.
Winds from across the meadow
Sprinkle the banks with down;
A torn apple tree's shadow
Falls on the muddy path;
The ground everywhere is strewn
With bits of brittle froth—
Of all things broken and lost
The porcelain troubles me most.

Before the first red tones
Begin to warm the sky
The earth wakes up, and moans.
It is the small sad cry
Of cups and saucers cracking,
The masters' precious dream
Of roses, of mowers raking
And shepherds on the lawn.
The black underground stream
Swallows the frozen swan.
This morning, as I walked past
The porcelain troubled me most.

The blackened plain spreads out
To where the horizon blurs
In a litter of handle and spout,
A lively pulp that stirs
And crunches under my feet.
Pretty, useless foam:
Your stained colors are sweet—
Some bloodstained, in dirty waves
Flecking the fresh black loam
In the mounds of these new graves.
In sorrow and pain and cost
The porcelain troubles me most.

Thomas Nashe

(1567–1601)

In Time of Plague

Adieu, farewell, earth's bliss!
This world uncertain is:
Fond are life's lustful joys,
Death proves them all but toys.
None from his darts can fly;
I am sick, I must die—
    Lord, have mercy on us.

Rich men, trust not in wealth,
Gold cannot buy you health;
Physic himself must fade;
All things to end are made;
The plague full swift goes by;
I am sick, I must die—
    Lord, have mercy on us.

Beauty is but a flower
Which wrinkles will devour;
Brightness falls from the hair;
Queens have died young and fair;
Dust hath closed Helen's eye;
I am sick, I must die—
    Lord, have mercy on us.

Strength stoops unto the grave,
Worms feed on Hector brave;
Swords may not fight with fate;

Earth still holds ope her gate;
Come, come! the bells do cry—
I am sick, I must die—
    Lord, have mercy on us.

Wit with his wantonness
Tasteth death's bitterness;
Hell's executioner
Hath no ears for to hear
What vain art can reply;
I am sick, I must die—
    Lord, have mercy on us.

Haste, therefore, each degree
To welcome destiny;
Heaven is our heritage;
Earth but a player's stage;
Mount we unto the sky;
I am sick, I must die—
    Lord, have mercy on us.

Edgar Allan Poe

(1809–1849)

Fairy-Land

Dim vales—and shadowy floods—
And cloudy-looking woods,
Whose forms we can't discover
For the tears that drip all over
Huge moons there wax and wane—
Again—again—again—
Every moment of the night—
Forever changing places—
And they put out the star-light
With the breath from their pale faces.
About twelve by the moon-dial
One more filmy than the rest
(A kind which, upon trial,
They have found to be the best)
Comes down—still down—and down
With its centre on the crown
Of a mountain's eminence,
While its wide circumference
In easy drapery falls
Over hamlets, over halls,
Wherever they may be—
O'er the strange woods—o'er the sea—
Over spirits on the wing—
Over every drowsy thing—
And buries them up quite
In a labyrinth of light—
And then, how deep!—O, deep!

Is the passion of their sleep.
In the morning they arise,
And their moony covering
Is soaring in the skies,
With the tempests as they toss,
Like—almost any thing—
Or a yellow Albatross.
They use that moon no more
For the same end as before—
Videlicet a tent—
Which I think extravagant:
Its atomies, however,
Into a shower dissever,
Of which those butterflies,
Of Earth, who seek the skies,
And so come down again
(Never-contented things!)
Have brought a specimen
Upon their quivering wings.

Sir Walter Raleigh

(1554–1618)

THE LIE

Go, Soul, the body's guest,
Upon a thankless arrant:
Fear not to touch the best;
The truth shall be thy warrant:
Go, since I needs must die,
And give the world the lie.

Say to the court, it glows
And shines like rotten wood;
Say to the church it shows
What's good, and doth no good:
If church and court reply,
Then give them both the lie.

Tell potentates, they live
Acting by others' action;
Not loved unless they give,
Not strong but by affection:
If potentates reply,
Give potentates the lie.

Tell men of high condition
That manage the estate,
Their purpose is ambition,
Their practice only hate:
And if they once reply,
Then give them all the lie.

Tell them that brave it most
They beg for more by spending,
Who, in their greatest cost,
Seek nothing but commending:
And if they make reply,
Then give them all the lie.

Tell zeal it wants devotion,
Tell love it is but lust;
Tell time it metes but motion,
Tell flesh it is but dust:
And wish them not reply,
For thou must give the lie.

Tell age it daily wasteth;
Tell honor how it alters;
Tell beauty how she blasteth;
Tell favor how it falters:
And as they shall reply,
Give every one the lie.

Tell wit how much it wrangles
In tickle points of niceness;
Tell wisdom she entangles
Herself in over-wiseness:
And when they do reply,
Straight give them both the lie.

Tell physic of her boldness;
Tell skill it is pretension;
Tell charity of coldness;
Tell law it is contention:
And as they do reply,
So give them still the lie.

Tell fortune of her blindness;
Tell nature of decay;

Tell friendship of unkindness;
Tell justice of delay:
And if they will reply,
Then give them all the lie.

Tell arts they have no soundness,
But vary by esteeming;
Tell schools they want profoundness,
And stand too much on seeming:
If arts and schools reply,
Give arts and schools the lie.

Tell faith it's fled the city;
Tell how the country erreth;
Tell manhood shakes off pity
And virtue least preferreth:
And if they do reply,
Spare not to give the lie.

So when thou hast, as I
Commanded thee, done blabbing
—Although to give the lie
Deserves no less than stabbing—
Stab at thee he that will,
No stab thy soul can kill.

Theodore Roethke

(1908–1963)

MY PAPA'S WALTZ

The whiskey on your breath
Could make a small boy dizzy;
But I hung on like death:
Such waltzing was not easy.

We romped until the pans
Slid from the kitchen shelf;
My mother's countenance
Could not unfrown itself.

The hand that held my wrist
Was battered on one knuckle;
At every step you missed
My right ear scraped a buckle.

You beat time on my head
With a palm caked hard by dirt,
Then waltzed me off to bed
Still clinging to your shirt.

WISH FOR A YOUNG WIFE

My lizard, my lively writher,
May your limbs never wither,
May the eyes in your face

Survive the green ice
Of envy's mean gaze;
May you live out your life
Without hate, without grief,
And your hair ever blaze,
In the sun, in the sun,
When I am undone,
When I am no one.

Charles Simic

(b. 1938)

NEEDLE
for Helen

1

Watch out for the needle,
She's the scent of a plant
The root of which is far and hidden.

She's the straw
From the nest
Where the blindfolded hand of your mother
Shelters her eggs.

She went out hunting
With your fathers in the old days.

Watch out for the emptiness
At the end of each of her tales,
The place where only a moment ago
She squinted.

2

Thread through her eye:
Two secret thoughts
A hair dipped in the ink of a spider
The silence of certain colors.

Stitch then that hole
Yawning toothless
From the back
Of my hanging shirt.

You'll hear the sound
Of nails growing
On sleeping men.

3

Do you keep losing your needles?
Tie in a handkerchief
A little salt, a little smoke,
It's time that you go looking for them.

When your little finger gets lost
In a forest, so that those
Who come later find only its ring
With thorns grown from the gold,
Know that you are near.

Close your eyes then.
If the needles open their doors,
They'll blind you.

4

Whenever a needle gets lost
She makes a perfect circle.
Her small eye becomes even smaller.

The match lit for her dies
In a noose of smoke. Every thread in the world
Turns black. The bent back of your mother
Is now an ancient stone.

Now under all that is soft,
Mellow and yielding,
Her sharp little tongue lies awake.

By and by
She'll make you shout
In your dream.

John Skelton

(1460–1529)

TO MISTRESS MARGERY WENTWORTH

With marjoram gentle,
　The flower of goodlihead,
Embroidered the mantle
　Is of your maidenhead.
Plainly I cannot glose;
　Ye be, as I divine,
The pretty primrose,
　The goodly columbine.
With marjoram gentle,
　The flower of goodlihead,
Embroidered the mantle
　Is of your maidenhead.
Benign, courteous, and meek,
　With wordës well devised;
In you, who list to seek,
　Be virtues well comprised.
With marjoram gentle,
　The flower of goodlihead,
Embroidered the mantle
　Is of your maidenhead.

May Swenson
(1913–1989)

QUESTION

Body my house
my horse my hound
what will I do
when you are fallen

Where will I sleep
How will I ride
What will I hunt

Where can I go
without my mount
all eager and quick
How will I know
in thicket ahead
is danger or treasure
when Body my good
bright dog is dead

How will it be
to lie in the sky
without roof or door
and wind for an eye

With cloud for shift
how will I hide?

George Turberville
(1540–ca. 1595)

To One That Had Little Wit

I thee advise
If thou be wise
To keep thy wit
Though it be small:
'Tis rare to get
And far to fet,
'Twas ever yit
Dearest ware of all.

William Carlos Williams

(1883–1963)

FINE WORK WITH PITCH AND COPPER

Now they are resting
in the fleckless light
separately in unison

like the sacks
of sifted stone stacked
regularly by twos

about the flat roof
ready after lunch
to be opened and strewn

The copper in eight
foot strips has been
beaten lengthwise

down the center at right
angles and lies ready
to edge the coping

One still chewing
picks up a copper strip
and runs his eye along it

POEM

As the cat
climbed over
the top of

the jamcloset
first the right
forefoot

carefully
then the hind
stepped down

into the pit of
the empty
flowerpot

TO WAKEN AN OLD LADY

Old age is
a flight of small
cheeping birds
skimming
bare trees
above a snow glaze.
Gaining and failing
they are buffeted
by a dark wind—
But what?
On harsh weedstalks
the flock has rested,
the snow

is covered with broken
seedhusks
and the wind tempered
by a shrill
piping of plenty.

William Butler Yeats

(1865–1939)

A Coat

I made my song a coat
Covered with embroideries
Out of old mythologies
From heel to throat;
But the fools caught it,
Wore it in the world's eyes
As though they'd wrought it.
Song, let them take it,
For there's more enterprise
In walking naked.

II

LONG LINES, STROPHES, PARALLELISMS

❖❖❖❖❖❖❖❖❖❖❖❖❖❖❖❖❖❖❖❖❖❖❖❖❖❖❖❖❖❖❖❖❖❖❖❖❖

THE FOLLOWING LINE, in the great sixteenth-century English translation of the Bible, has in its sound as well as its meaning the pressure of having much to say:

> And I gave my heart to seek and search out by wisdom
> concerning all *things* that are done under heaven: this
> sore travail hath God given to the sons of man to be
> exercised therewith.

Though the spatial limitations of a page, with its margins, require that the line be broken typographically, spatially, in some other significant sense we can recognize it as a single line. The unfolding cadences and meanings do not stop after "And I gave my heart to seek," for example, nor do they stop after "and search out by wisdom." Moreover, when the cadences and meanings *do* pause—after "things that are done under heaven"—the pause is part of the line.

That is, the giving of one's heart to seek and search out; the "by wisdom"; the encompassing of all things done under heaven—all these parts, in their meaning and rhythm, feel like they belong together as a unit. Also part of that same unit is the characterization, after the colon, of the heart's charge of knowledge-seeking as a sore God-given travail, a labor with which all sons of man will be exercised. These parts are one: they are beautiful and meaningful as one—just as surely as Thomas Campion's four lines (p. 15),

> Now winter night's enlarge
> The number of their hours;
> And clouds their storms discharge
> Upon the airy towers.

are four, and beautiful and meaningful as four.

Saying exactly how we know such things may be impossible. The line from Ecclesiastes conveys the energy of many things gathered into one prolonged gesture. In contrast, the lines by Campion convey the energy of weaving adeptly among things, disposing them in their relation. The feelings are distinct, and different.

A common-sense observation is that of course a longer unit will be made of shorter units. The second half of the biblical example can be divided into units similar to Campion's lines, and we could choose to express that fact typographically:

> This sore travail hath God
> given to the sons of man
> to be exercised therewith.

However, the typography merely blurs or partly camouflages the nature of the words as they were framed into a line by the English translators.

The formal rightness is even more clear in a larger context, giving more sense of the parallel constructions and repetitions among the lines, as well as echoes across lines. A bit after the line just quoted, another begins by repeating the same phrase, "And I gave my heart," along with some of the same words, as well as repeating some phrases from other lines in the passage:

> I have seen all the works that are done under the sun: and,
>   behold, all is vanity and vexation of spirit.
>
> That which is crooked cannot be made straight: and that which
>   is wanting cannot be numbered.

I communed with mine own heart, saying, Lo, I am come to
great estate, and have gotten more wisdom than all they that
have been before me in Jerusalem: yea, my heart had great
experience of wisdom and knowledge.

And I gave my heart to know wisdom, and to know madness
and folly: I perceived that this also is vexation of spirit.

For in much wisdom is much grief: and he that increaseth
knowledge increaseth sorrow.

The passage, with its returns to phrases and its return to a new move-
ment, recalls one of the terms used for such varying, extended units:
"strophe," from a Greek word meaning "to turn." "Verse" comes from
a Latin word meaning the same thing. The Greek is associated with a
movement by a chanting and dancing chorus.

The last line quoted above may have inspired the remarkable begin-
ning of the elegy (p. 65) composed by Fulke Greville—some scholars
say by Edward Dyer—for Philip Sidney:

Silence augmenteth grief, writing increaseth rage,
Staled are my thoughts, which loved and lost the wonder of our
age:
Yet quickened now with fire, though dead with frost ere now,
Enraged I write I know not what: dead, quick, I know not how.

The lines here are made systematically of shorter units, with an explo-
sive feeling of crashing ahead—quite different from the less symmetri-
cal feeling of Ecclesiastes. The opening of Walt Whitman's "Song of
Myself" (p. 95) creates still another different feeling by alternating lines
like Greville's with a more contained, musing pattern:

I celebrate myself,
And what I assume you shall assume,
For every atom belonging to me as good belongs to you.

I loafe and invite my soul,
I lean and loafe at my ease . . . . observing a spear of summer grass.

The rhythm and structure of the third and fifth lines here are more or less identical to certain lines of the elegy for Sidney.

A kind of line is a kind of feeling. It is notable that several of the examples in this section involve an explicit search for wisdom, with an emphasis on the past. In this way, Allen Ginsberg's strophes (p. 70) are profoundly traditional, in the best sense of the word:

> Where are we going, Walt Whitman? The doors close in an
> hour. Which way does your beard point tonight?
> (I touch your book and dream of our odyssey in the supermar-
> ket and feel absurd.)
> Will we walk all night through solitary streets? The trees add
> shade to shade, lights out in the houses, we'll both be lonely.
> Will we stroll dreaming of the lost America of love past blue
> automobiles in driveways, home to our silent cottage?
> Ah, dear father, graybeard, lonely old courage-teacher, what
> America did you have when Charon quit poling his ferry
> and you got out on a smoking bank and stood watching the
> boat disappear on the black waters of Lethe?

from Ecclesiastes: or, the Preacher (1–3)

Chapter 1

The words of the Preacher, the son of David, king in Jerusalem.

2 Vanity of vanities, saith the Preacher, vanity of vanities; all *is* vanity.

3 What profit hath a man of all his labour which he taketh under the sun?

4 *One* generation passeth away, and *another* generation cometh: but the earth abideth for ever.

5 The sun also ariseth, and the sun goeth down, and hasteth to his place where he arose.

6 The wind goeth toward the south, and turneth about unto the north; it whirleth about continually, and the wind returneth again according to his circuits.

7 All the rivers run into the sea; yet the sea *is* not full; unto the place from whence the rivers come, thither they return again.

8 All things *are* full of labour; man cannot utter *it*: the eye is not satisfied with seeing, nor the ear filled with hearing.

9 The thing that hath been, it *is that* which shall be; and that which is done *is* that which shall be done: and *there is* no new *thing* under the sun.

10 Is there *any* thing whereof it may be said, See, this *is* new? it hath been already of old time, which was before us.

11 *There is* no remembrance of former *things*; neither shall there be *any* remembrance of *things* that are to come with *those* that shall come after.

12 I the Preacher was king over Israel in Jerusalem.

13 And I gave my heart to seek and search out by wisdom concerning all *things* that are done under heaven: this sore

travail hath God given to the sons of man to be exercised therewith.

14 I have seen all the works that are done under the sun; and, behold, all *is* vanity and vexation of spirit.

15 *That which is* crooked cannot be made straight: and that which is wanting cannot be numbered.

16 I communed with mine own heart, saying, Lo, I am come to great estate, and have gotten more wisdom than all *they* that have been before me in Jerusalem: yea, my heart had great experience of wisdom and knowledge.

17 And I gave my heart to know wisdom, and to know madness and folly: I perceived that this also is vexation of spirit.

18 For in much wisdom *is* much grief: and he that increaseth knowledge increaseth sorrow.

Chapter 2

I said in mine heart, Go to now, I will prove thee with mirth, therefore enjoy pleasure: and, behold, this also *is* vanity.

2 I said of laughter, *It is* mad: and of mirth, What doeth it?

3 I sought in mine heart to give myself unto wine, yet acquaint-ing mine heart with wisdom; and to lay hold on folly, till I might see what *was* that good for the sons of men, which they should do under the heaven all the days of their life.

4 I made me great works; I builded me houses; I planted me vineyards:

5 I made me gardens and orchards, and I planted trees in them of all *kind of* fruits:

6 I made me pools of water, to water therewith the wood that bringeth forth trees:

7 I got *me* servants and maidens, and had servants born in my house; also I had great possessions of great and small cattle above all that were in Jerusalem before me:

8 I gathered me also silver and gold, and the peculiar treasure of kings and of the provinces: I gat me men singers and women singers, and the delights of the sons of men, *as* musical instruments, and that of all sorts.

9 So I was great, and increased more than all that were before me
in Jerusalem: also my wisdom remained with me.

10 And whatsoever mine eyes desired I kept not from them, I
withheld not my heart from any joy; for my heart rejoiced in
all my labour: and this was my portion of all my labour.

11 Then I looked on all the works that my hands had wrought,
and on the labour that I had laboured to do: and, behold,
all *was* vanity and vexation of spirit, and *there was* no profit
under the sun.

12 And I turned myself to behold wisdom, and madness, and folly:
for what *can* the man *do* that cometh after the king? *even*
that which hath been already done.

13 Then I saw that wisdom excelleth folly, as far as light excelleth
darkness.

14 The wise man's eyes *are* in his head; but the fool walketh in
darkness: and I myself perceived also that one event hap-
peneth to them all.

15 Then said I in my heart, As it happeneth to the fool, so it hap-
peneth even to me; and why was I then more wise? Then I
said in my heart, that this also *is* vanity.

16 For *there is* no remembrance of the wise more than of the fool
for ever; seeing that which now *is* in the days to come shall
all be forgotten. And how dieth the wise *man?* as the fool

17 Therefore I hated life; because the work that is wrought under
the sun *is* grievous unto me: for all *is* vanity and vexation of
spirit.

18 Yea, I hated all my labour which I had taken under the sun:
because I should leave it unto the man that shall be after me.

19 And who knoweth whether he shall be a wise *man* or a fool?
yet shall he have rule over all my labour wherein I have
laboured, and wherein I have showed myself wise under the
sun. This *is* also vanity.

20 Therefore I went about to cause my heart to despair of all the
labour which I took under the sun.

21 For there is a man whose labour *is* in wisdom, and in knowl-
edge, and in equity; yet to a man that hath not laboured

therein shall he leave it *for* his portion. This also *is* vanity and a great evil.

22 For what hath man of all his labour, and of the vexation of his heart, wherein he hath laboured under the sun?

23 For all his days *are* sorrows, and his travail grief; yea, his heart taketh not rest in the night. This is also vanity.

24 *There is* nothing better for a man, *than* that he should eat and drink, and *that* he should make his soul enjoy good in his labour. This also I saw, that it *was* from the hand of God.

25 For who can eat, or who else can hasten *hereunto*, more than I?

26 For *God* giveth to a man that *is* good in his sight wisdom, and knowledge, and joy: but to the sinner he giveth travail, to gather and to heap up, that he may give to *him that is* good before God. This also *is* vanity and vexation of spirit.

Chapter 3

To every *thing there is* a season, and a time to every purpose under the heaven:

2 A time to be born, and a time to die; a time to plant, and a time to pluck up *that which is* planted;

3 A time to kill, and a time to heal; a time to break down, and a time to build up;

4 A time to weep, and a time to laugh; a time to mourn, and a time to dance;

5 A time to cast away stones, and a time to gather stones together; a time to embrace, and a time to refrain from embracing;

6 A time to get, and a time to lose; a time to keep, and a time to cast away;

7 A time to rend, and a time to sew; a time to keep silence, and a time to speak;

8 A time to love, and a time to hate; a time of war, and a time of peace.

9 What profit hath he that worketh in that wherein he laboureth?

10 I have seen the travail, which God hath given to the sons of men to be exercised in it.

11 He hath made every *thing* beautiful in his time: also he hath

set the world in their heart, so that no man can find out the work that God maketh from the beginning to the end.

12 I know that *there is* no good in them, but for *a man* to rejoice, and to do good in his life.

13 And also that every man should eat and drink, and enjoy the good of all his labour, it *is* the gift of God.

14 I know that, whatsoever God doeth, it shall be for ever: nothing can be put to it, nor any thing taken from it: and God doeth *it*, that *men* should fear before him.

15 That which hath been is now; and that which is to be hath already been; and God requireth that which is past.

16 And moreover I saw under the sun the place of judgment, *that* wickedness *was* there; and the place of righteousness, *that* iniquity *was* there.

17 I said in mine heart, God shall judge the righteous and the wicked: for *there is* a time there for every purpose and for every work.

18 I said in mine heart concerning the estate of the sons of men, that God might manifest them, and that they might see that they themselves are beasts.

19 For that which befalleth the sons of men befalleth beasts; even one thing befalleth them: as the one dieth, so dieth the other; yea, they have all one breath so that a man hath no preeminence above a beast: for all *is* vanity.

20 All go unto one place; all are of the dust, and all turn to dust again.

21 Who knoweth the spirit of man that goeth upward, and the spirit of the beast that goeth downward to the earth?

22 Wherefore I perceive that *there is* nothing better, than that a man should rejoice in his own works; for that *is* his portion: for who shall bring him to see what shall be after him?

A. R. Ammons

(1926–2001)

THE CITY LIMITS

When you consider the radiance, that it does not withhold
itself but pours its abundance without selection into every
nook and cranny not overhung or hidden; when you consider

that birds' bones make no awful noise against the light but
lie low in the light as in a high testimony; when you consider
the radiance, that it will look into the guiltiest

swervings of the weaving heart and bear itself upon them,
not flinching into disguise or darkening; when you consider
the abundance of such resource as illuminates the glow-blue

bodies and gold-skeined wings of flies swarming the dumped
guts of a natural slaughter or the coil of shit and in no
way winces from its storms of generosity; when you consider

that air or vacuum, snow or shale, squid or wolf, rose or lichen,
each is accepted into as much light as it will take, then
the heart moves roomier, the man stands and looks about, the

leaf does not increase itself above the grass, and the dark
work of the deepest cells is of a tune with May bushes
and fear lit by the breadth of such calmly turns to praise.

Fulke Greville

(1554–1628)

Epitaph on Sir Philip Sidney

Silence augmenteth grief, writing increaseth rage,
Staled are my thoughts, which loved and lost the wonder of our
    age:
Yet quickened now with fire, though dead with frost ere now,
Enraged I write I know not what; dead, quick, I know not how.

Hard-hearted minds relent and rigour's tears abound,
And envy strangely rues his end, in whom no fault she found.
Knowledge her light hath lost; valour hath slain her knight.
Sidney is dead; dead is my friend; dead is the world's delight.

Place, pensive, wails his fall whose presence was her pride;
Time crieth out, "My ebb is come; his life was my spring tide."
Fame mourns in that she lost the ground of her reports;
Each living wight laments his lack, and all in sundry sorts.

He was (woe worth that word!) to each well-thinking mind
A spotless friend, a matchless man, whose virtue ever shined,
Declaring in his thoughts, his life, and that he writ,
Highest conceits, longest foresights, and deepest works of wit.

He, only like himself, was second unto none,
Whose death (though life) we rue, and wrong, and all in vain
    do moan.
Their loss, not him, wail they, that fill the world with cries,
Death slew not him, but he made death his ladder to the skies.

Now sink of sorrow I, who live, the more the wrong!
Who wishing death, whom death denies, whose thread is all
    too long;
Who tied to wretched life, who looks for no relief,
Must spend my ever dying days in never ending grief.

Heart's ease and only I, like parallels, run on,
Whose equal length keep equal breadth, and never meet in one;
Yet for not wronging him, my thoughts, my sorrow's cell,
Shall not run out, though leak they will, for liking him so well.

Farewell to you, my hopes, my wonted waking dreams,
Farewell, sometimes enjoyed joy; eclipsed are thy beams.
Farewell, self-pleasing thoughts, which quietness brings forth;
And farewell, friendship's sacred league, uniting minds of
    worth.

And farewell, merry heart, the gift of guiltless minds,
And all sports which for life's restore variety assigns;
Let all that sweet is void; in me no mirth may dwell.
Philip, the cause of all this woe, my life's content, farewell!

Now rhyme, the son of rage, which art no kin to skill,
And endless grief, which deads my life, yet knows not how to
    kill,
Go, seek that hapless tomb, which if ye hap to find,
Salute the stones, that keep the limbs, that held so good a mind.

W. S. Gilbert

(1836–1911)

WHEN YOU'RE LYING AWAKE WITH A DISMAL HEADACHE

Love, unrequited, robs me of my rest:
    Love, hopeless love, my ardent soul encumbers:
Love, nightmare-like, lies heavy on my chest,
    And weaves itself into my midnight slumbers!

When you're lying awake with a dismal headache, and repose is
    taboo'd by anxiety,
I conceive you may use any language you choose to indulge in,
    without impropriety;
For your brain is on fire—the bedclothes conspire of usual
    slumber to plunder you:
First your counterpane goes, and uncovers your toes, and your
    sheet slips demurely from under you;
Then the blanketing tickles—you feel like mixed pickles—so
    terribly sharp is the pricking,
And you're hot, and you're cross, and you tumble and toss till
    there's nothing 'twixt you and the ticking.
Then the bedclothes all creep to the ground in a heap, and you
    pick 'em all up in a tangle;
Next your pillow resigns and politely declines to remain at its
    usual angle!
Well, you get some repose in the form of a doze, with hot eye-
    balls and head ever aching,
But your slumbering teems with such horrible dreams that
    you'd very much better be waking:

For you dream you are crossing the Channel, and tossing about
    in a steamer from Harwich—
Which is something between a large bathing machine and a
    very small second-class carriage—
And you're giving a treat (penny ice and cold meat) to a party of
    friends and relations—
They're a ravenous horde—and they all came on board at
    Sloane Square and South Kensington Stations.
And bound on that journey you find your attorney (who started
    that morning from Devon);
He's a bit undersized, and you don't feel surprised when he tells
    you he's only eleven.
Well, you're driving like mad with this singular lad (by the by,
    the ship's now a four-wheeler),
And you're playing round games, and he calls you bad names
    when you tell him that "ties pay the dealer";
But this you can't stand, so you throw up your hand, and you
    find you're as cold as an icicle,
In your shirt and your socks (the black silk with gold clocks),
    crossing Salisbury Plain on a bicycle:
And he and the crew are on bicycles too—which they've some-
    how or other invested in—
And he's telling the tars all the particu*lars* of a company he's
    interested in—
It's a scheme of devices, to get at low prices all goods from
    cough mixtures to cables
(Which tickled the sailors), by treating retailers as though they
    were all veget*a*bles—
You get a good spadesman to plant a small tradesman (first take
    off his boots with a boot-tree),
And his legs will take root, and his fingers will shoot, and
    they'll blossom and bud like a fruit-tree—
From the greengrocer tree you get grapes and green pea, cauli-
    flower, pineapple, and cranberries,
While the pastrycook plant cherry brandy will grant, apple
    puffs, and three-corners, and Banburys—

The shares are a penny, and ever so many are taken by Roth-
schild and Baring,
And just as a few are allotted to you, you awake with a shudder
despairing—
You're a regular wreck, with a crick in your neck, and no
wonder you snore, for your head's on the floor, and you've
needles and pins from your soles to your shins, and your
flesh is a-creep, for your left leg's asleep, and you've cramp
in your toes, and a fly on your nose, and some fluff in your
lung, and a feverish tongue, and a thirst that's intense, and a
general sense that you haven't been sleeping in clover;
But the darkness has passed, and it's daylight at last, and the
night has been long—ditto ditto my song—and thank
goodness they're both of them over!

Allen Ginsberg

(1926–1997)

A SUPERMARKET IN CALIFORNIA

What thoughts I have of you tonight, Walt Whitman, for
I walked down the sidestreets under the trees with a headache
self-conscious looking at the full moon.

In my hungry fatigue, and shopping for images, I went into
the neon fruit supermarket, dreaming of your enumerations!

What peaches and what penumbras! Whole families shop-
ping at night! Aisles full of husbands! Wives in the avocados,
babies in the tomatoes!—and you, García Lorca, what were you
doing down by the watermelons?

I saw you, Walt Whitman, childless, lonely old grubber,
poking among the meats in the refrigerator and eyeing the
grocery boys.

I heard you asking questions of each: Who killed the pork
chops? What price bananas? Are you my Angel?

I wandered in and out of the brilliant stacks of cans follow-
ing you, and followed in my imagination by the store detective.

We strode down the open corridors together in our solitary
fancy tasting artichokes, possessing every frozen delicacy, and
never passing the cashier.

Where are we going, Walt Whitman? The doors close in an
hour. Which way does your beard point tonight?

(I touch your book and dream of our odyssey in the super-
market and feel absurd.)

Will we walk all night through solitary streets? The trees add
shade to shade, lights out in the houses, we'll both be lonely.

Will we stroll dreaming of the lost America of love past blue automobiles in driveways, home to our silent cottage?

Ah, dear father, graybeard, lonely old courage-teacher, what America did you have when Charon quit poling his ferry and you got out on a smoking bank and stood watching the boat disappear on the black waters of Lethe?

Thomas Hardy
(1840–1928)

AFTERWARDS

When the Present has latched its postern behind my tremulous stay,
    And the May month flaps its glad green leaves like wings,
Delicate-filmed as new-spun silk, will the neighbours say,
    "He was a man who used to notice such things?"

If it be in the dusk when, like an eyelid's soundless blink,
    The dewfall-hawk comes crossing the shades to alight
Upon the wind-warped upland thorn, a gazer may think,
    "To him this must have been a familiar sight."

If I pass during some nocturnal blackness, mothy and warm,
    When the hedgehog travels furtively over the lawn,
One may say, "He strove that such innocent creatures should come
        to no harm,
    But he could do little for them; and now he is gone."

If, when hearing that I have been stilled at last, they stand at the
        door,
    Watching the full-starred heavens that winter sees,
Will this thought rise on those who will meet my face no more,
    "He was one who had an eye for such mysteries."

And will any say when my bell of quittance is heard in the gloom,
    And a crossing breeze cuts a pause in its outrollings,
Till they swell again, as they were a new bell's boom,
    "He hears it not now, but used to notice such things?"

Gerard Manley Hopkins

(1844–1889)

SPELT FROM SIBYL'S LEAVES

Earnest, earthless, equal, attuneable, ' vaulty, voluminous, . . .
    stupendous
Evening strains to be tíme's vást, ' womb-of-all, home-of-all,
    hearse-of-all night.
Her fond yellow hornlight wound to the west, ' her wild hollow
    hoarlight hung to the height
Waste; her earliest stars, earlstars, ' stárs principal, overbend us,
Fíre-féaturing heaven. For earth ' her being has unbound; her
    dapple is at an end, as-
tray or aswarm, all throughther, in throngs; ' self ín self steepèd
    and páshed—qúite
Disremembering, dísmémbering ' áll now. Heart, you round
    me right
With: Óur évening is over us; óur night ' whélms, whélms, ánd
    will end us.
Only the beakleaved boughs dragonish ' damask the tool-
    smooth bleak light; black,
Ever so black on it. Óur tale, O óur oracle! ' Lét life, wáned, ah
    lét life wind
Off hér once skéined stained véined varíety ' upon, áll on twó
    spools; párt, pen, páck
Now her áll in twó flocks, twó folds—black, white; ' right,
    wrong; reckon but, reck but, mind
But thése two; wáre of a wórld where bút these ' twó tell, each
    off the óther; of a rack
Where, selfwrung, selfstrung, sheathe- and shelterless, '
    thóughts against thoughts ín groans grínd.

Kenneth Koch
(1925–2002)

PROVERB

Les morts vont vite, the dead go fast, the next day absent!
Et les vivants sont dingues, the living are haywire.
Except for a few who grieve, life rapidly readjusts itself
The milliner trims the hat not thinking of the departed
The horse sweats and throws his stubborn rider to the earth
Uncaring if he has killed him or not
The thrown man rises. But now he knows that he is not going,
Not going fast, though he was close to having been gone.
The day after Caesar's death, there was a new, bustling Rome
The moment after the racehorse's death, a new one is sought for
    the stable
The second after a moth's death there are one or two hundred
    other moths
The month after Einstein's death the earth is inundated with
    new theories
Biographies are written to cover up the speed with which we go:
No more presence in the bedroom or waiting in the hall
Greeting to say hello with mixed emotions. The dead go quickly
Not knowing why they go or where they go. To die is human,
To come back divine. Roosevelt gives way to Truman
Suddenly in the empty White House a brave new voice
    resounds
And the wheelchaired captain has crossed the great divide.
Faster than memories, faster than old mythologies, faster than
    the speediest train.

Alexander of Macedon, on time!
Prudhomme on time, Gorbachev on time, the beloved and the
    lover on time!
Les morts vont vite. We living stand at the gate
And life goes on.

D. H. Lawrence

(1885–1930)

Bavarian Gentians

Not every man has gentians in his house
in Soft September, at slow, sad Michaelmas.

Bavarian gentians, big and dark, only dark
darkening the daytime, torch-like with the smoking blueness of
    Pluto's gloom,
ribbed and torch-like, with their blaze of darkness spread blue
down flattening into points, flattened under the sweep of white
    day
torch-flower of the blue-smoking darkness, Pluto's dark-blue daze,
black lamps from the halls of Dis, burning dark blue,
giving off darkness, blue darkness, as Demeter's pale lamps give
    off light,
lead me then, lead the way.

Reach me a gentian, give me a torch!
let me guide myself with the blue, forked torch of this flower
down the darker and darker stairs, where blue is darkened on
    blueness
even where Persephone goes, just now, from the frosted September
to the sightless realm where darkness is awake upon the dark
and Persephone herself is but a voice
or a darkness invisible enfolded in the deeper dark
of the arms Plutonic, and pierced with the passion of dense
    gloom,
among the splendour of torches of darkness, shedding darkness on
    the lost bride and her groom.

Marianne Moore

(1887–1972)

-----❖-----

THE FISH

wade
through black jade.
   Of the crow-blue mussel-shells, one keeps
   adjusting the ash heaps;
      opening and shutting itself like

Illiteration

an
injured fan.
   The barnacles, which encrust the side
   of the wave cannot hide
      there, for the submerged shafts of the

sun,
split like spun
   glass, move themselves with spotlight swiftness
   into the crevices—
      in and out, illuminating _ *Assonance*

the
turquoise sea
   of bodies. The water drives a wedge
   of iron through the iron edge
      of the cliff; whereupon the stars,

pink
rice-grains, ink-
   bespattered jellyfish, crabs like green

       lilies, and submarine
          toadstools slide each on the other.

All
external
       marks of abuse are present on this
       defiant edifice—
          all the physical features of

ac-
cident—lack
       of cornice, dynamite grooves, burns, and
       hatchet strokes, these things stand
          out on it; the chasm side is

dead.
Repeated
       evidence has proved that it can live
       on what can not revive
          its youth. The sea grows old in it.

Ogden Nash

(1902–1971)

COLUMBUS

Once upon a time there was an Italian,
And some people thought he was a rapscallion,
But he wasn't offended,
Because other people thought he was splendid,
And he said the world was round,
And everybody made an uncomplimentary sound,
But his only reply was Pooh,
He replied, Isn't this fourteen ninety-two?
It's time for me to discover America if I know my chronology,
And if I discover America you owe me an apology,
So he went and tried to borrow some money from Ferdinand
But Ferdinand said America was a bird in the bush and he'd
    rather have a berdinand,
But Columbus' brain was fertile, it wasn't arid,
And he remembered that Ferdinand was unhappily married,
And he thought, there is no wife like a misunderstood one,
Because her husband thinks something is a terrible idea she is
    bound to think it a good one,
So he perfumed his handkerchief with bay rum and citronella,
And he went to see Isabella,
And he looked wonderful but he had never felt sillier,
And she said, I can't place the face but the aroma is familiar,
And Columbus didn't say a word,
All he said was, I am Columbus, the fifteenth-century Admiral
    Byrd,
And just as he thought, her disposition was very malleable,
And she said, Here are my jewels, and she wasn't penurious like

Cornelia the mother of the Gracchi, she wasn't referring to her children, no, she was referring to her jewels, which were very very valuable,

So Columbus said, somebody show me the sunset and somebody did and he set sail for it,

And he discovered America and they put him in jail for it,

And the fetters gave him welts,

And they named America after somebody else,

So the sad fate of Columbus ought to be pointed out to every child and every voter,

Because it has a very important moral, which is, Don't be a discoverer, be a promoter.

Thomas Nashe

(1567–1601)

Autumn Hath All the Summer's Fruitful Treasure

Autumn hath all the summer's fruitful treasure;
Gone is our sport, fled is poor Croydon's pleasure.
Short days, sharp days, long nights come on apace,—
Ah, who shall hide us from the winter's face?
Cold doth increase, the sickness will not cease,
And here we lie, God knows, with little ease.
    From winter, plague, and pestilence, good Lord deliver us!

London doth mourn, Lambeth is quite forlorn;
Trades cry, Woe worth that ever they were born.
The want of term is town and city's harm;
Close chambers we do want to keep us warm.
Long banished must we live from our friends;
This low-built house will bring us to our ends.
    From winter, plague, and pestilence, good Lord deliver us!

Ishmael Reed

(b. 1938)

I AM A COWBOY IN THE BOAT OF RA

"The devil must be forced to reveal any such physical evil
(potions, charms, fetishes, etc.) still outside the body
*and these must be burned." (*Rituale Romanum, *published*
1947, endorsed by the coat-of-arms and introductory
letter from Francis cardinal Spellman)

I am a cowboy in the boat of Ra,
sidewinders in the saloons of fools
bit my forehead   like   O
the untrustworthiness of Egyptologists
who do not know their trips. Who was that
dog-faced man?   they asked, the day I rode
from town.

School marms with halitosis cannot see
the Nefertiti   fake chipped on the run by slick
germans, the hawk behind Sonny Rollins'   head or
the ritual beard of his axe; a longhorn winding
its bells thru the Field of Reeds.

I am a cowboy in the boat of Ra. I bedded
down with Isis,   Lady of the Boogaloo, dove
down deep in her horny, stuck up her Wells-Far-ago
in daring midday getaway. "Start grabbing the
blue," I said from top of my double crown.

I am a cowboy in the boat of Ra. Ezzard Charles
of the Chisholm Trail.   Took up the bass but they

blew off my thumb. Alchemist in ringmanship but a
sucker for the right cross.

I am a cowboy in the boat of Ra. Vamoosed from
the temple I bide my time. The price on the wanted
poster was a-going down, outlaw alias copped my stance
and moody greenhorns were making me dance;
    while my mouth's
shooting iron got its chambers jammed.

I am a cowboy in the boat of Ra. Boning-up in
the ol West I bide my time. You should see
me pick off these tin cans whippersnappers. I
write the motown long plays for the comeback of
Osiris. Make them up when stars stare at sleeping
steer out here near the campfire. Women arrive
on the backs of goats and throw themselves on
my Bowie.

I am a cowboy in the boat of Ra. Lord of the lash,
the Loup Garou Kid. Half breed son of Pisces and
Aquarius. I hold the souls of men in my pot. I do
the dirty boogle with scorpions. I make the bulls
keep still and was the first swinger to grape the taste.

I am a cowboy in his boat. Pope Joan of the
Ptah Ra. C/mere a minute willya doll?
Be a good girl and
bring me my Buffalo horn of black powder
bring me my headdress of black feathers
bring me my bones of Ju-Ju snake
go get my eyelids of red paint.
Hand me my shadow

I'm going into town after Set

I am a cowboy in the boat of Ra

look out Set   here I come Set
to get Set   to sunset Set
to unseat Set   to Set down Set

usurper of the Royal couch
imposter Radio of Moses' bush
party pooper O hater of dance
vampire outlaw of the milky way

Christopher Smart

(1722–1771)

FROM JUBILATE AGNO

[MY CAT JEOFFRY]

For I will consider my Cat Jeoffry.

For he is the servant of the Living God duly and daily serving
him.

For at the first glance of the glory of God in the East he wor-
ships in his way

For is this done by wreathing his body seven times round with
elegant quickness.

For then he leaps up to catch the musk, wch is the blessing of
God upon his prayer.

For he rolls upon prank to work it in.

For having done duty and received blessing he begins to con-
sider himself

For this he performs in ten degrees.

For first he looks upon his fore-paws to see if they are clean.

For secondly he kicks up behind to clear away there.

For thirdly he works it upon stretch with the fore-paws
extended.

For fourthly he sharpens his paws by wood.

For fifthly he washes himself.

For Sixthly he rolls upon wash.

For Seventhly he fleas himself, that he may not be interrupted
upon the beat.

For Eighthly he rubs himself against a post.

For Ninthly he looks up for his instructions.

For Tenthly he goes in quest of food.

For having consider'd God and himself he will consider his
neighbor.

For if he meets another cat he will kiss her in kindness.

For when he takes his prey he plays with it to give it a chance.

For one mouse in seven escapes by his dallying.

For when his day's work is done his business more properly
begins.

For he keeps the Lord's watch in the night against the
adversary.

For he counteracts the powers of darkness by his electrical skin
& glaring eyes.

For he counteracts the Devil, who is death, by brisking about
the life.

For in his morning orisons he loves the sun and the sun loves
him.

For he is of the tribe of Tiger.

For the Cherub Cat is a term of the Angel Tiger.

For he has the subtlety and hissing of a serpent, which in good-
ness he suppresses.

For he will not do destruction if he is well-fed, neither will he
spit without provocation.

For he purrs in thankfulness, when God tells him he's a good
Cat.

For he is an instrument for the children to learn benevolence
upon.

For every house is incomplete without him & a blessing is
lacking in the spirit.

For the Lord commanded Moses concerning the cats at the
departure of the Children of Israel from Egypt.

For every family had one cat at least in the bag.

For the English Cats are the best in Europe.

For he is the cleanest in the use of his fore-paws of any
quadrupede.

For the dexterity of his defence is an instance of the love of God
to him exceedingly.

For he is the quickest to his mark of any creature.

For he is tenacious of his point.

For he is a mixture of gravity and waggery.

For he knows that God is his Saviour.

For there is nothing sweeter than his peace when at rest.

For there is nothing brisker than his life when in motion.

For he is of the Lord's poor and so indeed is he called by
benevolence perpetually—Poor Jeoffry! poor Jeoffry! the rat
has bit thy throat.

For I bless the name of the Lord Jesus that Jeoffry is better.

For the divine spirit comes about his body to sustain it in com-
pleat cat.

For his tongue is exceeding pure so that it has in purity what it
wants in music.

For he is docile and can learn certain things.

For he can set up with gravity which is patience upon
approbation.

For he can fetch and carry, which is patience in employment.

For he can jump over a stick which is patience upon proof
positive.

For he can spraggle upon waggle at the word of command.

For he can jump from an eminence into his master's bosom.

For he can catch the cork and toss it again.

For he is hated by the hypocrite and miser.

For the former is afraid of detection.

For the latter refuses the charge.

For he camels his back to bear the first notion of business.

For he is good to think on, if a man would express himself
neatly.

For he made a great figure in Egypt for his signal services.

For he killed the Icneumon-rat very pernicious by land.

For his ears are so acute that they sting again.

For from this proceeds the passing quickness of his attention.

For by stroking of him I have found out electricity.

For I perceived God's light about him both wax and fire.

For the Electrical fire is the spiritual substance, which God
sends from heaven to sustain the bodies both of man and
beast.

For God has blessed him in the variety of his movements.
For, though he cannot fly, he is an excellent clamberer.
For his motions upon the face of the earth are more than any
    other quadrupede.
For he can tread to all the measures upon the music.
For he can swim for life.
For he can creep.

George Turberville

(1540–1595)

The Lover Exhorteth His Lady to Take Time, While Time Is

Though brave your beauty be, and feature passing fair,
Such as Apelles to depaint might utterly despair,

Yet drowsy drooping Age, encroaching on apace,
With pensive plough will raze your hue, and Beauty's beams
    deface.

Wherefore in tender years how crooked Age doth haste
Revoke to mind, so shall you not your time consume in waste.

Whilst that you may, and youth in you is fresh and green,
Delight your self: for years do flit as fickle floods are seen;

For water slippèd by may not be called again,
And to revoke forepassèd hours were labor lost in vain.

Take time whilst time applies; with nimble foot it goes;
Nor to compare with passed prime thy after age suppose.

The holts that now are hoar, both bud and bloom I saw;
I wore a garland of the briar that puts me now in awe.

The time will be when thou that dost thy friends defy
A cold and crooked beldam shalt in loathsome cabin lie;

Nor with such nightly brawls thy postern gate shall sound,
Nor roses strewn affront thy door in dawning shall be found.

How soon are corpses, Lord, with filthy furrows filled?
How quickly Beauty, brave of late, and seemly shape is spilled?

Even thou that from thy youth to have been so, wilt swear;
With turn of hand in, all thy head shalt have gray powdered
    hair.

The snakes with shifted skins their loathsome age do way;
The buck doth hang his head on pale to live a longer day.

Your good without recure doth pass; receive the flower
Which if you pluck not from the stalk, will fall within this
    hour.

Charles Harper Webb

(b. 1952)

LIVER

Largest gland in the human body, three-pounds-plus of spongy
  red-brown meat
Shaped like a slug, or a fat, finless seal lodged in the abdomen's
  upper right quadrant,
Canopied by diaphragm, nudging stomach and guts—you taste
  so foul when cooked,
So musty and rotten, who would guess that you provide pro-
  tein, vitamins A, D, E, and B-complex,
Copper and iron? Who would guess the wealth of your accom-
  plishment: blood filter,
Storehouse for energy, aid to digestion, producer of antibodies,
  self-regenerator.
Doctors hacked out three-fourths of my friend Ken's liver in
  Hamburg, but it grew back.
Surgeons routinely take a chunk from an adult's liver and trans-
  plant it to a child.
The adult's liver grows back to its full size; the child's new liver
  grows as the child does.
Only vertebrates have livers. (Does this mean you house the
  soul?) No wonder
Ancients centered emotions in you—so much larger than the
  heart, more sanguine and substantial
Than the brain. No wonder, to Crow Indians, mountain man
  Jeremiah "Liver-Eatin'" Johnson
Was more powerful than if he'd been merely "Heart-Eatin',"
  "Lung-Eatin'," "Brain-Eatin'" Johnson.

Benedictions on the way blood percolates through you, Liver,
en route from the intestines to the heart.

Benedictions on the way you neutralize food additives, drugs,
poisons, germs, excess sex hormones (too much of a good
thing).

Benedictions on the way you store sugar as glycogen until it's
needed, then reconvert it to sugar for energy.

Benedictions on the way you boost the blood with *albumin*
(that keeps plasma from seeping

Through blood vessel walls), *fibrinogen* and *prothrombin* (that
help blood clot),

Heparin (that stops blood from clotting when it shouldn't),
globulin (that fights infections).

Benedictions on the way you convert ammonia to *urea*, dis-
charged in urine.

Benedictions on your production of bile: green liquid that,
despite medieval lies,

Improves the disposition, helping to break up globs of fat so
that intestinal

Enzymes can change them into glycerol and fatty acids the
body can use.

When red blood cells are destroyed in the bone marrow and
spleen, and their hemoglobin

Dumped back in the blood, bless you, Liver, for taking this
crimson dye and changing it

Into the folksily named red *bilirubin* and green *biliverdin* that
flow with the bile

To the intestines, giving feces the brown color that warns our
shoes away.

Astonishing, Liver, how you begin as a vestigal yolk sac.
Astonishing,

How a net of blood vessels, the *vitelline vessels*, develops in the
yolk sac's wall.

How the *umbilical vessels* develop to bring nourishment from
the uterus.

How both sets of vessels link behind the heart, and enter in like
  lovers holding hands.
How at their junction, capillaries create the *septum transversum*.
  How cells detach
From the "liver bay" in the gut, and the *mesothelium* that lines
  the body cavity,
Then migrate to the *septum transversum*, surround the capillar-
  ies, and become liver cells.
How each of the liver's four lobes is made of multisided
  lobules—50,000 to 100,000 per adult liver.
How each lobule is a central vein surrounded by bundles or
  sheets of liver cells.
How the *sinusoid* cavities separate the cells, making the liver
  spongy, helping it hold blood.
How the *sinusoids* drain into central veins, which join to form
  the *hepatic vein*, from which blood leaves the liver.
How the mature liver is a labyrinth of crooked hallways and
  long, thin, crooked rooms.

Forgive me, Liver, for the swill I've pumped through you. Please
  keep doing your fantastic work,
Dear red-brown friend. I'm so afraid of hepatitis, that inflames
  you and could kill me.
I'm so afraid of cirrhosis, that turns you into yellow scar tissue,
  making you contract and fail.
I'm so afraid of cancer that chews you from the inside out, and
  jaundice, when the blood
Contains too much *bilirubin*, causing yellowing of the skin and
  eyes, warning
Of worse trouble to come. I'm so afraid of dysentery, histoplas-
  mosis, t.b., and syphilis
That start elsewhere but take you over, Liver, the way kudzu has
  overrun the South.

You do much more for me every day than the Mayor. I think I
  should call you The Honorable Liver.

You do much more for me than the Governor. Liver for Gover-
nor. Liver for President—no, King!
I'd say "Liver for God," except you may already be. Our Liver,
who art in heaven. Hail Liver, full of grace.
Organ of life, playing better than Bach the toccatas and fugues
of good health and vitality,
Organ whose name contains the injunction "Live!"—O Liver,
great One-Who-Lives, so we can too.

Walt Whitman

(1819–1892)

FROM SONG OF MYSELF (1 & 52)

1

I celebrate myself,
And what I assume you shall assume,
For every atom belonging to me as good belongs to you.

I loafe and invite my soul,
I lean and loafe at my ease . . . . observing a spear of summer
    grass.

52

The spotted hawk swoops by and accuses me . . . . he complains
    of my gab and my loitering.

I too am not a bit tamed . . . . I too am untranslatable,
I sound my barbaric yawp over the roofs of the world.

The last scud of day holds back for me,
It flings my likeness after the rest and true as any on the shad-
    owed wilds,
It coaxes me to the vapor and the dusk.

I depart as air . . . . I shake my white locks at the runaway sun,
I effuse my flesh in eddies and drift it in lacy jags.

I bequeath myself to the dirt to grow from the grass I love
If you want me again look for me under your bootsoles.

You will hardly know who I am or what I mean,
But I shall be good health to you nevertheless,
And filter and fibre your blood.

Failing to fetch me at first keep encouraged,
Missing me one place search another,
I stop some where waiting for you.

C. K. Williams

(b. 1936)

THE DOG

Except for the dog, that she wouldn't have him put away,
　　wouldn't let him die, I'd have liked her.
She was handsome, busty, chunky, early middle-aged, very
　　black, with a stiff, exotic dignity
that flurried up in me a mix of warmth and sexual apprehension
　　neither of which, to tell the truth,
I tried very hard to nail down: she was that much older and in
　　those days there was still the race thing.
This was just at the time of civil rights: the neighborhood I was
　　living in was mixed.
In the narrow streets, the tiny three-floored houses they called
　　father-son-holy-ghosts
which had been servants' quarters first, workers' tenements,
　　then slums, still were, but enclaves of us,
beatniks and young artists, squatted there and commerce
　　between everyone was fairly easy.
Her dog, a grinning mongrel, rib and knob, gristle and grizzle,
　　wasn't terribly offensive.
The trouble was that he was ill, or the trouble more exactly was
　　that I had to know about it.
She used to walk him on a lot I overlooked, he must have had a
　　tumor or a blockage of some sort
because every time he moved his bowels, he shrieked, a chilling,
　　almost human scream of anguish.
It nearly always caught me unawares, but even when I'd see
　　them first, it wasn't better.

The limp leash coiled in her hand, the woman would be pro-
    filed to the dog, staring into the distance,
apparently oblivious, those breasts of hers like stone, while he,
    not a step away, laboring,
trying to eject the feeble, mucus-coated, blood-flecked chains
    that finally spurted from him,
would set himself on tiptoe and hump into a question mark,
    one quivering back leg grotesquely lifted.
Every other moment he'd turn his head, as though he wanted
    her, to no avail, to look at him,
then his eyes would dim and he'd drive his wounded anus in
    the dirt, keening uncontrollably,
lurching forward in a hideous, electric dance as though some-
    one were at him with a club.
When at last he'd finish, she'd wipe him with a tissue like a
    child; he'd lick her hand.
It was horrifying; I was always going to call the police; once I
    actually went out to chastise her—
didn't she know how selfish she was, how the animal was
    suffering?—she scared me off, though.
She was older than I'd thought, for one thing, her flesh was
    loosening, pouches of fat beneath the eyes,
and poorer, too, shabby, tarnished: I imagined smelling some-
    thing faintly acrid as I passed.
Had I ever really mooned for such a creature? I slunk around
    the block, chagrined, abashed.
I don't recall them too long after that. Maybe the dog died,
    maybe I was just less sensitive.
Maybe one year when the cold came and I closed my windows,
    I forgot them . . . then I moved.
Everything was complicated now, so many tensions, so much
    bothersome self-consciousness.
Anyway, those back streets, especially in bad weather when the
    ginkgos lost their leaves, were bleak.

It's restored there now, ivy, pointed brick, garden walls with
    broken bottles mortared on them,
but you'd get sick and tired then: the rubbish in the gutter, the
    general sense of dereliction.
Also, I'd found a girl to be in love with: all we wanted was to
    live together, so we did.

THE SINGING

I was walking home down a hill near our house on a balmy
    afternoon under the blossoms
Of the pear trees that go flamboyantly mad here every spring
    with their burgeoning forth

When a young man turned in from a corner singing no it was
    more of a cadenced shouting
Most of which I couldn't catch I thought because the young
    man was black speaking black

It didn't matter I could tell he was making his song up which
    pleased me he was nice-looking
Husky dressed in some style of big pants obviously full of him-
    self hence his lyrical flowing over

We went along in the same direction then he noticed me there
    almost beside him and "Big"
He shouted-sang "Big" and I thought how droll to have my
    height incorporated in his song

So I smiled but the face of the young man showed nothing he
    looked in fact pointedly away
And his song changed "I'm not a nice person" he chanted "I'm
    not I'm not a nice person"

No menace was meant I gathered no particular threat but he
    did want to be certain I knew
That if my smile implied I conceived of anything like concord
    between us I should forget it

That's all nothing else happened his song became indecipherable
    to me again he arrived
Where he was going a house where a girl in braids waited for
    him on the porch that was all

No one saw no one heard all the unasked and unanswered ques-
    tions were left where they were
It occurred to me to sing back "I'm not a nice person either" but
    I couldn't come up with a tune

Besides I wouldn't have meant it nor he have believed it both of
    us knew just where we were
In the duet we composed the equation we made the conventions
    to which we were condemned

Sometimes it feels even when no one is there that someone
    something is watching and listening
Someone to rectify redo remake this time again though no one
    saw nor heard no one was there

C. D. Wright

(b. 1949)

SELF PORTRAIT ON A ROCKY MOUNT

I am the goat. Caroline by name. Née 6 January. Domesticated since the sixth century before Jesus, a goat himself.

We have served as a source of meat, leather, milk, and hair. Our flesh is not widely loved. Yet our younger, under parts make fine gloves.

Out of our hair—pretty sweaters, wigs for magistrates. Our milk is good for cheese.

We share these gifts with Richard Milhous Nixon, who gained national prominence for his investigation of Mr. Hiss.

We're no sloth, full-time workers at the minimum wage. We had an annual income last year of $6,968, a little less than your average subway musician.

Our horoscope assures—we will be a great success socially and in some artistic calling.

We are surefooted, esp. on hills. We live on next-to-nothing. This week's victuals: ironing board covers and swollen paperbacks. Our small hills of filings fall under the heading of useful by-products. This we call Industrial Poetry. Both of us being Bearded, Mystic, Horned.

III

BALLADS, REPETITIONS, REFRAINS

IN POETRY, "BALLAD" traditionally indicates both a form, often set to music, often Scottish or North of England in origin, and a kind of content, often a luridly violent story told in bursts of dialogue and image, or in terse summary. The rapid narrative can be punctuated by a refrain, or repeated formulas that resemble a refrain. The refrains and repetitions—though this point may seem paradoxical—often heighten the economy, concentrating not just a lot of narrative, but a lot of impact, into a small space. Form achieves compression:

THE CRUEL MOTHER

She sat down below a thorn,
   Fine flowers in the valley;
And there she has her sweet babe born,
   And the green leaves they grow rarely.

"Smile na sae sweet, my bonnie babe,
   Fine flowers in the valley,
And ye smile sae sweet, ye'll smile me dead,"
   And the green leaves they grow rarely.

She's taen out her little penknife,
   Fine flowers in the valley,

And twinn'd the sweet babe o' its life,
And the green leaves they grow rarely.

She's howket a grave by the light o' the moon,
Fine flowers in the valley,
And there she's buried her sweet babe in,
And the green leaves they grow rarely.

As she was going to the church,
Fine flowers in the valley,
She saw a sweet babe in the porch,
And the green leaves they grow rarely.

"O sweet babe, and thou were mine,
Fine flowers in the valley,
I wad cleed thee in the silk so fine,"
And the green leaves they grow rarely.

"O mother dear, when I was thine,
Fine flowers in the valley,
"You did na prove to me sae kind,"
And the green leaves they grow rarely.

As magazine editors count, this ancient anonymous ballad (p. 106) contains just under two hundred words, including the title. The number of *different* words, the poem's entire vocabulary—reduced not only by the repeated refrain lines but by the repetitions of words like "babe," "sweet" and "she"—is not much over a hundred words: fewer than this editorial headnote has used so far.

As preachers and orators know, repetition can not only exert tremendous power: it can also be a form of variation, with each iteration transformed and transforming. In "The Cruel Mother" the springtime surging back to life of the flowers is first innocent and natural, then associated with the unwanted life of the pregnancy, then a counterpoint to killing, and then accompanies a supernatural return to life. The word "rarely" is not only from the Latin root *rarus* meaning "fine" or "unusual" but also from the Old English root *hrer* meaning "eager" or "first," as in meat that is snatched from the fire, cooked rare. One doesn't need that information about the word to sense conflicting emotions and meanings in the eager bursting of life in the refrain-lines.

A refrain is one kind of systematic repetition. The increasing chain of "The House That Jack Built" (p. 108) and the causal or temporal chain of "There Was a Man" (p. 111) are systematic in a different way. Alternating lines of four and three units, as in many ballads and in "Western Wind" (p. 112) and Elizabeth Bishop's "Chemin de Fer" (p. 122), involve systematic repetition of a pattern. These poems demonstrate how recurring sounds and words, systematic or random, can have primary significance: feeling their meaning precedes interpretations or clever summaries. "There Was a Man" is in different ways both enigmatic and clear.

When Edwin Arlington Robinson begins his "Eros Turannos" (p. 153) with a couple who are not identified, not yet put into much context, the intense, ballad-like rhymes, the lines of four units or three, the terse manner and singable quality all create the feeling. We hear and recognize that feeling in a deep, barely conscious form of recognition: the sounds put us in the story and its emotions:

> She fears him, and will always ask
> What fated her to choose him;
> She meets in his engaging mask
> All reasons to refuse him;
> But what she meets and what she fears
> Are less than are the downward years,
> Drawn slowly to the foamless weirs
> Of age, were she to lose him.

As with "The Cruel Mother," the sounds are arranged to create both the colors and the shadows of the story, and our attraction to the story: the desire to hear more.

Anonymous

The Cruel Mother

She sat down below a thorn,
  Fine flowers in the valley;
And there she has her sweet babe born,
  And the green leaves they grow rarely.

"Smile na sae sweet, my bonnie babe,
  Fine flowers in the valley,
And ye smile sae sweet, ye'll smile me dead,"
  And the green leaves they grow rarely.

She's taen out her little penknife,
  Fine flowers in the valley,
And twinn'd the sweet babe o' its life,
  And the green leaves they grow rarely.

She's howket a grave by the light o' the moon,
  Fine flowers in the valley,
And there she's buried her sweet babe in,
  And the green leaves they grow rarely.

As she was going to the church,
  Fine flowers in the valley,
She saw a sweet babe in the porch,
  And the green leaves they grow rarely.

"O sweet babe, and thou were mine,
  Fine flowers in the valley,

I wad cleed thee in the silk so fine,"
  And the green leaves they grow rarely.

"O mother dear, when I was thine,
  Fine flowers in the valley,
Ye did na prove to me sae kind,"
  And the green leaves they grow rarely.

Anonymous

The House That Jack Built

This is the house that Jack built.

This is the malt
That lay in the house that Jack built.

This is the rat,
That ate the malt
That lay in the house that Jack built.

This is the cat,
That killed the rat,
That ate the malt
That lay in the house that Jack built.

This is the dog,
That worried the cat,
That killed the rat,
That ate the malt
That lay in the house that Jack built.

This is the cow with the crumpled horn,
That tossed the dog,
That worried the cat,
That killed the rat,
That ate the malt
That lay in the house that Jack built.

This is the maiden all forlorn,
That milked the cow with the crumpled horn,

That tossed the dog,
That worried the cat,
That killed the rat,
That ate the malt
That lay in the house that Jack built.

This is the man all tattered and torn,
That kissed the maiden all forlorn,
That milked the cow with the crumpled horn,
That tossed the dog,
That worried the cat,
That killed the rat,
That ate the malt
That lay in the house that Jack built.

This is the priest all shaven and shorn,
That married the man all tattered and torn,
That kissed the maiden all forlorn,
That milked the cow with the crumpled horn,
That tossed the dog,
That worried the cat,
That killed the rat,
That ate the malt
That lay in the house that Jack built.

This is the cock that crowed in the morn,
That waked the priest all shaven and shorn,
That married the man all tattered and torn,
That kissed the maiden all forlorn,
That milked the cow with the crumpled horn,
That tossed the dog,
That worried the cat,
That killed the rat,
That ate the malt
That lay in the house that Jack built.

This is the farmer sowing the corn,
That kept the cock that crowed in the morn.
That waked the priest all shaven and shorn,
That married the man all tattered and torn,
That kissed the maiden all forlorn,
That milked the cow with the crumpled horn,
That tossed the dog,
That worried the cat,
That killed the rat,
That ate the malt
That lay in the house that Jack built.

Anonymous

---◦:◦---

THERE WAS A MAN

There was a man of double deed
Sewed his garden full of seed,
When the seed began to grow,
'Twas like a garden full of snow;
When the snow began to melt,
'Twas like a ship without a belt;
When the ship began to sail,
'Twas like a bird without a tail;
When the bird began to fly,
'Twas like an eagle in the sky;
When the sky began to roar,
'Twas like a lion at the door;
When the door began to crack,
'Twas like a stick across my back;
When my back began to smart,
'Twas like a penknife in my heart;
When my heart began to bleed,
'Twas death and death and death indeed.

Anonymous

WESTERN WIND

Western wind, when will thou blow,
    The small rain down can rain?
Christ, that my love were in my arms
    And I in my bed again!

John Ashbery

(b. 1927)

It Was Raining in the Capital

It was raining in the capital
And for many days and nights
The one they called the Aquarian
Had stayed alone with her delight.

What with the winter and its business
It had fallen to one side
And she had only recently picked it up
Where the other had died.

Between the pages of the newspaper
It smiled like a face.
Next to the drugstore on the corner
It looked to another place.

Or it would just hang around
Like sullen clouds over the sun.
But—this was the point—it was real
To her and to everyone.

For spring had entered the capital
Walking on gigantic feet.
The smell of witch hazel indoors
Changed to narcissus in the street.

She thought she had seen all this before:
Bundles of new, fresh flowers,

All changing, pressing upward
To the distant office towers.

Until now nothing had been easy,
Hemmed in by all that shit—
Horseshit, dogshit, birdshit, manshit—
Yes, she remembered having said it,

Having spoken in that way, thinking
There could be no road ahead,
Sobbing into the intractable presence of it
As one weeps alone in bed.

Its chamber was narrower than a seed
Yet when the doorbell rang
It reduced all that living to air
As "*kyrie eleison*" it sang.

Hearing that music he had once known
But now forgotten, the man,
The one who had waited casually in the dark
Turned to smile at the door's span.

He smiled and shrugged—a lesson
In the newspaper no longer
But fed by the ink and paper
Into a sign of something stronger

Who reads the news and takes the bus
Going to work each day
But who was never born of woman
Nor formed of the earth's clay.

Then what unholy bridegroom
Did the Aquarian foretell?
Or was such lively intelligence
Only the breath of hell?

It scarcely mattered at the moment
And it shall never matter at all
Since the moment will not be replaced
But stand, poised for its fall,

Forever. "This is what my learning
Teaches," the Aquarian said,
"To absorb life through the pores
For the life around you is dead."

The sun came out in the capital
Just before it set.
The lovely death's head shone in the sky
As though these two had never met.

Elizabeth Bishop

(1911–1979)

THE BURGLAR OF BABYLON

On the fair green hills of Rio
    There grows a fearful stain:
The poor who come to Rio
    And can't go home again.

On the hills a million people,
    A million sparrows, nest,
Like a confused migration
    That's had to light and rest,

Building its nests, or houses,
    Out of nothing at all, or air.
You'd think a breath would end them,
    They perch so lightly there.

But they cling and spread like lichen,
    And the people come and come.
There's one hill called the Chicken,
    And one called Catacomb;

There's the hill of Kerosene,
    And the hill of the Skeleton,
The hill of Astonishment,
    And the hill of Babylon.

Micuçú* was a burglar and killer,
　　An enemy of society.
He had escaped three times
　　From the worst penitentiary.

They don't know how many he murdered
　　(Though they say he never raped),
And he wounded two policemen
　　This last time he escaped.

They said, "He'll go to his auntie,
　　Who raised him like a son.
She has a little drink shop
　　On the hill of Babylon."

He did go straight to his auntie,
　　And he drank a final beer.
He told her, "The soldiers are coming,
　　And I've got to disappear.

"Ninety years they gave me.
　　Who wants to live that long?
I'll settle for ninety hours,
　　On the hill of Babylon.

"Don't tell anyone you saw me.
　　I'll run as long as I can.
You were good to me, and I love you,
　　But I'm a doomed man."

Going out, he met a *mulata*
　　Carrying water on her head.
"If you say you saw me, daughter,
　　You're just as good as dead."

---

* Micuçú (mē-coo-soo) is the folk name of a deadly snake, in the north.

There are caves up there, and hideouts,
    And an old fort, falling down.
They used to watch for Frenchmen
    From the hill of Babylon.

Below him was the ocean.
    It reached far up the sky,
Flat as a wall, and on it
    Were freighters passing by,

Or climbing the wall, and climbing
    Till each looked like a fly,
And then fell over and vanished;
    And he knew he was going to die.

He could hear the goats *baa-baa*-ing,
    He could hear the babies cry;
Fluttering kites strained upward;
    And he knew he was going to die.

A buzzard flapped so near him
    He could see its naked neck.
He waved his arms and shouted,
    "Not yet, my son, not yet!"

An Army helicopter
    Came nosing around and in.
He could see two men inside it,
    But they never spotted him.

The soldiers were all over,
    On all sides of the hill,
And right against the skyline
    A row of them, small and still.

Children peeked out of windows,
    And men in the drink shop swore,

And spat a little *cachaça*
　　At the light cracks in the floor.

But the soldiers were nervous, even
　　With tommy guns in hand,
And one of them, in a panic,
　　Shot the officer in command.

He hit him in three places;
　　The other shots went wild.
The soldier had hysterics
　　And sobbed like a little child.

The dying man said, "Finish
　　The job we came here for."
He committed his soul to God
　　And his sons to the Governor.

They ran and got a priest,
　　And he died in hope of Heaven
—A man from Pernambuco,
　　The youngest of eleven.

They wanted to stop the search,
　　But the Army said, "No, go on,"
So the soldiers swarmed again
　　Up the hill of Babylon.

Rich people in apartments
　　Watched through binoculars
As long as the daylight lasted.
　　And all night, under the stars,

Micuçú hid in the grasses
　　Or sat in a little tree,
Listening for sounds, and staring
　　At the lighthouse out at sea.

And the lighthouse stared back at him,
    Till finally it was dawn.
He was soaked with dew, and hungry,
    On the hill of Babylon.

The yellow sun was ugly,
    Like a raw egg on a plate—
Slick from the sea. He cursed it,
    For he knew it sealed his fate.

He saw the long white beaches
    And people going to swim,
With towels and beach umbrellas,
    But the soldiers were after him.

Far, far below, the people
    Were little colored spots,
And the heads of those in swimming
    Were floating coconuts.

He heard the peanut vendor
    Go *peep-peep* on his whistle,
And the man that sells umbrellas
    Swinging his watchman's rattle.

Women with market baskets
    Stood on the corners and talked,
Then went on their way to market,
    Gazing up as they walked.

The rich with their binoculars
    Were back again, and many
Were standing on the rooftops,
    Among TV antennae.

It was early, eight or eight-thirty.
    He saw a soldier climb,

Looking right at him. He fired,
    And missed for the last time.

He could hear the soldier panting,
    Though he never got very near.
Micuçú dashed for shelter.
    But he got it, behind the ear.

He heard the babies crying
    Far, far away in his head,
And the mongrels barking and barking.
    Then Micuçú was dead.

He had a Taurus revolver,
    And just the clothes he had on,
With two contos in the pockets,
    On the hill of Babylon.

The police and the populace
    Heaved a sigh of relief,
But behind the counter his auntie
    Wiped her eyes in grief.

"We have always been respected.
    My shop is honest and clean.
I loved him, but from a baby
    Micuçú was always mean.

"We have always been respected.
    His sister has a job.
Both of us gave him money.
    Why did he have to rob?

"I raised him to be honest,
    Even here, in Babylon slum."
The customers had another,
    Looking serious and glum.

But one of them said to another,
    When he got outside the door,
"He wasn't much of a burglar,
    He got caught six times—or more."

This morning the little soldiers
    Are on Babylon hill again;
Their gun barrels and helmets
    Shine in a gentle rain.

Micuçú is buried already.
    They're after another two,
But they say they aren't as dangerous
    As the poor Micuçú.

On the fair green hills of Rio
    There grows a fearful stain:
The poor who come to Rio
    And can't go home again.

There's the hill of Kerosene,
    And the hill of the Skeleton,
The hill of Astonishment,
    And the hill of Babylon.

CHEMIN DE FER

Alone on the railroad track
    I walked with pounding heart.
The ties were too close together
    or maybe too far apart.

The scenery was impoverished:
    scrub-pine and oak; beyond

its mingled gray-green foliage
    I saw the little pond

where the dirty hermit lives,
    lie like an old tear
holding onto its injuries
    lucidly year after year.

The hermit shot off his shot-gun
    and the tree by his cabin shook.
Over the pond went a ripple
    The pet hen went chook-chook.

"Love should be put into action!"
    screamed the old hermit.
Across the pond an echo
    tried and tried to confirm it.

Robert Bridges
(1844–1930)

LOW BAROMETER

The south-wind strengthens to a gale,
Across the moon the clouds fly fast,
The house is smitten as with a flail,
The chimney shudders to the blast.

On such a night, when Air has loosed
Its guardian grasp on blood and brain,
Old terrors then of god or ghost
Creep from their caves to life again;

And Reason kens he herits in
A haunted house. Tenants unknown
Assert their squalid lease of sin
With earlier title than his own.

Unbodied presences, the pack'd
Pollution and remorse of Time,
Slipp'd from oblivion reënact
The horrors of unhouseld crime.

Some men would quell the thing with prayer
Whose sightless footsteps pad the floor,
Whose fearful trespass mounts the stair
Or bursts the lock'd forbidden door.

Some have seen corpses long interr'd
Escape from hallowing control,

Pale charnel forms—nay ev'n have heard
The shrilling of a troubled soul,

That wanders till the dawn hath cross'd
The dolorous dark, or Earth hath wound
Closer her storm-spredd cloke, and thrust
The baleful phantoms underground.

Robert Burns

(1759–1796)

Green Grow the Rashes, O

Chorus
> Green grow the rashes, O;
> Green grow the rashes, O;
> The sweetest hours that e'er I spend,
> Are spent among the lasses, O.

I
> There's nought but care on ev'ry han',
> In every hour that passes, O:
> What signifies the life o' man,
> An't were nae for the lasses, O.

II
> The war'ly race may riches chase,
> An' riches still may fly them, O;
> An' tho' at last they catch them fast,
> Their hearts can ne'er enjoy them, O.

III
> But gie me a cannie hour at e'en,
> My arms about my dearie, O,
> An' war'ly cares an' war'ly men
> May a' gae tapsalteerie, O!

IV
> For you sae donce, ye sneer at this;
> Ye're nought but senseless asses, O;

The wisest man the warl' e'er saw,
    He dearly lov'd the lasses, O.

V

Auld Nature swears, the lovely dears
    Her noblest work she classes, O:
Her prentice han' she try'd on man,
    An' then she made the lasses, O.

Chorus

Green grow the rashes, O;
    Green grow the rashes, O;
The sweetest hours that e'er I spend,
    Are spent among the lasses, O.

Lewis Carroll

(1832–1898)

JABBERWOCKY

'Twas brillig, and the slithy toves
    Did gyre and gimble in the wabe:
All mimsy were the borogoves,
    And the mome raths outgrabe.

"Beware the Jabberwock, my son!
    The jaws that bite, the claws that catch!
Beware the Jubjub bird, and shun
    The frumious Bandersnatch!"

He took his vorpal sword in hand:
    Long time the manxome foe he sought—
So rested he by the Tumtum tree,
    And stood awhile in thought.

And, as in uffish thought he stood,
    The Jabberwock, with eyes of flame,
Came whiffling through the tulgey wood,
    And burbled as it came!

One, two! One, two! And through and through
    The vorpal blade went snicker-snack!
He left it dead, and with its head
    He went galumphing back.

"And hast thou slain the Jabberwock?
    Come to my arms, my beamish boy!

O frabjous day! Callooh! Callay!"
    He chortled in his joy.

'Twas brillig, and the slithy toves
    Did gyre and gimble in the wabe:
All mimsy were the borogoves,
    And the mome raths outgrabe.

William Cowper

(1731–1800)

Epitaph on a Hare

Here lies, whom hound did ne'er pursue,
    Nor swifter greyhound follow,
Whose foot ne'er tainted morning dew,
    Nor ear heard huntsman's hallo',

Old Tiney, surliest of his kind,
    Who, nursed with tender care,
And to domestic bounds confined,
    Was still a wild jack-hare.

Though duly from my hand he took
    His pittance every night,
He did it with a jealous look,
    And, when he could, would bite.

His diet was of wheaten bread,
    And milk, and oats, and straw,
Thistles, or lettuces instead,
    With sand to scour his maw.

On twigs of hawthorn he regaled,
    On pippins' russet peel;
And, when his juicy salads failed,
    Sliced carrot pleased him well.

A Turkey carpet was his lawn,
    Whereon he loved to bound,

To skip and gambol like a fawn,
    And swing his rump around.

His frisking was at evening hours,
    For then he lost his fear;
But most before approaching showers,
    Or when a storm drew near.

Eight years and five round-rolling moons
    He thus saw steal away,
Dozing out all his idle noons,
    And every night at play.

I kept him for his humor's sake,
    For he would oft beguile
My heart of thoughts that made it ache,
    And force me to a smile.

But now, beneath this walnut-shade
    He finds his long, last home,
And waits in snug concealment laid,
    Till gentler Puss shall come.

He, still more aged, feels the shocks
    From which no care can save,
And, partner once of Tiney's box,
    Must soon partake his grave.

Robert Creeley
(1926–2005)

IF YOU

If you were going to get a pet
what kind of animal would you get.

A soft bodied dog, a hen—
feathers and fur to begin it again.

When the sun goes down and it gets dark
I saw an animal in a park.

Bring it home, to give it to you.
I have seen animals break in two.

You were hoping for something soft
and loyal and clean and wondrously careful—

a form of otherwise vicious habit
can have long ears and be called a rabbit.

Dead. Died. Will die. Want.
Morning, midnight. I asked you

if you were going to get a pet
what kind of animal would you get.

Walter de la Mare

(1873–1956)

BUNCHES OF GRAPES

"Bunches of grapes," says Timothy;
"Pomegranates pink," says Elaine;
"A junket of cream and a cranberry tart
    For me," says Jane.

"Love-in-a-mist," says Timothy;
"Primroses pale," says Elaine;
"A nosegay of pinks and mignonette
    For me," says Jane.

"Chariots of gold," says Timothy;
"Silvery wings," says Elaine;
"A bumpity ride in a wagon of hay
    For me," says Jane.

Queen Elizabeth I

(1533–1603)

WHEN I WAS FAIR AND YOUNG

When I was fair and young, and favor gracéd me,
Of many was I sought, their mistress for to be;
But I did scorn them all, and answered them therefore,
    "Go, go, go seek some otherwhere!
      Importune me no more!"

How many weeping eyes I made to pine with woe,
How many sighing hearts, I have no skill to show;
Yet I the prouder grew, and answered them therefore,
    "Go, go, go seek some otherwhere!
      Importune me no more!"

Then spake fair Venus' son, that proud victorious boy,
And said, "Fine dame, since that you be so coy,
I will so pluck your plumes that you shall say no more,
    'Go, go, go seek some otherwhere!
      Importune me no more!'"

When he had spake these words, such change grew in my breast
That neither night nor day since that, I could take any rest.
Then lo! I did repent that I had said before,
    "Go, go, go seek some otherwhere!
      Importune me no more!"

Ralph Waldo Emerson

(1803–1882)

Concord Hymn

SUNG AT THE COMPLETION OF
THE BATTLE MONUMENT, JULY 4, 1837

By the rude bridge that arched the flood,
  Their flag to April's breeze unfurled,
Here once the embattled farmers stood
  And fired the shot heard round the world.

The foe long since in silence slept;
  Alike the conqueror silent sleeps;
And Time the ruined bridge has swept
  Down the dark stream which seaward creeps.

On this green bank, by this soft stream,
  We set to-day a votive stone;
That memory may their deed redeem,
  When, like our sires, our sons are gone.

Spirit, that made those heroes dare
  To die, and leave their children free,
Bid Time and Nature gently spare
  The shaft we raise to them and thee.

George Gascoigne

(1539–1577)

THE LULLABY OF A LOVER

Sing lullaby, as women do,
Wherewith they bring their babes to rest,
And lullaby can I sing too
As womanly as can the best.
With lullaby they still the child,
And if I be not much beguiled,
Full many wanton babes have I
Which must be stilled with lullaby.

First, lullaby my youthful years,
It is now time to go to bed,
For crooked age and hoary hairs
Have won the haven within my head;
With lullaby, then, youth be still,
With lullaby, content thy will,
Since courage quails and comes behind,
Go sleep, and so beguile thy mind.

Next, lullaby my gazing eyes,
Which wonted were to glance apace,
For every glass may now suffice
To shew the furrows in my face;
With lullaby, then, wink awhile,
With lullaby, your looks beguile,
Let no fair face nor beauty bright
Entice you eft with vain delight.

And lullaby, my wanton will,
Let reason's rule now reign thy thought,
Since all too late I find by skill
How dear I have thy fancies bought;
With lullaby, now take thine ease,
With lullaby, thy doubts appease;
For trust to this, if thou be still,
My body shall obey thy will.

Eke, lullaby my loving boy,
My little Robin, take thy rest;
Since age is cold and nothing coy,
Keep close thy coin, for so is best;
With lullaby, be thou content,
With lullaby, thy lusts relent;
Let others pay which have mo pence,
Thou art too poor for such expense.

Thus lullaby, my youth, mine eyes,
My will, my ware, and all that was!
I can no mo delays devise,
But welcome pain, let pleasure pass;
With lullaby, now take your leave,
With lullaby, your dreams deceive,
And when you rise with waking eye,
Remember, then, this lullaby.
                    Ever or Never

Thomas Hardy

(1840–1928)

The Darkling Thrush

I leant upon a coppice gate
    When Frost was spectre-gray,
And Winter's dregs made desolate
    The weakening eye of day.
The tangled bine-stems scored the sky
    Like strings of broken lyres,
And all mankind that haunted nigh
    Had sought their household fires.

The land's sharp features seemed to be
    The Century's corpse outleant,
His crypt the cloudy canopy,
    The wind his death-lament.
The ancient pulse of germ and birth
    Was shrunken hard and dry,
And every spirit upon earth
    Seemed fervourless as I.

At once a voice arose among
    The bleak twigs overhead
In a full-hearted evensong
    Of joy illimited;
An aged thrush, frail, gaunt, and small,
    In blast-beruffled plume,
Had chosen thus to fling his soul
    Upon the growing gloom.

So little cause for carolings
    Of such ecstatic sound
Was written on terrestrial things
    Afar or nigh around,
That I could think there trembled through
    His happy good-night air
Some blessed Hope, whereof he knew
    And I was unaware.

THE OXEN

Christmas Eve, and twelve of the clock.
    "Now they are all on their knees,"
An elder said as we sat in a flock
    By the embers in hearthside ease.

We pictured the meek mild creatures where
    They dwelt in their strawy pen,
Nor did it occur to one of us there
    To doubt they were kneeling then.

So fair a fancy few would weave
    In these years! Yet, I feel,
If someone said on Christmas Eve,
    "Come; see the oxen kneel,

"In the lonely barton by yonder coomb
    Our childhood used to know,"
I should go with him in the gloom,
    Hoping it might be so.

W. E. Henley

(1849–1903)

INVICTUS

Out of the night that covers me,
   Black as the Pit from pole to pole,
I thank whatever gods may be
   For my unconquerable soul.

In the fell clutch of circumstance
   I have not winced nor cried aloud.
Under the bludgeonings of chance
   My head is bloody, but unbowed.

Beyond this place of wrath and tears
   Looms but the Horror of the shade,
And yet the menace of the years
   Finds, and shall find, me unafraid.

It matters not how strait the gate,
   How charged with punishments the scroll,
I am the master of my fate;
   I am the captain of my soul.

Julia Ward Howe

(1819–1910)

Battle-Hymn of the Republic

Mine eyes have seen the glory of the coming of the Lord:
He is trampling out the vintage where the grapes of wrath are stored;
He hath loosed the fateful lightning of his terrible swift sword:
    His truth is marching on.

I have seen Him in the watch-fires of a hundred circling camps;
They have builded Him an altar in the evening dews and damps;
I can read His righteous sentence by the dim and flaring lamps.
    His day is marching on.

I have read a fiery gospel, writ in burnished rows of steel:
"As ye deal with my contemners, so with you my grace shall deal;
Let the Hero, born of woman, crush the serpent with his heel,
    Since God is marching on."

He has sounded forth the trumpet that shall never call retreat;
He is sifting out the hearts of men before his judgment-seat:
Oh! be swift, my soul, to answer Him! be jubilant, my feet!
    Our God is marching on.

In the beauty of the lilies Christ was born across the sea,
With a glory in his bosom that transfigures you and me:
As he died to make men holy, let us die to make men free,
    While God is marching on.

Attila József

translated by John Batki

(1905–1937)

THE SEVENTH

If you set out in this world,
better be born seven times.
Once, in a house on fire,
once, in a freezing flood,
once, in a wild madhouse,
once, in a field of ripe wheat,
once, in an empty cloister,
and once among pigs in a sty.
Six babes crying, not enough:
you yourself must be the seventh.

When you must fight to survive,
let your enemy see seven.
One, away from work on Sunday,
one, starting his work on Monday,
one, who teaches without payment,
one, who learned to swim by drowning,
one, who is the seed of a forest,
and one, whom wild forefathers protect,
but all their tricks are not enough:
you yourself must be the seventh.

If you want to find a woman,
let seven men go for her.
One, who gives his heart for words,

one, who takes care of himself,
one, who claims to be a dreamer,
one, who through her skirt can feel her,
one, who knows the hooks and snaps,
one, who steps upon her scarf:
let them buzz like flies around her.
You yourself must be the seventh.

If you write and can afford it,
let seven men write your poem.
One, who builds a marble village,
one, who was born in his sleep,
one, who charts the sky and knows it,
one, whom words call by his name,
one, who perfected his soul,
one, who dissects living rats.
Two are brave and four are wise;
you yourself must be the seventh.

And if all went as was written,
you will die for seven men.
One, who is rocked and suckled,
one, who grabs a hard young breast,
one, who throws down empty dishes,
one, who helps the poor to win,
one, who works till he goes to pieces,
one, who just stares at the moon.
The world will be your tombstone:
you yourself must be the seventh.

J. D. McClatchy
(b. 1945)

FADO

Suppose my heart had broken
Out of its cage of bone,
Its heaving grille of rumors—
    My metronome,

My honeycomb and crypt
Of jealousies long since
Preyed on, played out,
    My spoiled prince.

Suppose then I could hold it
Out towards you, could feel
Its growling hound of blood
    Brought to heel,

Its scarred skin grown taut
With anticipating your touch,
The tentative caress
    Or sudden clutch.

Suppose you could watch it burn,
A jagged crown of flames
Above the empty rooms
    Where counterclaims

Of air and anger feed
The fire's quickening flush

And into whose remorse
    Excuses rush.

Would you then stretch your hand
To take my scalding gift?
And would you kiss the blackened
    Hypocrite?

It's yours, it's yours—this gift,
This grievance embedded in each,
Where time will never matter
    And words can't reach.

Marilyn Nelson

(b. 1946)

The Ballad of Aunt Geneva

Geneva was the wild one.
Geneva was a tart.
Geneva met a blue-eyed boy
and gave away her heart.

Geneva ran a roadhouse.
Geneva wasn't sent
to college like the others:
Pomp's pride her punishment.

She cooked out on the river,
watching the shore slide by,
her lips pursed into hardness,
her deep-set brown eyes dry.

They say she killed a woman
over a good black man
by braining the jealous heifer
with an iron frying pan.

They say, when she was eighty,
she got up late at night
and sneaked her old, white lover in
to make love, and to fight.

First, they heard the tell-tale
singing of the springs,

then Geneva's voice rang out:
I need to buy some things,

So next time, bring more money.
And bring more moxie, too.
I ain't got no time to waste
on limp white mens like you.

Oh yeah? Well, Mister White Man,
it sure might be stone-white,
but my thing's white as it is.
And you know damn well I'm right.

Now listen: take your heart pills
and pay the doctor mind.
If you up and die on me,
I'll whip your white behind.

They tiptoed through the parlor
on heavy, time-slowed feet.
She watched him, from her front door,
walk down the dawnlit street.

Geneva was the wild one.
Geneva was a tart.
Geneva met a blue-eyed boy
and gave away her heart.

Michael Palmer

(b. 1943)

THE VILLAGE OF REASON

This is a glove
or a book from a book club

This is the sun
or a layer of mud

This is Monday,
this an altered word

This is the village of reason
and this an eye torn out

This is the father
or a number on a chart

This is a substitute,
this the thing you are

This is the varnished picture
or else an accepted response

This is the door
and this the word for door

This is a reflex caused by falling
and this a prisoner with an orange

This is a name you know
and this is the poison to make you well

This is the mechanism
and this the shadow of a bridge

This is a curve
and this its thirst

This is Monday,
this her damaged word

This is the trace
and this the term unmarked

This is the sonnet
and this its burning house

You are in this play
You are its landscape

This is an assumption
the length of an arm

This is a poppy,
this an epilogue

Robert Pinsky
(b. 1940)

SAMURAI SONG

When I had no roof I made
Audacity my roof. When I had
No supper my eyes dined.

When I had no eyes I listened.
When I had no ears I thought.
When I had no thought I waited.

When I had no father I made
Care my father. When I had
No mother I embraced order.

When I had no friend I made
Quiet my friend. When I had no
Enemy I opposed my body.

When I had no temple I made
My voice my temple. I have
No priest, my tongue is my choir.

When I have no means fortune
Is my means. When I have
Nothing, death will be my fortune.

Need is my tactic, detachment
Is my strategy. When I had
No lover I courted my sleep.

Sir Walter Raleigh

(1554–1618)

NATURE, THAT WASHED HER HANDS IN MILK

Nature, that washed her hands in milk,
    And had forgot to dry them,
Instead of earth took snow and silk,
    At Love's request to try them,
If she a mistress could compose
To please Love's fancy out of those.

Her eyes he would should be of light,
    A violet breath, and lips of jelly;
Her hair not black, nor overbright,
    And of the softest down her belly;
As for her inside he'd have it
Only of wantonness and wit.

At Love's entreaty such a one
    Nature made, but with her beauty
She hath framed a heart of stone;
    So as Love, by ill destiny,
Must die for her whom Nature gave him,
Because her darling would not save him.

But Time (which Nature doth despise,
    And rudely gives her love the lie,
Makes Hope a fool, and Sorrow wise)
    His hands do neither wash nor dry;
But being made of steel and rust,
Turns snow and silk and milk to dust.

The light, the belly, lips, and breath,
    He dims, discolors, and destroys;
With those he feeds but fills not death,
    Which sometimes were the food of joys.
Yea, Time doth dull each lively wit,
And dries all wantonness with it.

Oh, cruel Time! which takes in trust
    Our youth, our joys, and all we have,
And pays us but with age and dust;
    Who in the dark and silent grave
When we have wandered all our ways
Shuts up the story of our days.

Edwin Arlington Robinson

(1869–1935)

EROS TURANNOS

She fears him, and will always ask
    What fated her to choose him;
She meets in his engaging mask
    All reasons to refuse him;
But what she meets and what she fears
Are less than are the downward years,
Drawn slowly to the foamless weirs
    Of age, were she to lose him.

Between a blurred sagacity
    That once had power to sound him,
And Love, that will not let him be
    The Judas that she found him,
Her pride assuages her almost,
As if it were alone the cost.—
He sees that he will not be lost,
    And waits and looks around him.

A sense of ocean and old trees
    Envelops and allures him;
Tradition, touching all he sees,
    Beguiles and reassures him;
And all her doubts of what he says
Are dimmed with what she knows of days—
Till even prejudice delays
    And fades, and she secures him.

The falling leaf inaugurates
    The reign of her confusion;
The pounding wave reverberates
    The dirge of her illusion;
And home, where passion lived and died,
Becomes a place where she can hide,
While all the town and harbor side
    Vibrate with her seclusion.

We tell you, tapping on our brows,
    The story as it should be,—
As if the story of a house
    Were told, or ever could be;
We'll have no kindly veil between
Her visions and those we have seen,—
As if we guessed what hers have been,
    Or what they are or would be.

Meanwhile we do no harm; for they
    That with a god have striven,
Not hearing much of what we say,
    Take what the god has given;
Though like waves breaking it may be,
Or like a changed familiar tree,
Or like a stairway to the sea
    Where down the blind are driven.

MINIVER CHEEVY

Miniver Cheevy, child of scorn,
    Grew lean while he assailed the seasons;
He wept that he was ever born,
    And he had reasons.

Miniver loved the days of old
    When swords were bright and steeds were prancing;
The vision of a warrior bold
    Would set him dancing.

Miniver sighed for what was not,
    And dreamed, and rested from his labors;
He dreamed of Thebes and Camelot,
    And Priam's neighbors.

Miniver mourned the ripe renown
    That made so many a name so fragrant;
He mourned Romance, now on the town,
    And Art, a vagrant.

Miniver loved the Medici,
    Albeit he had never seen one;
He would have sinned incessantly
    Could he have been one.

Miniver cursed the commonplace
    And eyed a khaki suit with loathing;
He missed the mediæval grace
    Of iron clothing.

Miniver scorned the gold he sought,
    But sore annoyed was he without it;
Miniver thought, and thought, and thought,
    And thought about it.

Miniver Cheevy, born too late,
    Scratched his head and kept on thinking;
Miniver coughed, and called it fate,
    And kept on drinking.

Christina Rossetti
(1830–1894)

SONG

When I am dead, my dearest,
   Sing no sad songs for me;
Plant thou no roses at my head,
   Nor shady cypress tree:
Be the green grass above me
   With showers and dewdrops wet:
And if thou wilt, remember,
   And if thou wilt, forget.

I shall not see the shadows,
   I shall not feel the rain;
I shall not hear the nightingale
   Sing on as if in pain:
And dreaming through the twilight
   That doth not rise nor set,
Haply I may remember,
   And haply may forget.

UP-HILL

Does the road wind up-hill all the way?
   Yes, to the very end.
Will the day's journey take the whole long day?
   From morn to night, my friend.

But is there for the night a resting-place?
    A roof for when the slow dark hours begin.
May not the darkness hide it from my face?
    You cannot miss that inn.

Shall I meet other wayfarers at night?
    Those who have gone before.
Then must I knock, or call when just in sight?
    They will not keep you standing at that door.

Shall I find comfort, travel-sore and weak?
    Of labour you shall find the sum.
Will there be beds for me and all who seek?
    Yea, beds for all who come.

William Shakespeare

(1564–1616)

When that I was and a little tiny boy

When that I was and a little tiny boy,
    With hey, ho, the wind and the rain,
A foolish thing was but a toy,
    For the rain it raineth every day.

But when I came to man's estate,
    With hey, ho, the wind and the rain,
'Gainst knaves and thieves men shut their gate,
    For the rain it raineth every day.

But when I came, alas! to wive,
    With hey, ho, the wind and the rain,
By swaggering could I never thrive,
    For the rain it raineth every day.

But when I came unto my beds,
    With hey, ho, the wind and the rain,
With tosspots still had drunken heads,
    For the rain it raineth every day.

A great while ago the world begun,
    With hey, ho, the wind and the rain,
But that's all one, our play is done,
    And we'll strive to please you every day.

Charles Simic

(b. 1938)

BALLAD

What's that approaching like dusk like poverty
A little girl picking flowers in a forest
The migrant's fire of her long hair
Harm's way she comes and also the smile's round about way

In another life in another life
Aunt rain sewing orphan's buttons to each stone
Solitude's stitch
Let your horns out little stone

Screendoor screeching in the wind
Mother-hobble-gobble baking apples
Wooden spoons dancing ah the idyllic life of wooden spoons
I need a table to spread these memories on

Little girl fishing using me as bait
Me a gloomy woodcutter in the forest of words
I am going to say one thing and mean another
I'll tuck you in a matchbox like a hornet

In another life in another life
Dandelion and red poppy grow in the back yard
Shoes in the rain bark at the milkman
Little girl alone playing blindman's buff

The words want to bring back more—
You are *it* she says laughing and is gone

Divination by one's own heartbeat
Draw near to what doesn't say yes or no

And she had nothing under her dress
Star like an eye the gamecocks have overlooked
Tune up your fingers and whistle
On a trail lined with elms she hides herself behind a tree

I tread the sod you walked on with kindness
Not even the wind blew to remind me of time
Approaches that which they insist on calling happiness
The nightbird says its name

On a tripod made of limbs hoist this vision
At eveningtime when they examine you in love
Glancing back on the road long as sleep
Little girl skipping the owl's hushed way.

Alfred Tennyson

(1809–1892)

SONG FROM THE PRINCESS
(THE SPLENDOUR FALLS)

IV

The splendour falls on castle walls
    And snowy summits old in story:
The long light shakes across the lakes,
    And the wild cataract leaps in glory.
Blow, bugle, blow, set the wild echoes flying,
Blow, bugle; answer, echoes, dying, dying, dying.

O hark, O hear! how thin and clear,
    And thinner, clearer, farther going!
O sweet and far from cliff and scaur
    The horns of Elfland faintly blowing!
Blow, let us hear the purple glens replying:
Blow, bugle; answer, echoes, dying, dying, dying.

O love, they die in yon rich sky,
    They faint on hill or field or river:
Our echoes roll from soul to soul,
    And grow for ever and for ever.
Blow, bugle, blow, set the wild echoes flying,
And answer, echoes, answer, dying, dying, dying.

William Wordsworth

(1770–1850)

A Slumber Did My Spirit Seal

A slumber did my spirit seal;
    I had no human fears:
She seemed a thing that could not feel
    The touch of earthly years.

No motion has she now, no force;
    She neither hears nor sees;
Rolled round in earth's diurnal course,
    With rocks, and stones, and trees.

Thomas Wyatt

(1503–1542)

BLAME NOT MY LUTE

Blame not my lute, for he must sound
    Of these or that as liketh me;
For lack of wit the lute is bound
    To give such tunes as pleaseth me.
Though my songs be somewhat strange,
And speaks such words as touch thy change,
      Blame not my lute.

My lute, alas, doth not offend,
    Though that perforce he must agree
To sound such tunes as I intend
    To sing to them that heareth me;
Then though my songs be somewhat plain,
And toucheth some that use to feign,
      Blame not my lute.

My lute and strings may not deny,
    But as I strike they must obey;
Break not them then so wrongfully,
    But wreak thyself some wiser way;
And though the songs which I indite
Do quit thy change with rightful spite,
      Blame not my lute.

Spite asketh spite, and changing change,
    And falsèd faith must needs be known;
The fault so great, the case so strange,
    Of right it must abroad be blown;

Then since that by thine own desert
My songs do tell how true thou art,
  Blame not my lute.

Blame but the self that hast misdone
 And well deservëd to have blame;
Change thou thy way, so evil begone,
 And then my lute shall sound that same;
But if till then my fingers play
By thy desert their wonted way,
  Blame not my lute.

Farewell, unknown! for though thou break
 My strings in spite with great disdain,
Yet have I found out, for thy sake,
 Strings for to string my lute again.
And if, perchance, this foolish rime
Do make thee blush at any time,
  Blame not my lute.

IV

LOVE POEMS

A COMPELLING LOVE poem tells us something not only about love but also about the mind: how imagination or intellect or memory devises ways to make the familiar seem fresh and rediscovered:

HER TRIUMPH

I did the dragon's will until you came
Because I had fancied love a casual
Improvisation, or a settled game
That followed if I let the kerchief fall:
Those deeds were best that gave the minute wings
And heavenly music if they gave it wit;
And then you stood among the dragon-rings.
I mocked, being crazy, but you mastered it
And broke the chain and set my ankles free,
Saint George or else a pagan Perseus;
And now we stare astonished at the sea,
And a miraculous strange bird shrieks at us.

William Butler Yeats writes this poem (p. 237) in his sequence "A Woman Young and Old" on a theme treated countless times in songs, plays, movies, poems: I took love lightly until you came along. That standard sentiment is made mysterious and awesome anew by imagination: the "dragon's will" associated with the old, superficial days of imprisonment by a trivial notion of love and the "miraculous strange bird" of the new, liberated, and astonished time of discovery. The harsh or challenging quality of "shrieks" is part of that freshness.

In a similar way—regarding a quite different sort of love, in a quite different idiom—Paul Laurence Dunbar in "Little Brown Baby" (p. 191) calls up the fearsome nature of love: not only by affectionately teasing the child into a hug, but also by evoking fears for the child, a universe of loss implied by wishing the child could "stay jes' a chile." The dialect gives cultural and historical specificity to general or universal fear for a child's future: the context of race, affecting the innocence of the line that begins and ends the poem. The second stanza begins a transition, in its last two lines:

> Little brown baby wif spa'klin' eyes,
>> Who's pappy's darlin' an' who's pappy's chile?
> Who is it all de day nevah once tries
>> Fu' to be cross, er once loses dat smile?
> Whah did you git dem teef? My, you's a scamp!
>> Whah did dat dimple come f'om in yo' chin?
> Pappy do' know you—I b'lieves you's a tramp;
>> Mammy, dis hyeah's some ol' straggler got in!

Then the teasing becomes more elaborate, before it devolves into a new pitch of affection:

> Let's th'ow him outen de do' in de san',
>> We do' want stragglers a-layin' 'roun' hyeah;
> Let's gin him 'way to de big buggah-man;
>> I know he's hid in' erroun' hyeah right neah.
> Buggah-man, buggah-man, come in de do',
>> Hyeah's a bad boy you kin have fu' to eat.
> Mammy an' pappy do' want him no mo',
>> Swaller him down f'om his haid to his feet!

> Dah, now, I t'ought dat you'd hug me up close.
>> Go back, ol' buggah, you sha'n't have dis boy.

He ain't no tramp, ner no straggler, of co'se;
    He's pappy's pa'dner an' playmate an' joy.
Come to you' pallet now—go to yo' res';
    Wisht you could allus know ease an' cleah skies;
Wisht you could stay jes' a chile on my breas'—
    Little brown baby wif spa'klin' eyes!

The element of diversion or entertainment (along with the aggression) is part of the love-poem tradition: the child who curls into a parental embrace, like the lover who is hailed as a "pagan Perseus," understands that these mock-aggressive words resemble a present: a flattering display and a compliment.

As often as not, the compliment is paradoxical or oblique. Alan Dugan explains that he cannot crucify himself without a helpmeet (p. 189). Michael Drayton assumes that the one he loves and courts is clever and sophisticated enough to understand that his elaborate, hyperbolic insult (p. 187) is a showy, complimentary form of wooing. (The sight of the mythical basilisk was said to turn the viewer to stone; the cockatrice blinded the viewer.):

THREE SORTS OF SERPENTS DO RESEMBLE THEE

Three sorts of serpents do resemble thee:
That dangerous eye-killing cockatrice,
The enchanting siren, which doth so entice,
The weeping crocodile—these vile pernicious three.
The basilisk his nature takes from thee,
Who for my life in secret wait dost lie,
And to my heart sendst poison from thine eye:
Thus do I feel the pain, the cause, yet cannot see.
Fair-maid no more, but Mer-maid be thy name,
Who with thy sweet alluring harmony
Hast played the thief, and stolen my heart from me,
And like a tyrant makst my grief thy game:
    Thou crocodile, who when thou hast me slain,
    Lamentst my death, with tears of thy disdain.

The myth-making of dragons, the familial teasing of the "ol'straggler" and "buggah-man," the deadpan, courtly enumeration of monsters: in all three examples, the inward energy of love finds expression in the outward energy of invention: eloquence as courtship. Such similarities among a variety of large differences suggest the way that "love poem" denotes a form, as well as a subject.

Anna Akhmatova

translated by Jane Kenyon

(1889–1966)

N.V.N.

There is a sacred, secret line in loving
which attraction and even passion cannot cross,—
even if lips draw near in awful silence
and love tears at the heart.

Friendship is weak and useless here,
and years of happiness, exalted and full of fire,
because the soul is free and does not know
the slow luxuries of sensual life.

Those who try to come near it are insane
and those who reach it are shaken by grief.
So now you know exactly why
my heart beats no faster under your hand.

Matthew Arnold

(1822–1888)

DOVER BEACH

The sea is calm tonight.
The tide is full, the moon lies fair
Upon the straits—on the French coast the light
Gleams and is gone; the cliffs of England stand,
Glimmering and vast, out in the tranquil bay.
Come to the window, sweet is the night air!
Only, from the long line of spray
Where the sea meets the moon-blanched land,
Listen! you hear the grating roar
Of pebbles which the waves draw back, and fling,
At their return, up the high strand,
Begin, and cease, and then again begin,
With tremulous cadence slow, and bring
The eternal note of sadness in.

Sophocles long ago
Heard it on the Aegean, and it brought
Into his mind the turbid ebb and flow
Of human misery; we
Find also in the sound a thought,
Hearing it by this distant northern sea.

The Sea of Faith
Was once, too, at the full, and round earth's shore
Lay like the folds of a bright girdle furled.
But now I only hear
Its melancholy, long, withdrawing roar,

Retreating, to the breath
Of the night wind, down the vast edges drear
And naked shingles of the world.

Ah, love, let us be true
To one another! for the world, which seems
To lie before us like a land of dreams,
So various, so beautiful, so new,
Hath really neither joy, nor love, nor light,
Nor certitude, nor peace, nor help for pain;
And we are here as on a darkling plain
Swept with confused alarms of struggle and flight,
Where ignorant armies clash by night.

Margaret Atwood

(b. 1939)

VARIATION ON THE WORD *SLEEP*

I would like to watch you sleeping,
which may not happen.
I would like to watch you,
sleeping. I would like to sleep
with you, to enter
your sleep as its smooth dark wave
slides over my head

and walk with you through that lucent
wavering forest of bluegreen leaves
with its watery sun & three moons
towards the cave where you must descend,
towards your worst fear

I would like to give you the silver
branch, the small white flower, the one
word that will protect you
from the grief at the center
of your dream, from the grief
at the center. I would like to follow
you up the long stairway
again & become
the boat that would row you back
carefully, a flame
in two cupped hands
to where your body lies

beside me, and you enter
it as easily as breathing in

I would like to be the air
that inhabits you for a moment
only. I would like to be that unnoticed
& that necessary.

Frank Bidart

(b. 1939)

THE YOKE

don't worry   I know you're dead
but tonight

turn your face again
toward me

when I hear your voice there is now
no direction in which to turn

I sleep and wake and sleep and wake and sleep and wake and

but tonight
turn your face again

toward me

see   upon my shoulders is the yoke
that is not a yoke

don't worry   I know you're dead
but tonight

turn your face again

Eavan Boland

(b. 1944)

A Marriage for the Millennium

Do you believe
that Progress is a woman?
A spirit seeking for its opposite?
For a true marriage to ease her quick heartbeat?

I asked you this
as you sat with your glass of red wine
and your newspaper of yesterday's events.
You were drinking and reading, and did not hear me.

Then I closed the door
and left the house behind me and began
driving the whole distance of our marriage,
away from the suburb towards the city.

One by one
the glowing windows went out.
Television screens cooled down more slowly.
Ceramic turned to glass, circuits to transistors.

Old rowans were saplings.
Roads were no longer wide.
Children disappeared from their beds.
Wives, without warning, suddenly became children.

Computer games became codes again.
The codes were folded

back into the futures of their makers.
Their makers woke from sleep, weeping for milk.

When I came to the street we once lived on
with its iron edges out of another century
I stayed there only a few minutes.
Then I was in the car, driving again.

I was ready to tell you when I got home
that high above that street in a room
above the laid-out hedges and wild lilac
nothing had changed

them, nothing ever would:
The man with his creased copy of the newspaper.
Or the young woman talking to him. Talking to him.
Her heart eased by this.

Anne Bradstreet

(1612–1672)

To my Dear and loving Husband

If ever two were one, then surely we.
If ever man were lov'd by wife, then thee;
If ever wife was happy in a man,
Compare with me ye women if you can.
I prize thy love more then whole Mines of gold,
Or all the riches that the East doth hold.
My love is such that Rivers cannot quench,
Nor ought but love from thee, give recompence.
Thy love is such I can no way repay,
The heavens reward thee manifold I pray.
Then while we live, in love lets so persever,
That when we live no more, we may live ever.

Robert Browning

(1812–1889)

A Serenade at the Villa

I

That was I, you heard last night,
    When there rose no moon at all,
Nor, to pierce the strained and tight
    Tent of heaven, a planet small:
Life was dead and so was light.

II

Not a twinkle from the fly,
    Not a glimmer from the worm;
When the crickets stopped their cry,
    When the owls forbore a term,
You heard music; that was I.

III

Earth turned in her sleep with pain,
    Sultrily suspired for proof:
In at heaven and out again,
    Lightning!—where it broke the roof,
Bloodlike, some few drops of rain.

IV

What they could my words expressed,
    O my love, my all, my one!
Singing helped the verses best,
    And when singing's best was done,
To my lute I left the rest.

V

So wore night; the East was grey,
   White the broad-faced hemlock-flowers:
There would be another day;
   Ere its first of heavy hours
Found me, I had passed away.

VI

What became of all the hopes,
   Words and song and lute as well?
Say, this struck you—"When life gropes
   Feebly for the path where fell
Light last on the evening slopes,

VII

"One friend in that path shall be,
   To secure my step from wrong;
One to count night day for me,
   Patient through the watches long,
Serving most with none to see."

VIII

Never say—as something bodes—
   "So, the worst has yet a worse!"
When life halts 'neath double loads,
   Better the taskmaster's curse
Than such music on the roads!

IX

"When no moon succeeds the sun,
   Nor can pierce the midnight's tent
Any star, the smallest one,
   While some drops, where lightning rent,
Show the final storm begun—

X

"When the fire-fly hides its spot,
    When the garden-voices fail
In the darkness thick and hot,—
    Shall another voice avail,
That shape be where these are not?

XI

"Has some plague a longer lease,
    Proffering its help uncouth?
Can't one even die in peace?
    As one shuts one's eyes on youth,
Is that face the last one sees?"

XII

Oh how dark your villa was,
    Windows fast and obdurate!
How the garden grudged me grass
    Where I stood—the iron gate
Ground its teeth to let me pass!

Thomas Campion

(1567–1620)

Follow Your Saint

Follow your Saint, follow with accents sweet,
Haste you, sad noates, fall at her flying feete;
There, wrapt in cloud of sorrowe, pitie move,
And tell the ravisher of my soule I perish for her love.
But if she scorns my never-ceasing paine,
Then burst with sighing in her sight, and nere returne againe.

All that I soong still to her praise did tend,
Still she was first, still she my songs did end.
Yet she my love and Musicke both doeth flie,
The Musicke that her Eccho is, and beauties simpathie;
Then let my Noates pursue her scornefull flight:
It shall suffice that they were breath'd, and dyed, for her
    delight.

Constantine Cavafy

translated by Rae Dalven

(1863–1933)

BODY, REMEMBER . . .

Body, remember not only how much you were loved,
not only the beds on which you lay,
but also those desires for you
that glowed plainly in the eyes,
and trembled in the voice—and some
chance obstacle made futile.
Now that all of them belong to the past,
it almost seems as if you had yielded
to those desires—how they glowed,
remember, in the eyes gazing at you;
how they trembled in the voice, for you, remember, body.

John Donne

(1572–1631)

A Valediction: forbidding Mourning

As virtuous men pass mildly away,
   And whisper to their souls, to go,
Whilst some of their sad friends do say,
   The breath goes now, and some say, no:

So let us melt, and make no noise,
   No tear-floods, nor sigh-tempests move,
'Twere profanation of our joys
   To tell the laity our love.

Moving of th' earth brings harms and fears,
   Men reckon what it did and meant,
But trepidation of the spheres,
   Though greater far, is innocent.

Dull sublunary lovers' love
   (Whose soul is sense) cannot admit
Absence, because it doth remove
   Those things which elemented it.

But we by a love, so much refined,
   That our selves know not what it is,
Inter-assured of the mind,
   Care less, eyes, lips, and hands to miss.

Our two souls therefore, which are one,
   Though I must go, endure not yet

A breach, but an expansion,
    Like gold to aery thinness beat.

If they be two, they are two so
    As stiff twin compasses are two,
Thy soul the fixed foot, makes no show
    To move, but doth, if th' other do.

And though it in the centre sit,
    Yet when the other far doth roam,
It leans, and hearkens after it,
    And grows erect, as that comes home.

Such wilt thou be to me, who must
    Like th' other foot, obliquely run;
Thy firmness makes my circle just,
    And makes me end, where I begun.

THE GOOD MORROW

I wonder by my troth, what thou, and I
    Did, till we loved? were we not weaned till then,
But sucked on country pleasures, childishly?
    Or snorted we in the seven sleepers' den?
'Twas so; but this, all pleasures fancies be.
If ever any beauty I did see,
Which I desired, and got, 'twas but a dream of thee.

And now good morrow to our waking souls,
    Which watch not one another out of fear;
For love, all love of other sights controls,
    And makes one little room, an every where.
Let sea-discoverers to new worlds have gone,
Let maps to others, worlds on worlds have shown,
Let us possess one world, each hath one, and is one.

My face in thine eye, thine in mine appears,
  And true plain hearts do in the faces rest,
Where can we find two better hemispheres
  Without sharp north, without declining west?
What ever dies, was not mixed equally;
If our two loves be one, or, thou and I
Love so alike, that none do slacken, none can die.

John Dowland

(1563–1626)

FINE KNACKS FOR LADIES

Fine knacks for ladies, cheap, choice, brave and new!
Good pennyworths! but money cannot move.
I keep a fair but for the fair to view;
A beggar may be liberal of love.
Though all my wares be trash, the heart is true.

Great gifts are guiles and look for gifts again;
My trifles come as treasures from my mind.
It is a precious jewel to be plain;
Sometimes in shell the Orient's pearls we find.
Of others take a sheaf, of me a grain.

Within this pack pins, points, laces, and gloves,
And divers toys fitting a country fair.
But in my heart, where duty serves and loves,
Turtles and twins, court's brood, a heavenly pair.
Happy the heart that thinks of no removes!

Michael Drayton

(1563–1631)

How many paltry, foolish, painted things

(SONNET 6)

How many paltry, foolish, painted things,
That now in coaches trouble every street,
Shall be forgotten, whom no poet sings,
Ere they be well wrapped in their winding sheet?
Where I to thee eternity shall give,
When nothing else remaineth of these days,
And queens hereafter shall be glad to live
Upon the alms of thy superfluous praise.
Virgins and matrons, reading these my rhymes,
Shall be so much delighted with thy story
That they shall grieve they lived not in these times
To have seen thee, their sex's only glory;
So shalt thou fly above the vulgar throng,
Still to survive in my immortal song.

Three sorts of serpents do resemble thee

Three sorts of serpents do resemble thee:
That dangerous eye-killing cockatrice,
The enchanting siren, which doth so entice,
The weeping crocodile—these vile pernicious three.
The basilisk his nature takes from thee,
Who for my life in secret wait dost lie,

And to my heart sendst poison from thine eye:
Thus do I feel the pain, the cause, yet cannot see.
Fair-maid no more, but Mer-maid be thy name,
Who with thy sweet alluring harmony
Hast played the thief and stolen my heart from me,
And like a tyrant makst my grief thy game:
    Thou crocodile, who when thou hast me slain,
    Lamentst my death, with tears of thy disdain.

Alan Dugan
(1923–2003)

LOVE SONG: I AND THOU

Nothing is plumb, level, or square:
    the studs are bowed, the joists
are shaky by nature, no piece fits
    any other piece without a gap
or pinch, and bent nails
    dance all over the surfacing
like maggots. By Christ
    I am no carpenter. I built
the roof for myself, the walls
    for myself, the floors
for myself, and got
    hung up in it myself. I
danced with a purple thumb
    at this house-warming, drunk
with my prime whiskey: rage.
    Oh I spat rage's nails
into the frame-up of my work:
    it held. It settled plumb,
level, solid, square and true
    for that great moment. Then
it screamed and went on through,
    skewing as wrong the other way.
God damned it. This is hell,
    but I planned it, I sawed it,
I nailed it, and I
    will live in it until it kills me.

I can nail my left palm
    to the left-hand crosspiece but
I can't do everything myself.
    I need a hand to nail the right,
a help, a love, a you, a wife.

Paul Laurence Dunbar

(1872–1906)

LITTLE BROWN BABY

Little brown baby wif spa'klin' eyes,
    Come to yo' pappy an' set on his knee.
What you been doin', suh—makin' san' pies?
    Look at dat bib—you's ez du'ty ez me.
Look at dat mouf—dat's merlasses, I bet;
    Come hyeah, Maria, an' wipe off his han's.
Bees gwine to ketch you an' eat you up yit,
    Bein' so sticky an' sweet—goodness lan's!

Little brown baby wif spa'klin' eyes,
    Who's pappy's darlin' an' who's pappy's chile?
Who is it all de day nevah once tries
    Fu' to be cross, er once loses dat smile?
Whah did you git dem teef? My, you's a scamp!
    Whah did dat dimple come f'om in yo' chin?
Pappy do' know you—I b'lieves you's a tramp;
    Mammy, dis hyeah's some ol' straggler got in!

Let's th'ow him outen de do' in de san',
    We do' want stragglers a-layin' 'roun' hyeah;
Let's gin him 'way to de big buggah-man;
    I know he's hidin' erroun' hyeah right neah.
Buggah-man, buggah-man, come in de do',
    Hyeah's a bad boy you kin have fu' to eat.
Mammy an' pappy do' want him no mo',
    Swaller him down f'om his haid to his feet!

Dah, now, I t'ought dat you'd hug me up close.
    Go back, ol' buggah, you sha'n't have dis boy.
He ain't no tramp, ner no straggler, of co'se;
    He's pappy's pa'dner an' playmate an' joy.
Come to you' pallet now—go to yo' res';
    Wisht you could allus know ease an' cleah skies;
Wisht you could stay jes' a chile on my breas'—
    Little brown baby wif spa'klin' eyes!

Robert Frost

(1874–1963)

PUTTING IN THE SEED

You come to fetch me from my work tonight
When supper's on the table, and we'll see
If I can leave off burying the white
Soft petals fallen from the apple tree
(Soft petals, yes, but not so barren quite,
Mingled with these, smooth bean and wrinkled pea;)
And go along with you ere you lose sight
Of what you came for and become like me,
Slave to a springtime passion for the earth.
How Love burns through the Putting in the Seed
On through the watching for that early birth
When, just as the soil tarnishes with weed,
The sturdy seedling with arched body comes
Shouldering its way and shedding the earth crumbs.

Jack Gilbert

(b. 1925)

MEASURING THE TYGER

Barrels of chains. Sides of beef stacked in vans.
Water buffalo dragging logs of teak in the river mud
outside Mandalay. Pantocrater in the Byzantium dome.
The mammoth overhead crane bringing slabs of steel
through the dingy light and roar to the giant shear
that cuts the adamantine three-quarter-inch plates
and they flop down. The weight of the mind fractures
the girders and piers of the spirit, spilling out
the heart's melt. Incandescent ingots big as cars
trundling out of titanic mills, red slag scaling off
the brighter metal in the dark. The Monongahela River
below, night's sheen on its belly. Silence except
for the machinery clanging deeper in us. You will
love again, people say. Give it time. Me with time
running out. Day after day of the everyday.
What they call real life, made of eighth-inch gauge.
Newness strutting around as if it were significant.
Irony, neatness and rhyme pretending to be poetry.
I want to go back to that time after Michiko's death
when I cried every day among the trees. To the real.
To the magnitude of pain, of being that much alive.

Louise Glück

(b. 1943)

Mock Orange

It is not the moon, I tell you.
It is these flowers
lighting the yard.

I hate them.
I hate them as I hate sex,
the man's mouth
sealing my mouth, the man's
paralyzing body—

and the cry that always escapes,
the low, humiliating
premise of union—

In my mind tonight
I hear the question and pursuing answer
fused in one sound
that mounts and mounts and then
is split into the old selves,
the tired antagonisms. Do you see?
We were made fools of.
And the scent of mock orange
drifts through the window.

How can I rest?
How can I be content
when there is still
that odor in the world?

Thom Gunn

(1929–2004)

Yoko

All today I lie in the bottom of the wardrobe
feeling low but sometimes getting up
to moodily lumber across rooms
and lap from the toilet bowl, it is so sultry
and then I hear the noise of firecrackers again
all New York is jaggedy with firecrackers today
and I go back to the wardrobe gloomy
trying to void my mind of them.
I am confused, I feel loose and unfitted.

At last deep in the stairwell I hear a tread,
it is him, my leader, my love.
I run to the door and listen to his approach.
Now I can smell him, what a good man he is,
I love it when he has the sweat of work on him,
as he enters I yodel with happiness,
I throw my body up against his, I try to lick his lips,
I care about him more than anything.

After we eat we go for a walk to the piers.
I leap into the standing warmth, I plunge into
the combination of old and new smells.
Here on a garbage can at the bottom, so interesting,
what sister or brother I wonder left this message I sniff.
I too piss there, and go on.
Here a hydrant there a pole

here's a smell I left yesterday, well that's disappointing
but I piss there anyway, and go on.

I investigate so much that in the end
it is for form's sake only, only a drop comes out.

I investigate tar and rotten sandwiches, everything, and go on.

And here a dried old turd, so interesting
so old, so dry, yet so subtle and mellow.
I can place it finely, I really appreciate it,
a gold distant smell like packed autumn leaves in winter
reminding me how what is rich and fierce when excreted
becomes weathered and mild
                              but always interesting
and reminding me of what I have to do.

My leader looks on and expresses his approval.

I sniff it well and later I sniff the air well
a wind is meeting us after the close July day
rain is getting near too but first the wind.

Joy, joy,
being outside with you, active, investigating it all,
with bowels emptied, feeling your approval
and then running on, the big fleet Yoko,
my body in its excellent black coat never lets me down,
returning to you (as I always will, you know that)
and now
          filling myself out with myself, no longer confused,
my panting pushing apart my black lips, but unmoving,
I stand with you braced against the wind.

Robert Hass

(b. 1941)

THEN TIME

In winter, in a small room, a man and a woman
Have been making love for hours. Exhausted,
Very busy wringing out each other's bodies,
They look at one another suddenly and laugh.
"What is this?" he says. "I can't get enough of you,"
She says, a woman who thinks of herself as not given
To cliché. She runs her fingers across his chest,
Tentative touches, as if she were testing her wonder.
He says, "Me too." And she, beginning to be herself
Again, "You mean you can't get enough of you either?"
"I mean," he takes her arms in his hands and shakes them,
"Where does this come from?" She cocks her head
And looks into his face. "Do you really want to know?"
"Yes," he says. "Self-hatred," she says, "longing for God."
Kisses him again. "It's not what it is," a wry shrug,
"It's where it comes from." Kisses his bruised mouth
A second time, a third. Years later, in another city,
They're having dinner in a quiet restaurant near a park.
Fall. Earlier that day, hard rain: leaves, brass-colored
And smoky crimson, flying everywhere. Twenty years older,
She is very beautiful. An astringent person. She'd become,
She said, an obsessive gardener, her daughters grown.
He's trying not to be overwhelmed by love or pity
Because he sees she has no hands. He thinks
She must have given them away. He imagines,
Very clearly, how she wakes some mornings
(He has a vivid memory of her younger self, stirred

From sleep, flushed, just opening her eyes)
To momentary horror because she can't remember
What she did with them, why they were gone,
And then remembers, and calms herself, so that the day
Takes on its customary sequence once again.
She asks him if he thinks about her. "Occasionally,"
He says, smiling. "And you?" "Not much," she says,
"I think it's because we never existed inside time."
He studies her long fingers, a pianist's hands,
Or a gardener's, strong, much-used, as she fiddles
With her wineglass and he understands, vaguely,
That it must be his hands that are gone. Then
He's describing a meeting that he'd sat in all day,
Chaired by someone they'd felt, many years before,
Mutually superior to. "You know the expression
'A perfect fool,'" she'd said, and he had liked her tone
Of voice so much. She begins a story of the company
In Maine she orders bulbs from, begun by a Polish refugee
Married to a French-Canadian separatist from Quebec.
It's a story with many surprising turns and a rare
Chocolate-black lily at the end. He's listening,
Studying her face, still turning over her remark.
He decides that she thinks more symbolically
Than he does and that it seemed to have saved her,
For all her fatalism, from certain kinds of pain.
She finds herself thinking what a literal man he is,
Notices, as if she were recalling it, his pleasure
In the menu, and the cooking, and the architecture of the room.
It moves her—in the way that earnest limitation
Can be moving, and she is moved by her attraction to him.
Also by what he was to her. She sees her own avidity
To live then, or not to not have lived might be more accurate,
From a distance, the way a driver might see from the road
A startled deer running across an open field in the rain.
Wild thing. Here and gone. Death made it poignant, or,
If not death exactly, which she'd come to think of
As creatures seething in a compost heap, then time.

Robert Hayden

(1913–1980)

THOSE WINTER SUNDAYS

Sundays too my father got up early
and put his clothes on in the blueblack cold,
then with cracked hands that ached
from labor in the weekday weather made
banked fires blaze. No one ever thanked him.

I'd wake and hear the cold splintering, breaking.
When the rooms were warm, he'd call,
and slowly I would rise and dress,
fearing the chronic angers of that house,

Speaking indifferently to him,
who had driven out the cold
and polished my good shoes as well.
What did I know, what did I know
of love's austere and lonely offices?

Seamus Heaney

(1939)

THE SKUNK

Up, black, striped and damasked like the chasuble
At a funeral mass, the skunk's tail
Paraded the skunk. Night after night
I expected her like a visitor.

The refrigerator whinnied into silence.
My desk light softened beyond the verandah.
Small oranges loomed in the orange tree.
I began to be tense as a voyeur.

After eleven years I was composing
Love-letters again, broaching the word "wife"
Like a stored cask, as if its slender vowel
Had mutated into the night earth and air

Of California. The beautiful, useless
Tang of eucalyptus spelt your absence.
The aftermath of a mouthful of wine
Was like inhaling you off a cold pillow.

And there she was, the intent and glamorous,
Ordinary, mysterious skunk,
Mythologized, demythologized,
Snuffing the boards five feet beyond me.

It all came back to me last night, stirred
By the sootfall of your things at bedtime,
Your head-down, tail-up hunt in a bottom drawer
For the black plunge-line nightdress.

Lyn Hejinian
(b. 1941)

FAMILIARIZATION IS NOT GOOD—IT

Familiarization is not good—it
    causes passion
She won't divert herself
Two beings end up with
    the words of which they
    are composed
Two beings end up
That thing must be pleasant
    —it lacks occasion for distractions
It is all proportions
The features are handsome and
    brave
The breasts are stubborn and
    observant
Every person is born preceded
    by its desire
Love finds something there and
    wants to be its modifier
Forehead, nose—profound as sleep
As retrospection
Let me tell you that
    she's pleased again—when worried
The face is lucky, fingers
    have their own body, the
    tongue another

Robert Herrick

(1591–1674)

DELIGHT IN DISORDER

A sweet disorder in the dress
Kindles in clothes a wantonness:
A lawn about the shoulders thrown
Into a fine distraction:
An erring lace, which here and there
Enthrals the crimson stomacher:
A cuff neglectful, and thereby
Ribbands to flow confusedly:
A winning wave, deserving note,
In the tempestuous petticoat:
A careless shoe-string, in whose tie
I see a wild civility:
Do more bewitch me than when art
Is too precise in every part.

UPON JULIA'S CLOTHES

Whenas in silks my Julia goes,
Then, then, methinks, how sweetly flows
The liquefaction of her clothes!

Next, when I cast mine eyes and see
That brave vibration each way free,
—O how that glittering taketh me!

Ben Jonson

(1572–1637)

His Excuse for Loving

Let it not your wonder move,
Less your laughter, that I love.
Though I now write fifty years,
I have had, and have, my peers;
Poets, though divine, are men:
Some have loved as old again.
And it is not always face,
Clothes, or fortune gives the grace,
Or the feature, or the youth;
But the language, and the truth,
With the ardour and the passion,
Gives the lover weight and fashion.
If you will then read the story,
First prepare you to be sorry
That you never knew till now
Either whom to love, or how;
But be glad as soon with me,
When you know that this is she,
Of whose beauty it was sung,
She shall make the old man young,
Keep the middle age at stay,
And let nothing high decay,
Till she be the reason why
All the world for love may die.

My Picture Left in Scotland

I now think Love is rather deaf than blind,
    For else it could not be
           That she
Whom I adore so much should so slight me,
    And cast my love behind;
I'm sure my language to her was as sweet,
        And every close did meet
      In sentence of as subtle feet,
          As hath the youngest he
    That sits in shadow of Apollo's tree.

    Oh, but my conscious fears
      That fly my thoughts between,
      Tell me that she hath seen
      My hundred of grey hairs,
      Told seven-and-forty years,
    Read so much waste, as she cannot embrace
      My mountain belly, and my rocky face;
And all these through her eyes have stopped her ears.

Amy Lowell

(1874–1925)

THE GARDEN BY MOONLIGHT

A black cat among roses,
Phlox, lilac-misted under a first-quarter moon,
The sweet smells of heliotrope and night-scented stock.
The garden is very still,
It is dazed with moonlight,
Contented with perfume,
Dreaming the opium dreams of its folded poppies.
Firefly lights open and vanish
High as the tip buds of the golden glow
Low as the sweet alyssum flowers at my feet.
Moon-shimmer on leaves and trellises,
Moon-spikes shafting through the snow-ball bush.
Only the little faces of the ladies' delight are alert and staring,
Only the cat, padding between the roses,
Shakes a branch and breaks the chequered pattern
As water is broken by the falling of a leaf.
Then you come,
And you are quiet like the garden,
And white like the alyssum flowers,
And beautiful as the silent sparks of the fireflies.
Ah, Beloved, do you see those orange lilies?
They knew my mother,
But who belonging to me will they know
When I am gone.

THE LETTER

Little cramped words scrawling all over the paper
Like draggled fly's legs,
What can you tell of the flaring moon
Through the oak leaves?
Or of my uncurtained window and the bare floor
Spattered with moonlight?
Your silly quirks and twists have nothing in them
Of blossoming hawthorns,
And this paper is dull, crisp, smooth, virgin of loveliness
Beneath my hand.

I am tired, Beloved, of chafing my heart against
The want of you;
Of squeezing it into little inkdrops,
And posting it.
And I scald alone, here, under the fire
Of the great moon.

Andrew Marvell

(1621–1678)

To his Coy Mistress

Had we but world enough, and time,
This coyness lady were no crime.
We would sit down, and think which way
To walk, and pass our long love's day.
Thou by the Indian Ganges side
Should'st rubies find: I by the tide
Of Humber would complain. I would
Love you ten years before the flood:
And you should if you please refuse
Till the conversion of the Jews.
My vegetable love should grow
Vaster than empires, and more slow.
An hundred years should go to praise
Thine eyes, and on thy forehead gaze.
Two hundred to adore each breast:
But thirty thousand to the rest.
An age at least to every part,
And the last age should show your heart.
For lady you deserve this state;
Nor would I love at lower rate.
    But at my back I alwaies hear
Time's wingèd charriot hurrying near:
And yonder all before us lye
Desarts of vast eternity.
Thy beauty shall no more be found;
Nor, in thy marble vault, shall sound
My ecchoing song: then worms shall try

That long preserv'd virginity:
And your quaint honour turn to dust;
And into ashes all my Lust.
The grave's a fine and private place,
But none I think do there embrace.
   Now therefore, while the youthful hew
Sits on thy skin like morning dew,
And while thy willing soul transpires
At every pore with instant fires,
Now let us sport us while we may;
And now, like am'rous birds of prey,
Rather at once our time devour,
Than languish in his slow-chapt pow'r.
Let us roll all our strength, and all
Our sweetness, up into one ball:
And tear our pleasures with rough strife,
Thorough the iron gates of life.
Thus, though we cannot make our sun
Stand still, yet we will make him run.

James McMichael

(b. 1939)

She

    The back of her neck.
Crazy to think she'd like your

hand there sometime.
It would never happen that from way

inside her or from long ago she'd will that it be
your hand there and moving, the fingers

only at first and just the tips,
no impress, no

leverage from the knuckles. Until she
wants you to, until she strains invisibly

outward from her wanting toward your hand, you can't
alter her neck's exposure to the air,

you have to leave
entire and maiden each conjectured place her

skin starts on the way inside.
Proper to her body are its

lineaments and heat, its chroma, what she
ate this morning. As you greet her you

do something with your eyes and mouth
that shows you want her in your

arms now. She lets you see that that's all
right with her, she's

for that, and then her
shoulders are there, her clothes, it isn't

sexual, of course, how
could it be since where would

trust go if it were? Trust is
here with you both, you

feel it in her body,
she trusts that you'll be letting

go of her soon so you can
each of you start talking, there's usually

news enough, and isn't talking
just what the doctor ordered, isn't it grand?

She listens and talks.
She's as much herself as ever. It turns you

outside in, you're her
convert,

it's required of you that you keep doing
better since she's here to watch.

You're doing worse. The more
riotously you crave her,

the duller what you find to say. This
fluff you're telling: it's the anemic puling

child she filled you up with and you bore. Take it
away from her now forever. Hammer its sorry

brains out. Strangle or starve it. Fix its clock.
Don't let it grow up wanting.

John Milton

(1608–1674)

METHOUGHT I SAW MY LATE ESPOUSÈD SAINT

Methought I saw my late espousèd saint
    Brought to me like Alcestis from the grave,
    Whom Jove's great son to her glad husband gave,
    Rescued from death by force, though pale and faint.
Mine, as whom washed from spot of childbed taint
    Purification in the old law did save,
    And such as yet once more I trust to have
    Full sight of her in heaven without restraint,
Came vested all in white, pure as her mind.
    Her face was veiled; yet to my fancied sight
    Love, sweetness, goodness, in her person shined
So clear as in no face with more delight.
    But, oh! as to embrace me she inclined,
    I waked, she fled, and day brought back my night.

Lady Mary Wortley Montagu

(1689–1762)

THE LOVER: A BALLAD

At length by so much importunity press'd,
Take (Molly) at once the inside of my breast,
This stupid indifference so often you blame
Is not owing to nature, to fear, or to shame,
I am not as cold as a virgin in lead
Nor is Sunday's sermon so strong in my head,
I know but too well how time flys along,
That we live but few years and yet fewer are young.

But I hate to be cheated, and never will buy
Long years of repentance for moments of joy,
Oh was there a man (but where shall I find
Good sense, and good nature so equally joyn'd?)
Would value his pleasure, contribute to mine,
Not meanly would boast, nor lewdly design,
Not over severe, yet not stupidly vain,
For I would have the power tho not give the pain.

No pedant yet learnèd, not rakehelly gay
Or laughing because he has nothing to say,
To all my whole sex, obliging and free,
Yet never be fond of any but me.
In public preserve the decorums are just
And shew in his eyes he is true to his trust,
Then rarely approach, and respectfully bow,
Yet not fulsomely pert, nor yet foppishly low.

But when the long hours of public are past
And we meet with champagne and a chicken at last,
May every fond pleasure that hour endear,
Be banish'd afar both discretion and fear,
Forgetting or scorning the airs of the croud
He may cease to be formal, and I to be proud,
Till lost in the joy we confess that we live
And he may be rude, and yet I may forgive.

And that my delight may be solidly fix'd
Let the freind, and the lover be handsomly mix'd,
In whose tender bosom my soul might confide,
Whose kindness can sooth me, whose councel could guide,
From such a dear lover as here I describe
No danger should fright me, no millions should bribe,
But till this astonishing creature I know
As I long have liv'd chaste I will keep my selfe so.

I never will share with the wanton coquette
Or be caught by a vain affectation of wit.
The toasters, and songsters may try all their art
But never shall enter the pass of my heart;
I loath the lewd rake, the dress'd fopling despise,
Before such persuers the nice virgin flys,
And as Ovid has sweetly in parables told
We harden like trees, and like rivers are cold.

Carol Muske-Dukes

(b. 1945)

THE ILLUSION

After his death, I kept an illusion before me:
that I would find the key to him, the answer,
in the words of a play that he'd put to heart
years earlier. I'd find the secret place in him,

retracing lines he'd learned, tracking
his prints in snow. I'd discover, scrawled
in the margin of a script, a stage-note that
would clarify consciousness in a single gesture—

not only the playwright's imagery—but his,
the actor's, and his, the self's. Past thought's
proscenium: the slight tilt of Alceste's head or
his too-quick ironic bow; the long pause as Henry

Carr adjusts his straw boater; Salieri slumps at
the keyboard; Hotspur sinks into self-reflection—
where the actor disappears into physical inspiration.
Thought rises, a silent aria; thought glitters in the infinite

prism of representation. For love unrequited and tactical
hate, the shouted curse of a wretched son, a vengeful duke,
in that silent prescient dialogue—unspoken—he'd
show up in the ear, in a tone blue and sweetened as wood—

smoke, show up in these directions to the flesh: cues
like green shouts, the blood swimming with indicatives.

Look—the same smile he flashed at me
from the shaving mirror is here, right here—

but *realized:* I remember this path opening
in a deep forest outside Athens, the moon
shuddering into place—and no players as yet at hand.

Joyce Peseroff

(b. 1948)

THE HARDNESS SCALE

Diamonds are forever so I gave you quartz
which is #7 on the hardness scale
and it's hard enough to get to know anybody these days
if only to scratch the surface
and quartz will scratch six other mineral surfaces:
it will scratch glass
it will scratch gold
it will even
scratch your eyes out one morning—you can't be
too careful.
Diamonds are industrial so I bought
a ring of topaz
which is #8 on the hardness scale.
I wear it on my right hand, the way it was
supposed to be, right? No tears and fewer regrets
for reasons smooth and clear as glass. Topaz will scratch glass,
it will scratch your quartz,
and all your radio crystals. You'll have to be silent
the rest of your days
not to mention your nights. Not to mention
the night you ran away very drunk very
very drunk and you tried to cross the border
but couldn't make it across the lake.
Stirring up geysers with the oars you drove the red canoe
in circles, tried to pole it but
your left hand didn't know
what the right hand was doing.

You fell asleep
and let everyone know it when you woke up.
In a gin-soaked morning (hair of the dog) you went
hunting for geese,
shot three lake trout in violation of the game laws,
told me to clean them and that
my eyes were bright as sapphires
which is #9 on the hardness scale.
A sapphire will cut a pearl
it will cut stainless steel
it will cut vinyl and mylar and will probably
cut a record this fall
to be released on an obscure label known only to aficionados.
I will buy a copy.
I may buy you a copy
depending on how your tastes have changed.
I will buy copies for my friends
we'll get a new needle,
a diamond needle,
which is #10 on the hardness scale
and will cut anything.
It will cut wood and mortar,
plaster and iron,
it will cut the sapphires in my eyes and I will bleed
blind as 4 A.M. in the subways when even degenerates
are dreaming, blind as the time
you shot up the room with a new hunting rifle
blind drunk
as you were.
You were #11 on the hardness scale
later that night
apologetic as
you worked your way up
slowly from the knees
and you worked your way down
from the open-throated blouse.
Diamonds are forever so I give you softer things.

Katherine Philips

(1632–1664)

To My Excellent Lucasia,
on Our Friendship

I did not live until this time
    Crowned my felicity,
When I could say without a crime,
    I am not thine, but thee.

This carcass breathed, and walked, and slept,
    So that the world believed
There was a soul the motions kept;
    But they were all deceived.

For as a watch by art is wound
    To motion, such was mine:
But never had Orinda found
    A soul till she found thine;

Which now inspires, cures and supplies,
    And guides my darkened breast:
For thou art all that I can prize,
    My joy, my life, my rest.

No bridegroom's nor crown-conqueror's mirth
    To mine compared can be:
They have but pieces of the earth,
    I've all the world in thee.

Then let our flames still light and shine,
    And no false fear control,
As innocent as our design,
    Immortal as our soul.

Alexander Pope

(1688–1744)

EPISTLE TO MISS BLOUNT

ON HER LEAVING THE TOWN, AFTER THE CORONATION

As some fond virgin, whom her mother's care
Drags from the town to wholesome country air,
Just when she learns to roll a melting eye,
And hear a spark, yet think no danger nigh;
From the dear man unwilling she must sever,
Yet takes one kiss before she parts forever:
Thus from the world fair Zephalinda flew,
Saw others happy, and with sighs withdrew;
Not that their pleasures caused her discontent;
She sighed not that they stayed, but that she went.

She went, to plain-work, and to purling brooks,
Old-fashioned halls, dull aunts, and croaking rooks:
She went from opera, park, assembly, play,
To morning walks, and prayers three hours a day;
To part her time 'twixt reading and bohea,
To muse, and spill her solitary tea,
Or o'er cold coffee trifle with the spoon,
Count the slow clock, and dine exact at noon;
Divert her eyes with pictures in the fire,
Hum half a tune, tell stories to the squire;
Up to her godly garret after seven,
There starve and pray, for that's the way to heaven.

Some squire, perhaps, you take delight to rack,
Whose game is whist, whose treat a toast in sack;
Who visits with a gun, presents you birds,

Then gives a smacking buss, and cries—"No words!"
Or with his hounds comes hollowing from the stable,
Makes love with nods and knees beneath a table;
Whose laughs are hearty, though his jests are coarse,
And loves you best of all things—but his horse.
    In some fair evening, on your elbow laid,
You dream of triumphs in the rural shade;
In pensive thought recall the fancied scene,
See coronations rise on every green:
Before you pass the imaginary sights
Of lords and earls and dukes and gartered knights,
While the spread fan o'ershades your closing eyes;
Then give one flirt, and all the vision flies.
Thus vanish scepters, coronets, and balls,
And leave you in lone woods, or empty walls.
    So when your slave, at some dear idle time
(Not plagued with headaches or the want of rhyme)
Stands in the streets, abstracted from the crew,
And while he seems to study, thinks of you;
Just when his fancy points your sprightly eyes,
Or sees the blush of soft Parthenia rise,
Gay pats my shoulder, and you vanish quite;
Streets, chairs, and coxcombs rush upon my sight;
Vexed to be still in town, I knit my brow,
Look sour, and hum a tune—as you may now.

Ezra Pound

(1885–1972)

THE RIVER-MERCHANT'S WIFE: A LETTER

While my hair was still cut straight across my forehead
I played about the front gate, pulling flowers.
You came by on bamboo stilts, playing horse,

You walked about my seat, playing with blue plums.
And we went on living in the village of Chokan:
Two small people, without dislike or suspicion.

At fourteen I married My Lord you.
I never laughed, being bashful.
Lowering my head, I looked at the wall.
Called to, a thousand times, I never looked back.

At fifteen I stopped scowling,
I desired my dust to be mingled with yours
Forever and forever and forever.
Why should I climb the look out?

At sixteen you departed,
You went into far Ku-tō-en, by the river of swirling eddies,
And you have been gone five months.
The monkeys make sorrowful noise overhead.

You dragged your feet when you went out.
By the gate now, the moss is grown, the different mosses,
Too deep to clear them away!
The leaves fall early this autumn, in wind.

The paired butterflies are already yellow with August
Over the grass in the West garden;
They hurt me. I grow older.
If you are coming down through the narrows of the river
    Kiang,
Please let me know beforehand,
And I will come out to meet you
                As far as Chō-fū-Sa.

Sappho

translated by Jim Powell

(ca. 612–570 B.C.E.)

ARTFULLY ADORNED APHRODITE

Artfully adorned Aphrodite, deathless
child of Zeus and weaver of wiles I beg you
please don't hurt me, don't overcome my spirit,
    goddess, with longing,

but come here, if ever at other moments
hearing these my words from afar you listened
and responded: leaving your father's house, all
    golden, you came then,

hitching up your chariot: lovely sparrows
drew you quickly over the dark earth, whirling
on fine beating wings from the heights of heaven
    down through the sky and

instantly arrived—and then O my blessed
goddess with a smile on your deathless face you
asked me what the matter was *this* time, what I
    called you for this time,

what I now most wanted to happen in my
raving heart: "Whom *this* time should I persuade to
lead you back again to her love? Who *now*, oh
    Sappho, who wrongs you?

If she flees you now, she will soon pursue you;
if she won't accept what you give, she'll give it;
if she doesn't love you, she'll love you soon now,
    even unwilling."

Come to me again, and release me from this
want past bearing. All that my heart desires to
happen—make it happen. And stand beside me,
    goddess, my ally.

William Shakespeare

(1564–1616)

WHEN TO THE SESSIONS OF
SWEET SILENT THOUGHT

(SONNET 30)

When to the sessions of sweet silent thought
I summon up remembrance of things past,
I sigh the lack of many a thing I sought,
And with old woes new wail my dear time's waste:
Then can I drown an eye, unused to flow,
For precious friends hid in death's dateless night,
And weep afresh love's long since canceled woe,
And moan the expense of many a vanished sight:
Then can I grieve at grievances foregone,
And heavily from woe to woe tell o'er
The sad account of fore-bemoaned moan,
Which I new pay as if not paid before.
    But if the while I think on thee, dear friend,
    All losses are restored and sorrows end.

WHAT IS YOUR SUBSTANCE,
WHEREOF ARE YOU MADE

(SONNET 53)

What is your substance, whereof are you made,
That millions of strange shadows on you tend?

Since every one hath, every one, one shade,
And you, but one, can every shadow lend.
Describe Adonis, and the counterfeit
Is poorly imitated after you.
On Helen's cheek all art of beauty set,
And you in Grecian tires are painted new.
Speak of the spring and foison of the year,
The one doth shadow of your beauty show,
The other as your bounty doth appear,
And you in every blessèd shape we know.
    In all external grace you have some part,
    But you like none, none you, for constant heart.

To me, fair friend, you never can be old

(SONNET 104)

To me, fair friend, you never can be old,
For as you were when first your eye I eyed,
Such seems your beauty still. Three winters cold
Have from the forests shook three summers' pride,
Three beauteous springs to yellow autumn turned
In process of the seasons have I seen,
Three April perfumes in three hot Junes burned,
Since first I saw you fresh, which yet are green.
Ah, yet doth beauty, like a dial hand,
Steal from his figure, and no pace perceived.
So your sweet hue, which methinks still doth stand,
Hath motion, and mine eye may be deceived.
    For fear of which, hear this, thou age unbred—
    Ere you were born was beauty's summer dead.

Philip Sidney

(1554–1586)

My True Love Hath My Heart
and I Have His

My true love hath my heart and I have his,
By just exchange one for the other giv'n.
I hold his dear, and mine he cannot miss:
There never was a better bargain driv'n.
   His heart in me keeps me and him in one,
My heart in him his thoughts and senses guides:
He loves my heart for once it was his own;
I cherish his because in me it bides.

His heart his wound received from my sight;
My heart was wounded with his wounded heart,
For as from me on him his hurt did light,
So still methought in me his hurt did smart.
   Both equal hurt, in this change sought our bliss:
My true love hath my heart and I have his.

Wallace Stevens
(1879–1955)

FINAL SOLILOQUY OF THE INTERIOR PARAMOUR

Light the first light of evening, as in a room
In which we rest and, for small reason, think
The world imagined is the ultimate good.

This is, therefore, the intensest rendezvous.
It is in that thought that we collect ourselves,
Out of all the indifferences, into one thing:

Within a single thing, a single shawl
Wrapped tightly round us, since we are poor, a warmth,
A light, a power, the miraculous influence.

Here, now, we forget each other and ourselves.
We feel the obscurity of an order, a whole,
A knowledge, that which arranged the rendezvous.

Within its vital boundary, in the mind.
We say God and the imagination are one . . .
How high that highest candle lights the dark.

Out of this same light, out of the central mind,
We make a dwelling in the evening air,
In which being there together is enough.

William Carlos Williams

(1883–1963)

Love Song

I lie here thinking of you:—

the stain of love
is upon the world!
Yellow, yellow, yellow
it eats into the leaves,
smears with saffron
the horned branches that lean
heavily
against a smooth purple sky!
There is no light
only a honey-thick stain
that drips from leaf to leaf
and limb to limb
spoiling the colors
of the whole world—

you far off there under
the wine-red selvage of the west!

SAPPHO

That man is peer of the gods, who
face to face sits listening
to your sweet speech and lovely
          laughter.

It is this that rouses a tumult
in my breast. At mere sight of you
my voice falters, my tongue
          is broken.

Straightway, a delicate fire runs in
my limbs; my eyes
are blinded and my ears
          thunder.

Sweat pours out: a trembling hunts
me down. I grow
paler than grass and lack little
          of dying.

Mary Wroth
(1587–ca. 1651)

MY MUSE NOW HAPPY, LAY THYSELF TO REST

(SONNET 103)

My muse now happy, lay thyself to rest,
    Sleep in the quiet of a faithful love,
    Write you no more, but let these fancies move
    Some other hearts, wake not to new unrest.

But if you study, be those thoughts addressed
    To truth, which shall eternal goodness prove;
    Enjoying of true joy, the most, and best,
    The endless gain which never will remove.

Leave the discourse of Venus, and her son
    To young beginners, and their brains inspire
    With stories of great love, and from that fire
    Get heat to write the fortunes they have won.

And thus leave off, what's past shows you can love,
Now let your constancy your honor prove.

Thomas Wyatt
(1503–1542)

MADAM, WITHOUTEN MANY WORDS

Madam, withouten many words,
    Once I am sure ye will or no;
And if ye will, then leave your bourdes,
    And use your wit and show it so.

And with a beck ye shall me call;
    And if of one that burneth alway
Ye have any pity at all,
    Answer him fair with yea or nay.

If it be yea, I shall be fain;
    If it be nay, friends as before;
Ye shall another man obtain,
    And I mine own, and yours no more.

THEY FLEE FROM ME

They flee from me, that sometime did me seek
    With naked foot, stalking in my chamber.
I have seen them gentle, tame, and meek
    That now are wild, and do not remember
    That sometime they put themselves in danger
To take bread at my hand; and now they range
Busily seeking with a continual change.

Thankëd be fortune it hath been otherwise
    Twenty times better; but once, in speciál,
In thin array, after a pleasant guise,
    When her loose gown from her shoulders did fall,
    And she me caught in her arms long and small,
Therewith all sweetly did me kiss,
And softly said, "Dear heart, how like you this?"

It was no dream: I lay broad waking.
    But all is turnëd, through my gentleness,
Into a strange fashion of forsaking;
    And I have leave to go of her goodness,
    And she also to use newfangleness.
But since that I so kindly am served,
I would fain know what she hath deserved.

William Butler Yeats

(1865–1939)

HER TRIUMPH

I did the dragon's will until you came
Because I had fancied love a casual
Improvisation, or a settled game
That followed if I let the kerchief fall:
Those deeds were best that gave the minute wings
And heavenly music if they gave it wit;
And then you stood among the dragon-rings.
I mocked, being crazy, but you mastered it
And broke the chain and set my ankles free,
Saint George or else a pagan Perseus;
And now we stare astonished at the sea,
And a miraculous strange bird shrieks at us.

CRAZY JANE GROWN OLD LOOKS
AT THE DANCERS

I found that ivory image there
Dancing with her chosen youth,
But when he wound her coal-black hair
As though to strangle her, no scream
Or bodily movement did I dare,
Eyes under eyelids did so gleam;
Love is like the lion's tooth.

When she, and though some said she played
I said that she had danced heart's truth,
Drew a knife to strike him dead,
I could but leave him to his fate;
For no matter what is said
They had all that had their hate;
Love is like the lion's tooth.

Did he die or did she die?
Seemed to die or died they both?
God be with the times when I
Cared not a thraneen for what chanced
So that I had the limbs to try
Such a dance as there was danced—
Love is like the lion's tooth.

V

STORIES

❧❧

POSSIBLY ALL STORIES proceed by referring to other stories, for
example, a movie that refers to others in its genre; formulas like
"once upon a time" or "in a new development"; the narrative
bards who tell stories within epics like the *Iliad* and *Beowulf*; conven-
tions like the present-tense of jokes ("a guy goes into a bar"). A ballad
like "The Cruel Mother" (p. 106) or a sonnet like "Three sorts of serpent
do resemble thee" (p. 187) makes itself clear and forceful partly by plac-
ing itself within a form.

In this section, Elizabeth Bishop's "The Man-Moth" (p. 242) pro-
ceeds by referring to a newspaper misprint. In Heather McHugh's
"What He Thought" (p. 285) the poet tells a story about herself in which
a character tells a very old true story that turns out to be the center of
the poem. "Harlem Happiness" (p. 246) by Sterling Brown portrays the
happiness of two lovers by alluding all but directly to the many movies
where lovers, late at night, in the city, have benign encounters with vari-
ous ethnic types, all beaming at the joyful couple—though in Brown's
poem the Harlem setting brings something like a reversal to the story.

The poems by Terrance Hayes (p. 272) and James Wright (p. 318)
combine a furious welter of many stories: an excess of narrative is
part of the feeling each of those poems conveys. Yvor Winters retells
the story of "Sir Gawaine and the Green Knight" (p. 316) compactly,
directly, with an implicit personal significance. Sharon Olds (p. 288)
also retells an old story, but with explicit commentary and reflection.
Extremely singular and unified is "Tichborne's Elegy" (p. 309)—which

scholars say may be a fiction, written by some brilliant deviser, and not what its subtitle says:

TICHBORNE'S ELEGY

WRITTEN WITH HIS OWN HAND IN THE
TOWER BEFORE HIS EXECUTION

My prime of youth is but a frost of cares,
My feast of joy is but a dish of pain,
My crop of corn is but a field of tares,
And all my good is but vain hope of gain;
The day is past, and yet I saw no sun,
And now I live, and now my life is done.

My tale was heard and yet it was not told,
My fruit is fallen and yet my leaves are green,
My youth is spent and yet I am not old,
I saw the world and yet I was not seen;
My thread is cut and yet it is not spun,
And now I live, and now my life is done.

I sought my death and found it in my womb,
I looked for life and saw it was a shade,
I trod the earth and knew it was my tomb,
And now I die, and now I was but made;
My glass is full, and now my glass is run,
And now I live, and now my life is done.

The story that the young man wrote the poem the night before he was executed may be a legend rather than a fact. Either way, the plain, stony simplicity of that story has considerable power. The sense of symmetrical, unyielding walls with no unexpected exit is emphasized by the refrain and by the plainness of the writing. The expression "explain it in words of one syllable" is usually figurative, a demand for unornamented, direct clarity. In this poem, the words are literally of one syllable—nearly all of them, and all of them if one pronounces "fallen" as "fall'n." That severe, demanding simplicity demonstrates how the story-teller's art may be in an apparent absence of art.

Longfellow's "Paul Revere's Ride" (p. 279), in contrast, pretty openly sets out to create a national and nationalist legend. The poem was for many decades memorized by American students. (Senator Edward Kennedy, for example, can recite it.) Longfellow saw a need for legends and myths, and his poem is a brilliant, sophisticated writer's effort to supply a simple, heroic tale—to be handed down to children, as the first line declares. Ernest Lawrence Thayer's "Casey at the Bat" (p. 306), with its subtitle, "A Ballad of the Republic, Sung in the Year 1888," undertakes a similar role.

Without scorning either of those works, one can understand them as exemplifying a background for modernism: T. S. Eliot's "The Love Song of J. Alfred Prufrock" (p. 256) and William Carlos Williams' "Dedication for a Plot of Ground" (p. 311) fill an appetite for reality, and for real stories, accounts of fear and courage, partial defeats and bitter victories, utterly different from the legends of Paul Revere and Casey.

The story of being one person—not a multitude or a legend, but a quiet enigma—is memorably told by Mark Strand, with yet another kind of plainness, and another kind of narrated solitude (p. 300):

OLD MAN LEAVES PARTY

It was clear when I left the party
That though I was over eighty I still had
A beautiful body. The moon shone down as it will
On moments of deep introspection. The wind held its breath.
And look, somebody left a mirror leaning against a tree.
Making sure that I was alone, I took off my shirt.
The flowers of bear grass nodded their moonwashed heads.
I took off my pants and the magpies circled the redwoods.
Down in the valley the creaking river was flowing once more.
How strange that I should stand in the wilds alone with my
    body.
I know what you are thinking. I was like you once. But now
With so much before me, so many emerald trees, and
Weed-whitened fields, mountains and lakes, how could I not
Be only myself, this dream of flesh, from moment to moment?

Elizabeth Bishop
(1911–1979)

THE MAN-MOTH*

       Here, above,
cracks in the buildings are filled with battered moonlight.
The whole shadow of Man is only as big as his hat.
It lies at his feet like a circle for a doll to stand on,
and he makes an inverted pin, the point magnetized to the
      moon.
He does not see the moon; he observes only her vast properties,
feeling the queer light on his hands, neither warm nor cold,
of a temperature impossible to record in thermometers.

       But when the Man-Moth
pays his rare, although occasional, visits to the surface,
the moon looks rather different to him. He emerges
from an opening under the edge of one of the sidewalks
and nervously begins to scale the faces of the buildings.
He thinks the moon is a small hole at the top of the sky,
proving the sky quite useless for protection.
He trembles, but must investigate as high as he can climb.

       Up the façades,
his shadow dragging like a photographer's cloth behind him,
he climbs fearfully, thinking that this time he will manage
to push his small head through that round clean opening
and be forced through, as from a tube, in black scrolls on the
      light.

* Newspaper misprint for "mammoth."

(Man, standing below him, has no such illusions.)
But what the Man-Moth fears most he must do, although
he fails, of course, and falls back scared but quite unhurt.

      Then he returns
to the pale subways of cement he calls his home. He flits,
he flutters, and cannot get aboard the silent trains
fast enough to suit him. The doors close swiftly.
The Man-Moth always seats himself facing the wrong way
and the train starts at once at its full, terrible speed,
without a shift in gears or a gradation of any sort.
He cannot tell the rate at which he travels backwards.

      Each night he must
be carried through artificial tunnels and dream recurrent
    dreams.
Just as the ties recur beneath his train, these underlie
his rushing brain. He does not dare look out the window,
for the third rail, the unbroken draught of poison,
runs there beside him. He regards it as a disease
he has inherited the susceptibility to. He has to keep
his hands in his pockets, as others must wear mufflers.

      If you catch him,
hold up a flashlight to his eye. It's all dark pupil,
an entire night itself, whose haired horizon tightens
as he stares back, and closes up the eye. Then from the lids
one tear, his only possession, like the bee's sting, slips.
Slyly he palms it, and if you're not paying attention
he'll swallow it. However, if you watch, he'll hand it over,
cool as from underground springs and pure enough to drink.

William Blake

(1757–1827)

A Poison Tree

I was angry with my friend:
I told my wrath, my wrath did end.
I was angry with my foe:
I told it not, my wrath did grow.

And I watered it in fears.
Night and morning with my tears:
And I sunned it with smiles.
And with soft deceitful wiles.

And it grew both day and night.
Till it bore an apple bright.
And my foe beheld it shine.
And he knew that it was mine.

And into my garden stole.
When the night had veild the pole;
In the morning glad I see;
My foe outstretchd beneath the tree.

THE CHIMNEY-SWEEPER

(FROM SONGS OF INNOCENCE)

When my mother died I was very young,
And my father sold me while yet my tongue
Could scarcely cry, "weep weep weep weep."
So your chimneys I sweep and in soot I sleep.

There's little Tom Dacre, who cried when his head,
That curled like a lamb's back, was shaved, so I said:
"Hush Tom, never mind it, for when your head's bare,
You know that the soot cannot spoil your white hair."

And so he was quiet, and that very night,
As Tom was a-sleeping, he had such a sight:
That thousands of sweepers, Dick, Joe, Ned and Jack,
Were all of them locked up in coffins of black,

And by came an angel who had a bright key,
And he opened the coffins and set them all free.
Then down a green plain leaping, laughing they run,
And wash in a river and shine in the sun.

Then naked and white, all their bags left behind,
They rise upon clouds, and sport in the wind.
And the angel told Tom if he'd be a good boy,
He'd have God for his father and never want joy.

And so Tom awoke, and we rose in the dark,
And got with our bags and our brushes to work.
Though the morning was cold, Tom was happy and warm.
So if all do their duty, they need not fear harm.

Sterling Brown
(1901–1989)

HARLEM HAPPINESS

I think there is in this the stuff for many lyrics:—
A dago fruit stand at three A.M.; the wop asleep, his woman
Knitting a tiny garment, laughing when we approached her,
Flashing a smile from white teeth, then weighing out the grapes,
Grapes large as plums, and tart and sweet as—well we know the
    lady
And purplish red and firm, quite as this lady's lips are. . . .
We laughed, all three when she awoke her swarthy, snoring Pietro
To make us change, which we, rich paupers, left to help the
    garment.
We swaggered off; while they two stared, and laughed in
    understanding,
And thanked us lovers who brought back an old Etrurian
    springtide.
Then, once beyond their light, a step beyond their pearly smiling
We tasted grapes and tasted lips, and laughed at sleepy Harlem,
And when the huge Mick cop stomped by, a'swingin' of his billy
You nodded to him gaily, and I kissed you with him looking,
Beneath the swinging light that weakly fought against the mist
That settled on Eighth Avenue, and curled around the houses.
And he grinned too and understood the wisdom of our madness.
That night at least the world was ours to spend, nor were we
    misers.
Ah, Morningside with Maytime awhispering in the foliage!
Alone, atop the city,—the tramps were still in shelter—
And moralizing lights that peered up from the murky distance

Seemed soft as our two cigarette ends burning slowly, dimly,
And careless as the jade stars that winked upon our gladness. . . .

And when I flicked my cigarette, and we watched it falling,
    falling,
It seemed a shooting meteor, that we, most proud creators
Sent down in gay capriciousness upon a trivial Harlem—

And then I madly quoted lyrics from old kindred masters,
Who wrote of you, unknowing you, for far more lucky me—
And you sang broken bits of song, and we both slept in snatches,
And so the night sped on too swift, with grapes, and words and
    kisses,
And numberless cigarette ends glowing in the darkness
Old Harlem slept regardless, but a motherly old moon—
Shone down benevolently on two happy wastrel lovers. . . .

Robert Browning

(1812–1889)

My Last Duchess

FERRARA

That's my last Duchess painted on the wall,
Looking as if she were alive. I call
That piece a wonder, now: Frà Pandolf's hands
Worked busily a day, and there she stands.
Will't please you sit and look at her? I said
"Frà Pandolf" by design, for never read
Strangers like you that pictured countenance,
The depth and passion of its earnest glance,
But to myself they turned (since none puts by
The curtain I have drawn for you, but I)
And seemed as they would ask me, if they durst,
How such a glance came there; so, not the first
Are you to turn and ask thus. Sir, 't was not
Her husband's presence only, called that spot
Of joy into the Duchess' cheek: perhaps
Frà Pandolf chanced to say "Her mantle laps
"Over my lady's wrist too much," or "Paint
"Must never hope to reproduce the faint
"Half-flush that dies along her throat": such stuff
Was courtesy, she thought, and cause enough
For calling up that spot of joy. She had
A heart—how shall I say?—too soon made glad,
Too easily impressed; she liked whate'er
She looked on, and her looks went everywhere.
Sir, 't was all one! My favour at her breast,

The dropping of the daylight in the West,
The bough of cherries some officious fool
Broke in the orchard for her, the white mule
She rode with round the terrace—all and each
Would draw from her alike the approving speech,
Or blush, at least. She thanked men,—good! but thanked
Somehow—I know not how—as if she ranked
My gift of a nine-hundred-years-old name
With anybody's gift. Who'd stoop to blame
This sort of trifling? Even had you skill
In speech—(which I have not)—to make your will
Quite clear to such an one, and say, "Just this
"Or that in you disgusts me; here you miss,
"Or there exceed the mark"—and if she let
Herself be lessoned so, nor plainly set
Her wits to yours, forsooth, and made excuse,
—E'en then would be some stooping; and I choose
Never to stoop. Oh sir, she smiled, no doubt,
Whene'er I passed her; but who passed without
Much the same smile? This grew; I gave commands;
Then all smiles stopped together. There she stands
As if alive. Will't please you rise? We'll meet
The company below, then. I repeat,
The Count your master's known munificence
Is ample warrant that no just pretence
Of mine for dowry will be disallowed;
Though his fair daughter's self, as I avowed
At starting, is my object. Nay, we'll go
Together down, sir. Notice Neptune, though,
Taming a sea-horse, thought a rarity,
Which Claus of Innsbruck cast in bronze for me!

Constantine Cavafy

translated by E. Keeley and P. Sherrard

(1864–1933)

WAITING FOR THE BARBARIANS

What are we waiting for, assembled in the forum?

    The barbarians are due here today.

Why isn't anything going on in the senate?
Why are the senators sitting there without legislating?

    Because the barbarians are coming today.
    What's the point of senators making laws now?
    Once the barbarians are here, they'll do the legislating.

Why did our emperor get up so early,
and why is he sitting enthroned at the city's main gate,
in state, wearing the crown?

    Because the barbarians are coming today
    and the emperor's waiting to receive their leader.
    He's even got a scroll to give him,
    loaded with titles, with imposing names.

Why have our two consuls and praetors come out today
wearing their embroidered, their scarlet togas?
Why have they put on bracelets with so many amethysts,
rings sparkling with magnificent emeralds?

Why are they carrying elegant canes
beautifully worked in silver and gold?

    Because the barbarians are coming today
    and things like that dazzle the barbarians.

Why don't our distinguished orators turn up as usual
to make their speeches, say what they have to say?

    Because the barbarians are coming today
    and they're bored by rhetoric and public speaking.

Why this sudden bewilderment, this confusion?
(How serious people's faces have become.)
Why are the streets and squares emptying so rapidly,
everyone going home lost in thought?

    Because night has fallen and the barbarians haven't come.
    And some of our men just in from the border say
    there are no barbarians any longer.

Now what's going to happen to us without barbarians?
Those people were a kind of solution.

John Clare

(1793–1864)

BADGER

When midnight comes a host of dogs and men
Go out and track the badger to his den,
And put a sack within the hole, and lie
Till the old grunting badger passes by.
He comes and hears—they let the strongest loose.
The old fox hears the noise and drops the goose.
The poacher shoots and hurries from the cry,
And the old hare half wounded buzzes by.
They get a forkéd stick to bear him down
And clap the dogs and take him to the town,
And bait him all the day with many dogs,
And laugh and shout and fright the scampering hogs.
He runs along and bites at all he meets:
They shout and hollo down the noisy streets.

He turns about to face the loud uproar
And drives the rebels to their very door.
The frequent stone is hurled where'er they go;
When badgers fight, then everyone's a foe.
The dogs are clapped and urged to join the fray;
The badger turns and drives them all away.
Though scarcely half as big, demure and small,
He fights with dogs for hours and beats them all.
The heavy mastiff, savage in the fray,
Lies down and licks his feet and turns away.
The bulldog knows his match and waxes cold,
The badger grins and never leaves his hold.

He drives the crowd and follows at their heels
And bites them through—the drunkard swears and reels.

The frighted women take the boys away,
The blackguard laughs and hurries on the fray.
He tries to reach the woods, an awkward race,
But sticks and cudgels quickly stop the chase.
He turns again and drives the noisy crowd
And beats the many dogs in noises loud.
He drives away and beats them every one,
And then they loose them all and set them on.
He falls as dead and kicked by boys and men,
Then starts and grins and drives the crowd again;
Till kicked and torn and beaten out he lies
And leaves his hold and crackles, groans, and dies.

Stephen Dobyns

(b. 1941)

TOMATOES

A woman travels to Brazil for plastic
surgery and a face-lift. She is sixty
and has the usual desire to stay pretty.
Once she is healed, she takes her new face
out on the streets of Rio. A young man
with a gun wants her money. Bang, she's dead.
The body is shipped back to New York,
but in the morgue there is a mix-up. The son
is sent for. He is told that his mother
is one of these ten different women.
Each has been shot. Such is modern life.
He studies them all but can't find her.
With her new face, she has become a stranger.
Maybe it's this one, maybe it's that one.
He looks at their breasts. Which ones nursed him?
He presses their hands to his cheek.
Which ones consoled him? He even tries
climbing into their laps to see which
feels most familiar but the coroner stops him.
Well, says the coroner, which is your mother?
They all are, says the young man, let me
take them as a package. The coroner hesitates,
then agrees. Actually, it solved a lot of problems.
The young man has the ten women shipped home,
then cremates them all together. You've seen
how some people have a little urn on the mantel?
This man has a huge silver garbage can.

In the spring, he drags the garbage can
out to the garden and begins working the teeth,
the ash, the bits of bone into the soil.
Then he plants tomatoes. His mother loved tomatoes.
They grow straight from seed, so fast and big
that the young man is amazed. He takes the first
ten into the kitchen. In their roundness,
he sees his mother's breasts. In their smoothness,
he finds the consoling touch of her hands.
Mother, mother, he cries, and he flings himself
on the tomatoes. Forget about the knife, the fork,
the pinch of salt. Try to imagine the filial
starvation, think of his ravenous kisses.

T. S. Eliot

(1888–1965)

THE LOVE SONG OF J. ALFRED PRUFROCK

S'io credesse che mia risposta fosse
A persona che mai tornasse al mondo,
Questa fiamma staria senza piu scosse.
Ma perciocche giammai di questo fondo
Non torno vivo alcun, s'i'odo il vero,
Senza tema d'infamia ti rispondo.

Let us go then, you and I,
When the evening is spread out against the sky
Like a patient etherized upon a table;
Let us go, through certain half-deserted streets,
The muttering retreats
Of restless nights in one-night cheap hotels
And sawdust restaurants with oyster-shells:
Streets that follow like a tedious argument
Of insidious intent
To lead you to an overwhelming question . . .
Oh, do not ask, "What is it?"
Let us go and make our visit.

    In the room the women come and go
Talking of Michelangelo.

    The yellow fog that rubs its back upon the window-panes,
The yellow smoke that rubs its muzzle on the window-panes
Licked its tongue into the corners of the evening,
Lingered upon the pools that stand in drains,

Let fall upon its back the soot that falls from chimneys,
Slipped by the terrace, made a sudden leap,
And seeing that it was a soft October night,
Curled once about the house, and fell asleep.

And indeed there will be time
For the yellow smoke that slides along the street,
Rubbing its back upon the window-panes;
There will be time, there will be time
To prepare a face to meet the faces that you meet;
There will be time to murder and create,
And time for all the works and days of hands
That lift and drop a question on your plate;
Time for you and time for me,
And time yet for a hundred indecisions,
And for a hundred visions and revisions,
Before the taking of a toast and tea.

In the room the women come and go
Talking of Michelangelo.

And indeed there will be time
To wonder, "Do I dare?" and, "Do I dare?"
Time to turn back and descend the stair,
With a bald spot in the middle of my hair—
[They will say: "How his hair is growing thin!"]
My morning coat, my collar mounting firmly to the chin,
My necktie rich and modest, but asserted by a simple pin—
[They will say: "But how his arms and legs are thin!"]
Do I dare
Disturb the universe?
In a minute there is time
For decisions and revisions which a minute will reverse.

For I have known them all already, known them all—
Have known the evenings, mornings, afternoons,
I have measured out my life with coffee spoons;

I know the voices dying with a dying fall
Beneath the music from a farther room.
    So how should I presume?

    And I have known the eyes already, known them all—
The eyes that fix you in a formulated phrase,
And when I am formulated, sprawling on a pin,
When I am pinned and wriggling on the wall,
Then how should I begin
To spit out all the butt-ends of my days and ways?
    And how should I presume?

    And I have known the arms already, known them all—
Arms that are braceleted and white and bare
[But in the lamplight, downed with light brown hair!]
Is it perfume from a dress
That makes me so digress?
Arms that lie along a table, or wrap about a shawl.
    And should I then presume?
    And how should I begin?

                    . . . . .

Shall I say, I have gone at dusk through narrow streets
And watched the smoke that rises from the pipes
Of lonely men in shirt-sleeves, leaning out of windows? . . .

    I should have been a pair of ragged claws
Scuttling across the floors of silent seas.

                    . . . . .

And the afternoon, the evening, sleeps so peacefully!
Smoothed by long fingers,
Asleep . . . tired . . . or it malingers,
Stretched on the floor, here beside you and me.
Should I, after tea and cakes and ices,
Have the strength to force the moment to its crisis?
But though I have wept and fasted, wept and prayed,

Though I have seen my head [grown slightly bald] brought in
    upon a platter,
I am no prophet—and here's no great matter;
I have seen the moment of my greatness flicker,
And I have seen the eternal Footman hold my coat, and snicker,
And in short, I was afraid.

    And would it have been worth it, after all,
After the cups, the marmalade, the tea,
Among the porcelain, among some talk of you and me,
Would it have been worth while,
To have bitten off the matter with a smile,
To have squeezed the universe into a ball
To roll it toward some overwhelming question,
To say: "I am Lazarus, come from the dead,
Come back to tell you all, I shall tell you all"—
If one, settling a pillow by her head,
    Should say: "That is not what I meant at all.
    That is not it, at all."

    And would it have been worth it, after all,
Would it have been worth while,
After the sunsets and the dooryards and the sprinkled streets,
After the novels, after the teacups, after the skirts that trail
    along the floor—
And this, and so much more?—
It is impossible to say just what I mean!
But as if a magic lantern threw the nerves in patterns on a
    screen:
Would it have been worth while
If one, settling a pillow or throwing off a shawl,
And turning toward the window, should say:
    "That is not it at all,
    That is not what I meant, at all."

        · · · · ·

No! I am not Prince Hamlet, nor was meant to be;
Am an attendant lord, one that will do

To swell a progress, start a scene or two,
Advise the prince; no doubt, an easy tool,

Deferential, glad to be of use,
Politic, cautious, and meticulous;
Full of high sentence, but a bit obtuse;
At times, indeed, almost ridiculous—
Almost, at times, the Fool.

I grow old . . . I grow old . . .
I shall wear the bottoms of my trousers rolled.

Shall I part my hair behind? Do I dare to eat a peach?
I shall wear white flannel trousers, and walk upon the beach.
I have heard the mermaids singing, each to each.

I do not think that they will sing to me.

I have seen them riding seaward on the waves
Combing the white hair of the waves blown back
When the wind blows the water white and black.

We have lingered in the chambers of the sea
By sea-girls wreathed with seaweed red and brown
Till human voices wake us, and we drown.

Ralph Waldo Emerson

(1803–1882)

DAYS

Daughters of Time, the hypocritic Days,
Muffled and dumb like barefooted dervishes,
And marching single in an endless file,
Bring diadems and fagots in their hands.
To each they offer gifts after his will,
Bread, kingdom, stars, and sky that holds them all.
I, in my pleachéd garden, watched the pomp,
Forgot my mourning wishes, hastily
Took a few herbs and apples, and the Day
Turned and departed silent. I, too late,
Under her solemn fillet saw the scorn.

David Ferry
(b. 1924)

Gilgamesh, I: The Story

of him who knew the most of all men know;
who made the journey; heartbroken; reconciled;

who knew the way things were before the Flood,
the secret things, the mystery; who went

to the end of the earth, and over; who returned,
and wrote the story on a tablet of stone.

He built Uruk. He built the keeping place
of Anu and Ishtar. The outer wall

shines in the sun like brightest copper; the inner
wall is beyond the imagining of kings.

Study the brickwork, study the fortification;
climb the great ancient staircase to the terrace;

study how it is made; from the terrace see
the planted and fallow fields, the ponds and orchards.

This is Uruk, the city of Gilgamesh
the Wild Ox, son of Lugalbanda, son

of the Lady Wildcow Ninsun, Gilgamesh
the vanguard and the rear guard of the army,

Shadow of Darkness over the enemy field,
the Web, the Flood that rises to wash away

the walls of alien cities, Gilgamesh
the strongest one of all, the perfect, the terror.

It is he who opened passes through the mountains;
and he who dug deep wells on the mountainsides;

who measured the world; and sought out Utnapishtim
beyond the world; it is he who restored the shrines;

two-thirds a god, one-third a man, the king.
Go to the temple of Anu and Ishtar:

open the copper chest with the iron locks;
the tablet of lapis lazuli tells the story.

Robert Frost

(1874–1963)

HOME BURIAL

He saw her from the bottom of the stairs
Before she saw him. She was starting down,
Looking back over her shoulder at some fear.
She took a doubtful step and then undid it
To raise herself and look again. He spoke
Advancing toward her: "What is it you see
From up there always? — for I want to know."
She turned and sank upon her skirts at that,
And her face changed from terrified to dull.
He said to gain time: "What is it you see?"
Mounting until she cowered under him.
"I will find out now — you must tell me, dear."
She, in her place, refused him any help,
With the least stiffening of her neck and silence.
She let him look, sure that he wouldn't see,
Blind creature; and awhile he didn't see.
But at last he murmured, "Oh," and again, "Oh."

"What is it — what?" she said.

                              "Just that I see."

"You don't," she challenged. "Tell me what it is."

"The wonder is I didn't see at once.
I never noticed it from here before.
I must be wonted to it — that's the reason.

The little graveyard where my people are!
So small the window frames the whole of it.
Not so much larger than a bedroom, is it?
There are three stones of slate and one of marble,
Broad-shouldered little slabs there in the sunlight
On the sidehill. We haven't to mind *those.*
But I understand: it is not the stones,
But the child's mound —— "

                            "Don't, don't, don't,
don't," she cried.

She withdrew, shrinking from beneath his arm
That rested on the banister, and slid downstairs;
And turned on him, with such a daunting look,
He said twice over before he knew himself:
"Can't a man speak of his own child he's lost?"

"Not you! — Oh, where's my hat? Oh, I don't need it!
I must get out of here. I must get air. —
I don't know rightly whether any man can."

"Amy! Don't go to someone else this time.
Listen to me. I won't come down the stairs."
He sat and fixed his chin between his fists.
"There's something I should like to ask you, dear."

"You don't know how to ask it."

                            "Help me, then."

Her fingers moved the latch for all reply.

"My words are nearly always an offense.
I don't know how to speak of anything
So as to please you. But I might be taught,
I should suppose. I can't say I see how.
A man must partly give up being a man

With womenfolk. We could have some arrangement
By which I'd bind myself to keep hands off
Anything special you're a-mind to name.
Though I don't like such things 'twixt those that love.
Two that don't love can't live together without them.
But two that do can't live together with them."
She moved the latch a little. "Don't — don't go.
Don't carry it to someone else this time.
Tell me about it if it's something human.
Let me into your grief. I'm not so much
Unlike other folks as your standing there
Apart would make me out. Give me my chance.
I do think, though, you overdo it a little.
What was it brought you up to think it the thing
To take your mother-loss of a first child
So inconsolably — in the face of love.
You'd think his memory might be satisfied ——"

"There you go sneering now!"
                                            "I'm not. I'm not!
You make me angry. I'll come down to you.
God, what a woman! And it's come to this,
A man can't speak of his own child that's dead."

"You can't because you don't know how to speak.
If you had any feeling, you that dug
With your own hand — how could you? — his little grave;
I saw you from that very window there,
Making the gravel leap and leap in air,
Leap up, like that, like that, and land so lightly
And roll back down the mound beside the hole.
I thought, who is that man? I didn't know you.
And I crept down the stairs and up the stairs
To look again, and still your spade kept lifting.
Then you came in. I heard your rumbling voice

Out in the kitchen, and I don't know why,
But I went near to see with my own eyes.

You could sit there with the stains on your shoes
Of the fresh earth from your own baby's grave
And talk about your everyday concerns.
You had stood the spade up against the wall
Outside there in the entry, for I saw it."

"I shall laugh the worst laugh I ever laughed.
I'm cursed. God, if I don't believe I'm cursed."

"I can repeat the very words you were saying:
'Three foggy mornings and one rainy day
Will rot the best birch fence a man can build.'
Think of it, talk like that at such a time!
What had how long it takes a birch to rot
To do with what was in the darkened parlor?
You *couldn't* care! The nearest friends can go
With anyone to death, comes so far short
They might as well not try to go at all.
No, from the time when one is sick to death,
One is alone, and he dies more alone.
Friends make pretense of following to the grave,
But before one is in it, their minds are turned
And making the best of their way back to life
And living people, and things they understand.
But the world's evil. I won't have grief so
If I can change it. Oh, I won't, I won't!"

"There, you have said it all and you feel better.
You won't go now. You're crying. Close the door.
The heart's gone out of it: why keep it up?
Amy! There's someone coming down the road!"

"*You* — oh, you think the talk is all. I must go —
Somewhere out of this house. How can I make you —— "

"If — you — do!" She was opening the door wider.
"Where do you mean to go? First tell me that.
I'll follow and bring you back by force. I *will*! — "

Louise Glück

(b. 1943)

TRIBUTARIES

All the roads in the village unite at the fountain.
Avenue of Liberty, Avenue of the Acacia Trees—
The fountain rises at the center of the plaza;
on sunny days, rainbows in the piss of the cherub.

In summer, couples sit at the pool's edge.
There's room in the pool for many reflections;
the plaza's nearly empty, the acacia trees don't get this far.
And the Avenue of Liberty is barren and austere; its image
doesn't crowd the water.

Interspersed with the couples, mothers with their younger children.
Here's where they come to talk to one another, maybe
meet a young man, see if there's anything left of their beauty.
When they look down, it's a sad moment: the water isn't
    encouraging.

The husbands are off working, but by some miracle
all the amorous young men are always free;
they sit at the edge of the fountain, splashing their sweethearts
with fountain water.

Around the fountain, there are clusters of metal tables.
This is where you sit when you're old,
beyond the intensities of the fountain.
The fountain is for the young, who still want to look at themselves.
Or for the mothers, who need to keep their children diverted.

A few old people linger at the tables.
Life is simple now: one day cognac, one day coffee and a cigarette.
To the couples, it's clear who's on the outskirts of life, who's at the
    center.

The children cry, they sometimes fight over toys.
But the water's there, to remind the mothers that they love these
    children,
that for them to drown would be terrible.

The mothers are tired constantly, the children are always fighting,
the husbands at work or angry. No young man comes.
The couples are like an image from some faraway time, an echo
    coming
very faint from the mountains.

They're alone at the fountain, in a dark well.
They've been exiled by the world of hope,
which is the world of action,
but the world of thought hasn't as yet opened to them.
When it does, everything will change.

Darkness is falling, the plaza empties.
The first leaves of autumn litter the fountain.
The roads don't gather here anymore;
the fountain sends them away, back into the hills they came from.

Avenue of Broken Faith, Avenue of Disappointment,
Avenue of the Acacia Trees, of Olive Trees,
the wind filling with silver leaves,

Avenue of Lost Time, Avenue of Liberty that ends in stone,
not at the field's edge but at the foot of the mountain.

Robert Hass

(b. 1941)

A STORY ABOUT THE BODY

The young composer, working that summer at an artist's colony, had watched her for a week. She was Japanese, a painter, almost sixty, and he thought he was in love with her. He loved her work, and her work was like the way she moved her body, used her hands, looked at him directly when she made amused and considered answers to his questions. One night, walking back from a concert, they came to her door and she turned to him and said, "I think you would like to have me. I would like that too, but I must tell you that I have had a double mastectomy," and when he didn't understand, "I've lost both my breasts." The radiance that he had carried around in his belly and chest cavity—like music—withered very quickly, and he made himself look at her when he said, "I'm sorry. I don't think I could." He walked back to his own cabin through the pines, and in the morning he found a small blue bowl on the porch outside his door. It looked to be full of rose petals, but he found when he picked it up that the rose petals were on top; the rest of the bowl—she must have swept them from the corners of her studio—was full of dead bees.

Robert Hayden

(1913–1980)

FREDERICK DOUGLASS

When it is finally ours, this freedom, this liberty, this beautiful
and terrible thing, needful to man as air,
usable as earth; when it belongs at last to all,
when it is truly instinct, brain matter, diastole, systole,
reflex action; when it is finally won; when it is more
than the gaudy mumbo jumbo of politicians:
this man, this Douglass, this former slave, this Negro
beaten to his knees, exiled, visioning a world
where none is lonely, none hunted, alien,
this man, superb in love and logic, this man
shall be remembered. Oh, not with statues' rhetoric,
not with legends and poems and wreaths of bronze alone,
but with the lives grown out of his life, the lives
fleshing his dream of the beautiful, needful thing.

Terrance Hayes

(b. 1971)

WOOFER (WHEN I CONSIDER
THE AFRICAN-AMERICAN)

When I consider the much discussed dilemma
of the African-American, I think not of the diasporic
middle passing, unchained, juke, jock, and jiving
sons and daughters of what sleek dashikied poets
and tether fisted Nationalists commonly call Mother
Africa, but of an ex-girlfriend who was the child
of a black-skinned Ghanaian beauty and Jewish-
American, globetrotting ethnomusicologist.
I forgot all my father's warnings about meeting women
at bus stops (which is the way he met my mother)
when I met her waiting for the rush hour bus in October
because I have always been a sucker for deep blue denim
and Afros and because she spoke so slowly
when she asked the time. I wrote my phone number
in the back of the book of poems I had and said
something like "You can return it when I see you again"
which has to be one of my top two or three best
pickup lines ever. If you have ever gotten lucky
on a first date you can guess what followed: her smile
twizzling above a tight black v-neck sweater, chatter
on my velvet couch and then the two of us wearing nothing
but shoes. When I think of African-American rituals
of love, I think not of young, made-up unwed mothers
who seek warmth in the arms of any brother
with arms because they never knew their fathers
(though that could describe my mother), but of that girl

and me in the basement of her father's four story Victorian
making love among the fresh blood and axe
and chicken feathers left after the Thanksgiving slaughter
executed by a 3-D witchdoctor houseguest (his face
was starred by tribal markings) and her ruddy American
poppa while drums drummed upstairs from his hi-fi woofers
because that's the closest I've ever come to anything
remotely ritualistic or African, for that matter.
We were quiet enough to hear their chatter
between the drums and the scraping of their chairs
at the table above us and the footsteps of anyone
approaching the basement door and it made
our business sweeter, though I'll admit I wondered
if I'd be cursed for making love under her father's nose
or if the witchdoctor would sense us and then cast a spell.
I have been cursed, broken hearted, stunned, frightened
and bewildered, but when I consider the African-American
I think not of the tek nines of my generation deployed
by madness or that we were assigned some lousy fate
when God prescribed job titles at the beginning of Time
or that we were too dumb to run the other way
when we saw the wide white sails of the ships
since given the absurd history of the world, everyone
is a descendant of slaves (which makes me wonder
if outrunning your captors is not the real meaning of Race?).
I think of the girl's bark colored, bi-continental nipples
when I consider the African-American.
I think of a string of people connected one to another
and including the two of us there in the basement
linked by a hyphen filled with blood;
linked by a blood filled baton in one great historical relay.

George Herbert
(1593–1633)

LOVE UNKNOWN

Dear Friend, sit down, the tale is long and sad:
And in my faintings I presume your love
Will more comply than help. A Lord I had,
And have, of whom some grounds, which may improve,
I hold for two lives, and both lives in me.
To him I brought a dish of fruit one day,
And in the middle placed my heart. But he
           (I sigh to say)
Looked on a servant, who did know his eye
Better than you know me, or (which is one)
Than I myself. The servant instantly
Quitting the fruit, seized on my heart alone,
And threw it in a font, wherein did fall
A stream of blood, which issued from the side
Of a great rock: I well remember all,
And have good cause: there it was dipped and dyed,
And washed, and wrung: the very wringing yet
Enforceth tears. *Your heart was foul, I fear.*
Indeed 'tis true. I did and do commit
Many a fault more than my lease will bear;
Yet still asked pardon, and was not denied.
But you shall hear. After my heart was well,
And clean and fair, as I one even-tide
           (I sigh to tell)
Walked by myself abroad, I saw a large
And spacious furnace flaming, and thereon
A boiling cauldron, round about whose verge

Was in great letters set *AFFLICTION*.
The greatness showed the owner. So I went
To fetch a sacrifice out of my fold,
Thinking with that, which I did thus present,
To warm his love, which I did fear grew cold.
But as my heart did tender it, the man,
Who was to take it from me, slipped his hand,
And threw my heart into the scalding pan;
My heart, that brought it (do you understand?)
The offerer's heart. *Your heart was hard, I fear.*
Indeed it's true. I found a callous matter
Began to spread and to expatiate there:
But with a richer drug than scalding water
I bathed it often, ev'n with holy blood,
Which at a board, while many drunk bare wine,
A friend did steal into my cup for good,
Ev'n taken inwardly, and most divine
To supple hardnesses. But at the length
Out of the cauldron getting, soon I fled
Unto my house, where to repair the strength
Which I had lost, I hasted to my bed.
But when I thought to sleep out all these faults
                (I sigh to speak)
I found that some had stuffed the bed with thoughts,
I would say *thorns*. Dear, could my heart not break,
When with my pleasures ev'n my rest was gone?
Full well I understood, who had been there:
For I had giv'n the key to none, but one:
It must be he. *Your heart was dull, I fear.*
Indeed a slack and sleepy state of mind
Did oft possess me, so that when I prayed,
Though my lips went, my heart did stay behind.
But all my scores were by another paid,
Who took the debt upon him. *Truly, Friend,*
For ought I hear, your Master shows to you
More favour than you wot of. Mark the end.
The Font did only, what was old, renew:

The Cauldron suppled, what was grown too hard:
The Thorns did quicken, what was grown too dull:
All did but strive to mend, what you had marred.
Wherefore be cheered, and praise him to the full
Each day, each hour, each moment of the week,
Who fain would have you be new, tender, quick.

Robinson Jeffers

(1887–1962)

VULTURE

I had walked since dawn and lay down to rest on a bare hillside
Above the ocean. I saw through half-shut eyelids a vulture
    wheeling high up in heaven,
And presently it passed again, but lower and nearer, its orbit
    narrowing, I understood then
That I was under inspection. I lay death-still and heard the
    flight-feathers
Whistle above me and make their circle and come nearer.
I could see the naked red head between the great wings
Bear downward staring. I said, "My dear bird, we are wasting
    time here.
These old bones will still work; they are not for you." But how
    beautiful he looked, gliding down
On those great sails; how beautiful he looked, veering away in
    the sea-light over the precipice. I tell you solemnly
That I was sorry to have disappointed him. To be eaten by that
    beak and become part of him, to share those wings and
    those eyes—
What a sublime end of one's body, what an enskyment; what a
    life after death.

Walter Savage Landor

(1775–1864)

DYING SPEECH OF AN OLD PHILOSOPHER

I strove with none, for none was worth my strife:
    Nature I loved, and, next to Nature, Art:
I warm'd both hands before the fire of Life;
    It sinks; and I am ready to depart.

Henry Wadsworth Longfellow
(1807–1882)

Paul Revere's Ride

Listen, my children, and you shall hear
Of the midnight ride of Paul Revere,
On the eighteenth of April, in Seventy-five;
Hardly a man is now alive
Who remembers that famous day and year.

He said to his friend, "If the British march
By land or sea from the town to-night,
Hang a lantern aloft in the belfry arch
Of the North Church tower as a signal light,—
One, if by land, and two, if by sea;
And I on the opposite shore will be,
Ready to ride and spread the alarm
Through every Middlesex village and farm,
For the country-folk to be up and to arm."

Then he said "Good night!" and with muffled oar
Silently rowed to the Charlestown shore,
Just as the moon rose over the bay,
Where swinging wide at her moorings lay
The Somerset, British man-of-war;
A phantom ship, with each mast and spar
Across the moon like a prison bar,
And a huge black hulk, that was magnified
By its own reflection in the tide.

Meanwhile, his friend, through alley and street,
Wanders and watches with eager ears,
Till in the silence around him he hears
The muster of men at the barrack door,
The sound of arms, and the tramp of feet,
And the measured tread of the grenadiers,
Marching down to their boats on the shore.

Then he climbed the tower of the Old North Church,
By the wooden stairs, with stealthy tread,
To the belfry-chamber overhead,
And startled the pigeons from their perch
On the sombre rafters, that round him made
Masses and moving shapes of shade,—
By the trembling ladder, steep and tall,
To the highest window in the wall,
Where he paused to listen and look down
A moment on the roofs of the town,
And the moonlight flowing over all.

Beneath, in the churchyard, lay the dead,
In their night-encampment on the hill,
Wrapped in silence so deep and still
That he could hear, like a sentinel's tread,
The watchful night-wind, as it went
Creeping along from tent to tent,
And seeming to whisper, "All is well!"
A moment only he feels the spell
Of the place and the hour, and the secret dread
Of the lonely belfry and the dead;
For suddenly all his thoughts are bent
On a shadowy something far away,
Where the river widens to meet the bay,—
A line of black that bends and floats
On the rising tide, like a bridge of boats.

Meanwhile, impatient to mount and ride,
Booted and spurred, with a heavy stride
On the opposite shore walked Paul Revere.
Now he patted his horse's side,
Now gazed at the landscape far and near,
Then, impetuous, stamped the earth,
And turned and tightened his saddle-girth;
But mostly he watched with eager search
The belfry-tower of the Old North Church,
As it rose above the graves on the hill,
Lonely and spectral and sombre and still.
And lo! as he looks, on the belfry's height
A glimmer, and then a gleam of light!
He springs to the saddle, the bridle he turns,
But lingers and gazes, till full on his sight
A second lamp in the belfry burns!

A hurry of hoofs in a village street,
A shape in the moonlight, a bulk in the dark,
And beneath, from the pebbles, in passing, a spark
Struck out by a steed flying fearless and fleet:
That was all! And yet, through the gloom and the light,
The fate of a nation was riding that night;
And the spark struck out by that steed, in his flight,
Kindled the land into flame with its heat.

He has left the village and mounted the steep,
And beneath him, tranquil and broad and deep,
Is the Mystic, meeting the ocean tides;
And under the alders, that skirt its edge,
Now soft on the sand, now loud on the ledge,
Is heard the tramp of his steed as he rides.

It was twelve by the village clock
When he crossed the bridge into Medford town.
He heard the crowing of the cock,
And the barking of the farmer's dog,

And felt the damp of the river fog,
That rises after the sun goes down.

It was one by the village clock,
When he galloped into Lexington.
He saw the gilded weathercock
Swim in the moonlight as he passed,
And the meeting-house windows, black and bare,
Gaze at him with a spectral glare,
As if they already stood aghast
At the bloody work they would look upon.

It was two by the village clock,
When he came to the bridge in Concord town.
He heard the bleating of the flock,
And the twitter of birds among the trees,
And felt the breath of the morning breeze
Blowing over the meadow, brown.
And one was safe and asleep in his bed
Who at the bridge would be first to fall,
Who that day would be lying dead,
Pierced by a British musket-ball.

You know the rest. In the books you have read,
How the British Regulars fired and fled, —
How the farmers gave them ball for ball,
From behind each fence and farm-yard wall,
Chasing the red-coats down the lane,
Then crossing the fields to emerge again
Under the trees at the turn of the road,
And only pausing to fire and load.

So through the night rode Paul Revere;
And so through the night went his cry of alarm
To every Middlesex village and farm, —
A cry of defiance and not of fear,
A voice in the darkness, a knock at the door,

And a word that shall echo forevermore!
For, borne on the night-wind of the Past,
Through all our history, to the last,
In the hour of darkness and peril and need,
The people will waken and listen to hear
The hurrying hoof-beats of that steed,
And the midnight message of Paul Revere.

Gail Mazur

(b. 1937)

MICHELANGELO: TO GIOVANNI DA PISTOIA WHEN THE AUTHOR WAS PAINTING THE VAULT OF THE SISTINE CHAPEL

—1509

I've already grown a goiter from this torture,
hunched up here like a cat in Lombardy
(or anywhere else where the stagnant water's poison).
My stomach's squashed under my chin, my beard's
pointing at heaven, my brain's crushed in a casket,
my breast twists like a harpy's. My brush,
above me all the time, dribbles paint
so my face makes a fine floor for droppings!

My haunches are grinding into my guts,
my poor ass strains to work as a counterweight,
every gesture I make is blind and aimless.
My skin hangs loose below me, my spine's
all knotted from folding over itself.
I'm bent taut as a Syrian bow.

Because I'm stuck like this, my thoughts
are crazy, perfidious tripe:
anyone shoots badly through a crooked blowpipe.

My painting is dead.
Defend it for me, Giovanni, protect my honor.
I am not in the right place—I am not a painter.

Heather McHugh

(b. 1948)

WHAT HE THOUGHT
for Fabbio Doplicher

We were supposed to do a job in Italy
and, full of our feeling for
ourselves (our sense of being
Poets from America) we went
from Rome to Fano, met
the mayor, mulled
a couple matters over (what's
cheap date, they asked us; what's
flat drink). Among Italian literati

we could recognize our counterparts:
the academic, the apologist,
the arrogant, the amorous,
the brazen and the glib—and there was one

administrator (the conservative), in suit
of regulation gray, who like a good tour guide
with measured pace and uninflected tone narrated
sights and histories the hired van hauled us past.
Of all, he was most politic and least poetic,
so it seemed. Our last few days in Rome
(when all but three of the New World Bards had flown)
I found a book of poems this
unprepossessing one had written: it was there
in the *pensione* room (a room he'd recommended)
where it must have been abandoned by

the German visitor (was there a bus of *them?*)
to whom he had inscribed and dated it a month before.
I couldn't read Italian, either, so I put the book
back into the wardrobe's dark. We last Americans

were due to leave tomorrow. For our parting evening then
our host chose something in a family restaurant, and there
we sat and chatted, sat and chewed,
till, sensible it was our last
big chance to be poetic, make
our mark, one of us asked
                    "What's poetry?
Is it the fruits and vegetables and
marketplace of Campo dei Fiori, or
the statue there?" Because I was

the glib one, I identified the answer
instantly, I didn't have to think—"The truth
is both, it's both," I blurted out. But that
was easy. That was easiest to say. What followed
taught me something about difficulty,
for our underestimated host spoke out,
all of a sudden, with a rising passion, and he said:

The statue represents Giordano Bruno,
brought to be burned in the public square
because of his offense against
authority, which is to say
the Church. His crime was his belief
the universe does not revolve around
the human being: God is no
fixed point or central government, but rather is
poured in waves through all things. All things
move. "If God is not the soul itself, He is
the soul of the soul of the world." Such was
his heresy. The day they brought him
forth to die, they feared he might

incite the crowd (the man was famous
for his eloquence). And so his captors
placed upon his face
an iron mask, in which

he could not speak. That's
how they burned him. That is how
he died: without a word, in front
of everyone.
          And poetry—
                  (we'd all
put down our forks by now, to listen to
the man in gray; he went on
softly)—
              poetry is what
he thought, but did not say.

Sharon Olds

(b. 1942)

BIBLE STUDY: 71 B.C.E.

After Marcus Licinius Crassus
defeated the army of Spartacus,
he crucified 6,000 men.
That is what the records say,
as if he drove in the 18,000
nails himself. I wonder how
he felt, that day, if he went outside
among them, if he walked that human
woods. I think he stayed in his tent
and drank, and maybe copulated,
hearing the singing being done for him,
the woodwind-tuning he was doing at one
remove, to the six-thousandth power.
And maybe he looked out, sometimes,
to see the rows of instruments,
his orchard, the earth bristling with it
as if a patch in his brain had itched
and this was his way of scratching it
directly. Maybe it gave him pleasure,
and a sense of balance, as if he had suffered,
and now had found redress for it,
and voice for it. I speak as a monster,
someone who today has thought at length
about Crassus, his ecstasy of feeling
nothing while so much is being
felt, his hot lightness of spirit
in being free to walk around

while others are nailed above the earth.
It may have been the happiest day
of his life. If he had suddenly cut
his hand on a wineglass, I doubt he would
have woken up to what he was doing.
It is frightening to think of him suddenly
seeing what he was, to think of him running
outside, to try to take them down,
one man to save 6,000.
If he could have lowered one,
and seen the eyes when the level of pain
dropped like a sudden soaring into pleasure,
wouldn't that have opened in him
the wild terror of understanding
the other? But then he would have had
5,999
to go. Probably it almost never
happens, that a Marcus Crassus
wakes. I think he dozed, and was roused
to his living dream, lifted the flap
and stood and looked out, at the rustling, creaking
living field—his, like an external
organ, a heart.

Wilfred Owen

(1893–1918)

DULCE ET DECORUM EST

Bent double, like old beggars under sacks,
Knock-kneed, coughing like hags, we cursed through sludge,
Till on the haunting flares we turned our backs
And towards our distant rest began to trudge.
Men marched asleep. Many had lost their boots
But limped on, blood-shod. All went lame; all blind;
Drunk with fatigue; deaf even to the hoots
Of tired, outstripped Five-Nines that dropped behind.

Gas! GAS! Quick, boys!—An ecstasy of fumbling,
Fitting the clumsy helmets just in time;

But someone still was yelling out and stumbling,
And flound'ring like a man in fire or lime . . .
Dim, through the misty panes and thick green light,
As under a green sea, I saw him drowning.

In all my dreams, before my helpless sight,
He plunges at me, guttering, choking, drowning.

If in smothering dreams you too could pace
Behind the wagon that we flung him in,
And watch the white eyes writhing in his face,
His hanging face, like a devil's sick of sin;
If you could hear, at every jolt, the blood
Come gargling from the froth-corrupted lungs,
Obscene as cancer, bitter as the cud

Of vile, incurable sores on innocent tongues,—
My friend, you would not tell with such high zest
To children ardent for some desperate glory,
The old Lie: Dulce et decorum est
Pro patria mori.

Edgar Allan Poe

(1809–1849)

ALONE

From childhood's hour I have not been
As others were—I have not seen
As others saw—I could not bring
My passions from a common spring—
From the same source I have not taken
My sorrow—I could not awaken
My heart to joy at the same tone—
And all I lov'd—*I* lov'd alone.
Then—in my childhood—in the dawn
Of a most stormy life—was drawn
From ev'ry depth of good and ill
The mystery which binds me still—
From the torrent, or the fountain—
From the red cliff of the mountain—
From the sun that round me roll'd
In its autumn tint of gold—
From the lightning in the sky
As it pass'd me flying by—
From the thunder, and the storm—
And the cloud that took the form
(When the rest of Heaven was blue)
Of a demon in my view.

John Crowe Ransom

(1888–1974)

CAPTAIN CARPENTER

Captain Carpenter rose up in his prime
Put on his pistols and went riding out
But had got wellnigh nowhere at that time
Till he fell in with ladies in a rout.

It was a pretty lady and all her train
That played with him so sweetly but before
An hour she'd taken a sword with all her main
And twined him of his nose for evermore.

Captain Carpenter mounted up one day
And rode straightway into a stranger rogue
That looked unchristian but be that as may
The Captain did not wait upon prologue.

But drew upon him out of his great heart
The other swung against him with a club
And cracked his two legs at the shinny part
And let him roll and stick like any tub.

Captain Carpenter rode many a time
From male and female took he sundry harms
He met the wife of Satan crying "I'm
The she-wolf bids you shall bear no more arms."

Their strokes and counters whistled in the wind
I wish he had delivered half his blows

But where she should have made off like a hind
The bitch bit off his arms at the elbows.

And Captain Carpenter parted with his ears
To a black devil that used him in this wise
O Jesus ere his threescore and ten years
Another had plucked out his sweet blue eyes.

Captain Carpenter got up on his roan
And sallied from the gate in hell's despite
I heard him asking in the grimmest tone
If any enemy yet there was to fight?

"To any adversary it is fame
If he risk to be wounded by my tongue
Or burnt in two beneath my red heart's flame
Such are the perils he is cast among.

"But if he can he has a pretty choice
From an anatomy with little to lose
Whether he cut my tongue and take my voice
Or whether it be my round red heart he choose."

It was the neatest knave that ever was seen
Stepping in perfume from his lady's bower
Who at this word put in his merry mien
And fell on Captain Carpenter like a tower.

I would not knock old fellows in the dust
But there lay Captain Carpenter on his back
His weapons were the old heart in his bust
And a blade shook between rotten teeth alack.

The rogue in scarlet and grey soon knew his mind
He wished to get his trophy and depart
With gentle apology and touch refined
He pierced him and produced the Captain's heart.

God's mercy rest on Captain Carpenter now
I thought him Sirs an honest gentleman
Citizen husband soldier and scholar enow
Let jangling kites eat of him if they can.

But God's deep curses follow after those
That shore him of his goodly nose and ears
His legs and strong arms at the two elbows
And eyes that had not watered seventy years.

The curse of hell upon the sleek upstart
That got the Captain finally on his back
And took the red red vitals of his heart
And made the kites to whet their beaks clack clack.

Michael Ryan

(b. 1946)

DICKHEAD

A man who's trying to be a good man
but isn't, because he can't not take
whatever's said to him as judgement.
It causes him, as he puts it, to *react*.
His face and neck redden and bloat,
a thick blue vein bulges up his forehead
and bisects his bald pate, scaring his children
but provoking hilarity at work
where one guy likes to get his goat
by pasting pro-choice bumper stickers
on his computer screen while he's in the john,
then gathers a group into the next cubicle
to watch when he comes back.
He has talked to his minister and to his wife
about learning how not to *react*,
to make a joke, and he has tried to make jokes,
but his voice gets tense, they come out flat,
so even his joke becomes a joke at his expense,
another thing to laugh at him about.
He has thought to turn to them and ask,
Why don't you like me? What have I done to you?
But he has been told already all his life:
self-righteous goody two-shoes, a stick up your ass.
They are right. He has never never never gotten along.
He says nothing this time, just peels off the bumper sticker,
crumples it gently, places it gently
by his mousepad to dispose of later properly,

comparing his suffering to Christ's in Gethsemane
spat upon and mocked (his minister's advice),
and tries a smile that twists into a grimace,
which starts the hot blood rising into his face.
This is what they came for, to see Dickhead,
the bulging vein, the skull stoplight-red,
and indeed it is remarkable how gorged it gets
as if his torso had become a helium pump,
so, except for him whose eyes are shut tight,
they burst into laughter together exactly at the moment
cruelty turns into astonishment.

Percy Bysshe Shelley
(1792–1822)

OZYMANDIAS

I met a traveller from an antique land
Who said: "Two vast and trunkless legs of stone
Stand in the desert. Near them, on the sand,
Half sunk, a shattered visage lies, whose frown,
And wrinkled lip, and sneer of cold command,
Tell that its sculptor well those passions read
Which yet survive, stamped on these lifeless things,
The hand that mocked them and the heart that fed.
And on the pedestal these words appear—
'My name is Ozymandias, king of kings:
Look on my works, ye Mighty, and despair!'
Nothing beside remains. Round the decay
Of that colossal wreck, boundless and bare
The lone and level sands stretch far away."

Stevie Smith

(1902–1971)

Not Waving but Drowning

Nobody heard him, the dead man,
But still he lay moaning:
I was much further out than you thought
And not waving but drowning.

Poor chap, he always loved larking
And now he's dead
It must have been too cold for him his heart gave way,
They said.

Oh, no no no, it was too cold always
(Still the dead one lay moaning)
I was much too far out all my life
And not waving but drowning.

Mark Strand

(b. 1934)

OLD MAN LEAVES PARTY

It was clear when I left the party
That though I was over eighty I still had
A beautiful body. The moon shone down as it will
On moments of deep introspection. The wind held its breath.
And look, somebody left a mirror leaning against a tree.
Making sure that I was alone, I took off my shirt.
The flowers of bear grass nodded their moonwashed heads.
I took off my pants and the magpies circled the redwoods.
Down in the valley the creaking river was flowing once more.
How strange that I should stand in the wilds alone with my
    body.
I know what you are thinking. I was like you once. But now
With so much before me, so many emerald trees, and
Weed-whitened fields, mountains and lakes, how could I not
Be only myself, this dream of flesh, from moment to moment?

James Tate

(b. 1943)

The Lost Pilot

for my father, 1922–1944

Your face did not rot
like the others—the co-pilot,
for example, I saw him

yesterday. His face is corn-
mush: his wife and daughter,
the poor ignorant people, stare

as if he will compose soon.
He was more wronged than Job.
But your face did not rot

like the others—it grew dark,
and hard like ebony;
the features progressed in their

distinction. If I could cajole
you to come back for an evening,
down from your compulsive

orbiting, I would touch you,
read your face as Dallas,
your hoodlum gunner, now,

with the blistered eyes, reads
his braille editions. I would
touch your face as a disinterested

scholar touches an original page.
However frightening, I would
discover you, and I would not

turn you in; I would not make
you face your wife, or Dallas,
or the co-pilot, Jim. You

could return to your crazy
orbiting, and I would not try
to fully understand what

it means to you. All I know
is this: when I see you,
as I have seen you at least

once every year of my life,
spin across the wilds of the sky
like a tiny, African god,

I feel dead. I feel as if I were
the residue of a stranger's life,
that I should pursue you.

My head cocked toward the sky,
I cannot get off the ground,
and, you, passing over again,

fast, perfect, and unwilling
to tell me that you are doing
well, or that it was mistake

that placed you in that world,
and me in this; or that misfortune
placed these worlds in us.

Alfred Tennyson

(1809–1892)

ULYSSES

It little profits that an idle king,
By this still hearth, among these barren crags,
Matched with an aged wife, I mete and dole
Unequal laws unto a savage race,
That hoard, and sleep, and feed, and know not me.

I cannot rest from travel: I will drink
Life to the lees: all times I have enjoyed
Greatly, have suffered greatly, both with those
That loved me, and alone; on shore, and when
Through scudding drifts the rainy Hyades
Vext the dim sea: I am become a name;
For always roaming with a hungry heart
Much have I seen and known; cities of men
And manners, climates, councils, governments,
Myself not least, but honored of them all;
And drunk delight of battle with my peers,
Far on the ringing plains of windy Troy.
I am a part of all that I have met;
Yet all experience is an arch wherethrough
Gleams that untravelled world whose margin fades
For ever and for ever when I move.
How dull it is to pause, to make an end,
To rust unburnished, not to shine in use!
As though to breathe were life! Life piled on life
Were all too little, and of one to me
Little remains: but every hour is saved

From that eternal silence, something more,
A bringer of new things; and vile it were
For some three suns to store and hoard myself,
And this gray spirit yearning in desire
To follow knowledge like a sinking star,
Beyond the utmost bound of human thought.

    This is my son, mine own Telemachus,
To whom I leave the scepter and the isle—
Well-loved of me, discerning to fulfill
This labor, by slow prudence to make mild
A rugged people, and through soft degrees
Subdue them to the useful and the good.
Most blameless is he, centered in the sphere
Of common duties, decent not to fail
In offices of tenderness, and pay
Meet adoration to my household gods,
When I am gone. He works his work, I mine.

    There lies the port; the vessel puffs her sail:
There gloom the dark, broad seas. My mariners,
Souls that have toiled, and wrought, and thought with me—
That ever with a frolic welcome took
The thunder and the sunshine, and opposed
Free hearts, free foreheads—you and I are old;
Old age hath yet his honor and his toil;
Death closes all: but something ere the end,
Some work of noble note, may yet be done,
Not unbecoming men that strove with Gods.
The lights begin to twinkle from the rocks:
The long day wanes: the slow moon climbs: the deep
Moans round with many voices. Come, my friends,
'Tis not too late to seek a newer world.
Push off, and sitting well in order smite
The sounding furrows; for my purpose holds
To sail beyond the sunset, and the baths
Of all the western stars, until I die.

It may be that the gulfs will wash us down:
It may be we shall touch the Happy Isles,
And see the great Achilles, whom we knew.
Though much is taken, much abides; and though
We are not now that strength which in old days
Moved earth and heaven; that which we are, we are,
One equal temper of heroic hearts,
Made weak by time and fate, but strong in will
To strive, to seek, to find, and not to yield.

Ernest Lawrence Thayer

(1863–1940)

CASEY AT THE BAT

A BALLAD OF THE REPUBLIC, SUNG IN THE YEAR 1888

The outlook wasn't brilliant for the Mudville nine that day;
The score stood four to two with but one inning more to play.
And then when Cooney died at first, and Barrows did the same,
A sickly silence fell upon the patrons of the game.

A straggling few got up to go in deep despair. The rest
Clung to that hope which springs eternal in the human breast;
They thought if only Casey could but get a whack at that—
We'd put up even money now with Casey at the bat.

But Flynn preceded Casey, as did also Jimmy Blake,
And the former was a lulu and the latter was a cake;
So upon that stricken multitude grim melancholy sat,
For these seemed but little chance of Casey's getting to the bat.

But Flynn let drive a single, to the wonderment of all,
And Blake, the much despised, tore the cover off the ball;
And when the dust had lifted, and the men saw what had
    occurred,
There was Jimmy safe at second and Flynn a-hugging third.

Then from 5,000 throats and more there rose a lusty yell;
It rumbled through the valley, it rattled in the dell;
It knocked upon the mountain and recoiled upon the flat,
For Casey, mighty Casey, was advancing to the bat.

There was ease in Casey's manner as he stepped into his place;
There was pride in Casey's bearing and a smile on Casey's face.
And when, responding to the cheers, he lightly doffed his hat,
No stranger in the crowd could doubt 'twas Casey at the bat.

Ten thousand eyes were on him as he rubbed his hands with
    dirt;
Five thousand tongues applauded when he wiped them on his
    shirt.
Then while the writhing pitcher ground the ball into his hip,
Defiance gleamed in Casey's eye, a sneer curled Casey's lip.

And now the leather-covered sphere came hurtling through the
    air,
And Casey stood a-watching it in haughty grandeur there.
Close by the sturdy batsman the ball unheeded sped—
"That ain't my style," said Casey. "Strike one," the umpire said.

From the benches, black with people, there went up a muffled
    roar,
Like the beating of the storm-waves on a stern and distant
    shore.
"Kill him! Kill the umpire!" shouted some one on the stand;
And it's likely they'd have killed him had not Casey raised his
    hand.

With a smile of Christian charity great Casey's visage shone;
He stilled the rising tumult; he bade the game go on;
He signaled to the pitcher, and once more the spheroid flew;
But Casey still ignored it, and the umpire said, "Strike two."

"Fraud!" cried the maddened thousands, and echo answered
    fraud;
But one scornful look from Casey and the audience was awed.
They saw his face grow stern and cold, they saw his muscles
    strain,
And they knew that Casey wouldn't let that ball go by again.

The sneer is gone from Casey's lip, his teeth are clinched in
    hate;
He pounds with cruel violence his bat upon the plate.
And now the pitcher holds the ball, and now he lets it go,
And now the air is shattered by the force of Casey's blow.

Oh, somewhere in this favored land the sun is shining bright;
The band is playing somewhere, and somewhere hearts are light,
And somewhere men are laughing, and somewhere children
    shout;
But there is no joy in Mudville — mighty Casey has struck out.

Chidiock Tichborne

(1558–1586)

Tichborne's Elegy

WRITTEN WITH HIS OWN HAND
IN THE TOWER BEFORE HIS EXECUTION

My prime of youth is but a frost of cares,
My feast of joy is but a dish of pain,
My crop of corn is but a field of tares,
And all my good is but vain hope of gain;
The day is past, and yet I saw no sun,
And now I live, and now my life is done.

My tale was heard and yet it was not told,
My fruit is fallen and yet my leaves are green,
My youth is spent and yet I am not old,
I saw the world and yet I was not seen;
My thread is cut and yet it is not spun,
And now I live, and now my life is done.

I sought my death and found it in my womb,
I looked for life and saw it was a shade,
I trod the earth and knew it was my tomb,
And now I die, and now I was but made;
My glass is full, and now my glass is run,
And now I live, and now my life is done.

Ellen Voigt

(b. 1943)

THE HEN

The neck lodged under a stick,
the stick under her foot,
she held the full white breast
with both hands, yanked up and out,
and the head was delivered of the body.
Brain stuck like a lens; the profile
fringed with red feathers.
Deposed, abstracted,
the head lay on the ground like a coin.
But the rest, released into the yard,
language and direction wrung from it,
flapped the insufficient wings
and staggered forward, convulsed, instinctive—
I thought it was sobbing to see it hump the dust,
pulsing out those muddy juices,
as if something, deep in the gizzard,
in the sack of soft nuggets,
drove it toward the amputated member.
Even then, watching it litter the ground
with snowy refusals, I knew it was this
that held life, gave life,
and not the head with its hard contemplative eye.

William Carlos Williams

(1883–1963)*

DEDICATION FOR A PLOT OF GROUND

This plot of ground
facing the waters of this inlet
is dedicated to the living presence of
Emily Dickinson Wellcome
who was born in England; married;
lost her husband and with
her five year old son
sailed for New York in a two-master;
was driven to the Azores;
ran adrift on Fire Island shoal,
met her second husband
in a Brooklyn boarding house,
went with him to Puerto Rico
bore three more children, lost
her second husband, lived hard
for eight years in St. Thomas,
Puerto Rico, San Domingo, followed
the oldest son to New York,
lost her daughter, lost her "baby,"
seized the two boys of
the oldest son by the second marriage
mothered them—they being
motherless—fought for them
against the other grandmother
and the aunts, brought them here

* See *Variations on a Theme by William Carlos Williams* on page 452.

summer after summer, defended
herself here against thieves,
storms, sun, fire,
against flies, against girls
that came smelling about, against
drought, against weeds, storm-tides,
neighbors, weasels that stole her chickens,
against the weakness of her own hands,
against the growing strength of
the boys, against wind, against
the stones, against trespassers,
against rents, against her own mind.

She grubbed this earth with her own hands,
domineered over this grass plot,
blackguarded her oldest son
into buying it, lived here fifteen years,
attained a final loneliness and—

If you can bring nothing to this place
but your carcass, keep out.

This Is Just to Say

I have eaten
the plums
that were in
the icebox

and which
you were probably
saving
for breakfast

Forgive me
they were delicious
so sweet
and so cold

Anne Winters

(b. 1939)

Night Wash

All seas are seas in the moon to these
lonely and full of light.
High above laundries and rooftops
the pinstriped silhouettes speak nightmare
as do the faces full of fire and orange peel.
Every citizen knows what's the trouble: *America's longest
river is—New York; that's what they say, and I say so.*

Wonderful thing, electricity,
all these neons and nylons spun dry by a dime
in the Fifth Street Laundromat. The city
must be flying a thousand kites tonight
with its thousands of different keys.
—Sir, excuse me, *sir?*
Excuse me interfering, but you don't want
to put that in—it's got a rubber backing, see? Oh, not at all . . .

Piles of workshirts, piles of leopard underthings,
it's like fishing upside down all night long, and then the moon
    rises
like armfuls of thready sleeves. Her voice
rising and falling, her boys folded sideways asleep on the bench:
—Listen, that old West Indian cleaning lady?
Ask anyone here, she never has change.
Come on, she's too wise . . .

Down in the Tombs
the prisoner's knuckles climb like stripes
of paint in the light. He dreams he hears
the voice of a pig he used to slop for his uncles.
It pokes its head
through the bars and says
"Have you brought any beet greens?"

—You can never leave them alone at night. Like today
the stitching overseer says to me
If you can't keep the rhythm missus . . .
I says to him fire
me all you want, I don't take that shit
off anybody. That was a scare though—
you can't always get back on a day shift.

In the moonlight
the city rides serenely enough, its thousand light moorings
the hunted news in their eyes. Even the rivers
are tidal, as sailors and bankers know.
The glass bank of the Chase Manhattan stands dark
over the Harbor. One last
light slowly moving around the top floor.

—No washing machines in the basement, that's
what's the trouble. The laundry would dry overnight
on the roof, in the wind. Well a month ago
you know, some big boys took this twelveyearold
little Spanish girl up there. Then they killed her, they
threw her, six stories down. Listen, the stone age or something
running around on those roofs. So this cop said to me
Your street is the bottom, he actually
said that to me. So what could I say—that it's great?

On the folding table the same
gestures repeat, smoothing and folding
the same ancient shirt. Or the old West Indian cleaning lady

pretending to finger her pockets for change. At midnight she'll
    prop
her grey spaghetti mop and glide toward you
in her black cotton trousers, her black
lavender face tilted up. Very clearly
she says to the world in dream-language
I mean to live.

Yvor Winters

(1900–1968)

SIR GAWAINE AND THE GREEN KNIGHT

Reptilian green the wrinkled throat,
Green as a bough of yew the beard;
He bent his head, and so I smote;
Then for a thought my vision cleared.

The head dropped clean; he rose and walked;
He fixed his fingers in the hair;
The head was unabashed and talked;
I understood what I must dare.

His flesh, cut down, arose and grew.
He bade me wait the season's round,
And then, when he had strength anew,
To meet him on his native ground.

The year declined; and in his keep
I passed in joy a thriving yule;
And whether waking or in sleep,
I lived in riot like a fool.

He beat the woods to bring me meat.
His lady, like a forest vine,
Grew in my arms; the growth was sweet;
And yet what thoughtless force was mine!

By practice and conviction formed,
With ancient stubbornness ingrained,

Although her body clung and swarmed,
My own identity remained.

Her beauty, lithe, unholy, pure,
Took shapes that I had never known;
And had I once been insecure,
Had grafted laurel in my bone.

And then, since I had kept the trust,
Had loved the lady, yet was true,
The knight withheld his giant thrust
And let me go with what I knew.

I left the green bark and the shade,
Where growth was rapid, thick, and still;
I found a road that men had made
And rested on a drying hill.

James Wright

(1927–1980)

Ars Poetica: Some Recent Criticism

1

I loved my country,
When I was a little boy.
Agnes is my aunt,
And she doesn't even know
If I love any thing
On this God's
Green little apple.

I have no idea why Uncle Sherman
Who is dead
Fell in with her.
He wasn't all that drunk.
He longed all life long
To open a package store,
And he never did anything,
But he fell in with Agnes.
She is no more to me
Than my mind is,
Which I bless. She was a homely woman
In the snow, alone.

Sherman sang bad,
But he could sing.
I too have fallen in
With a luminous woman.

There must be something.

The only bright thing
Agnes ever did
That I know of
Was to get hurt and angry.
When Sherman met my other uncle
Emerson Buchanan, who thinks he is not dead,

At the wedding of Agnes
Uncle Emerson smirked:
"What's the use buying a cow,
When you can get the milk free?"

She didn't weep.
She got mad.
Mad means something.
"You guys are makin' fun
Out of me."

2

She stank.
Her house stank.
I went down to see Uncle Sherman
One evening.
I had a lonely furlough
Out of the army.
He must have been
One of the heroes
Of love, because he lay down
With my Aunt Agnes
Twice at least.
Listen, lay down there,
Even when she went crazy.
She wept two weeping daughters,
But she did not cry.
I think she was too lonely
To weep for herself.

3

I gather my Aunt Agnes
Into my veins.
I could tell you,
If you have read this far,
That the nut house in Cambridge
Where Agnes is dying
Is no more Harvard
Than you could ever be.
And I want to gather you back to my Ohio.
You could understand Aunt Agnes,
Sick, her eyes blackened,
Her one love dead.

4

Why do I care for her,
That slob,
So fat and stupid?
One afternoon,
At Aetnaville, Ohio,
A broken goat escaped
From a carnival,
One of the hooch dances
They used to hold
Down by my river.
Scrawny the goat panicked
Down Agnes's alley,
Which is my country,
If you haven't noticed,
America,
Which I loved when I was young.

5

That goat ran down the alley,
And many boys giggled
While they tried to stone our fellow
Goat to death.

And my Aunt Agnes,
Who stank and lied,
Threw stones back at the boys
And gathered the goat,
Nuts as she was,
Into her sloppy arms.

6

Reader,
We had a lovely language,
We would not listen.

I don't believe in your god.
I don't believe my Aunt Agnes is a saint.
I don't believe the little boys
Who stoned the poor
Son of a bitch goat
Are charming Tom Sawyers.

I don't believe in the goat either.

7

When I was a boy
I loved my country.

Ense petit placidam
Sub libertate quietem.

Hell, I ain't got nothing.
Ah, you bastards,

How I hate you.

VI

ODES, COMPLAINTS, AND CELEBRATIONS

T HIS MAY BE the most basic of poetic categories: every poem, by definition, says *here is an occasion worth making a poem about.* A certain element in poetry resembles pre-verbal sounds: a cheer or a sigh or a groan—or a subdued, wordless murmur of awe, as in Walter Savage Landor's response to seeing a hair of Lucretia Borgia's (p. 384). (The centuries-old lock of hair was said to have been stolen from a museum by Edward John Trelawny, a rapscallion friend of the Romantic poets.) Landor marvels both at the vanishing of the once-powerful, half-legendary Borgia and at the rather beautiful relic of her life that is in front of him:

ON SEEING A HAIR OF LUCRETIA BORGIA

Borgia, thou once wert almost too august
And high for adoration; now thou'rt dust.
All that remains of thee these plaits unfold,
Calm hair, meandering in pellucid gold.

The slow, lush rhythm of the last line makes an audible gesture that indicates both object and feeling: the strands of hair and the sense of marvel; the curvilinear shimmer of gold and the long perspective of time. This kind of feeling used to be called "wonder."

Wonder can be part of a complaint, too. Wallace Stevens in "Madame La Fleurie" (p. 414) sings a kind of complaint related to the notions that the earth is our mother, that the earth is flowered, that we are made of earth and return to earth. We may think that the earth reflects our "crisp" human ways of thinking and knowing, but:

> Now, he brings all that he saw into the earth, to the waiting
> parent.
> His crisp knowledge is devoured by her, beneath a dew.

Stevens' imagery of ancient myth or modern horror film is so exuberant, so elaborately imagined, that as in the movies or mythology dread becomes a triumph of the imagination:

> His grief is that his mother should feed on him, himself and
> what he saw,
> In that distant chamber, a bearded queen, wicked in her dead
> light.

In these lines, the feeling of wonder emerges from language that is like an equivalent of special effects.

Wonder is implicit in the second-person of the ode form—John Keats addressing Autumn or a Nightingale or an Urn (pp. 380, 377, 376); Robert Herrick addressing his dead friend and master in poetry Ben Jonson (p. 364); George Herbert addressing the day, the rose, the spring (p. 362); Hart Crane addressing the Brooklyn Bridge (p. 344); Allen Ginsberg addressing America (p. 357). Calling anything at all "you," asking it or commanding it to listen, or even to behave certain ways, is such a basic move that it can seem hackneyed or corny. On the other hand, the second-person imperatives generate tremendous emotion and grace in George Peele's poem, a song in the voice of the biblical Bathsheba, imagined as fearful at the consequences of beauty (p. 401):

BETHSABE'S SONG

Hot sun, cool fire, tempered with sweet air,
Black shade, fair nurse, shadow my white hair;

Shine, sun; burn, fire; breathe, air, and ease me;
Black shade, fair nurse, shroud me and please me:
Shadow, my sweet nurse, keep me from burning,
Make not my glad cause cause of mourning.

The requests made directly to sun, shade, air, fire are part of a braided-together pathos and marveling, held in balance by the rhymes and the plaintive, halting rhythm of pauses.

Wonder has many keys, and can be part of many different emotions. (It may be a surprise to find that the poem we know as "Twinkle, Twinkle, Little Star," with its explicit "I wonder," has an author—Jane Taylor—and five stanzas [p. 417].) Ben Jonson in "An Ode to Himself" (p. 374) marvels complainingly about his own failure to write: "Where dost thou careless lie / Buried in ease and sloth?" He urges himself to ignore the fools who, like little fishes, gorge themselves on fake poetry; his rhetorical questions marvel at the power of the world's defects—how can we let such things bother us?

What though the greedy fry
     Be taken with false baits
Of worded balladry,
And think it poesy?
     They die with their conceits,
And only piteous scorn upon their folly waits.

Grousing at himself for taking the "greedy fry" to heart, Jonson manages to complain about them quite vigorously, while urging himself to pay them no attention.

W. S. Merwin creates the feeling of wonder partly by changing tense from the past to the present, between the second and third stanza of his four-stanza poem "The Drunk in the Furnace" (p. 392):

They were afterwards astonished
To confirm, one morning, a twist of smoke like a pale
Resurrection, staggering out of its chewed hole,
And to remark then other tokens that someone,
Cosily bolted behind the eye-holed iron

Door of the drafty burner, had there established
　　His bad castle.

　　Where he gets his spirits
It's a mystery. But the stuff keeps him musical:
Hammer-and-anviling with poker and bottle
To his jugged bellowings, till the last groaning clang
As he collapses onto the rioting
Springs of a litter of car-seats ranged on the grates,
　　To sleep like an iron pig.

The astonishment of the good citizens who discover that the drunk
has moved into an abandoned furnace is part of the narrative. When
the next stanza ponders his ongoing, musical being in the present, the
astonishment becomes a degree or two closer to the poet and the reader.
The clattering and bellowing of the musical drunk persist, happening in
the present: in that immediacy, akin to the voice embedded in a poem.

Anna Laetitia Barbauld

(1743–1825)

THE RIGHTS OF WOMAN

Yes, injured Woman! rise, assert thy right!
Woman! too long degraded, scorned, opprest;
O born to rule in partial Law's despite,
Resume thy native empire o'er the breast!

Go forth arrayed in panoply divine;
That angel pureness which admits no stain;
Go, bid proud Man his boasted rule resign,
And kiss the golden scepter of thy reign.

Go, gird thyself with grace; collect thy store
Of bright artillery glancing from afar;
Soft melting tones thy thundering cannon's roar,
Blushes and fears thy magazine of war.

Thy rights are empire: urge no meaner claim,—
Felt, not defined, and if debated, lost;
Like sacred mysteries, which withheld from fame,
Shunning discussion, are revered the most.

Try all that wit and art suggest to bend
Of thy imperial foe the stubborn knee;
Make treacherous Man thy subject, not thy friend;
Thou mayst command, but never canst be free.

Awe the licentious, and restrain the rude;
Soften the sullen, clear the cloudy brow:

Be, more than princes' gifts, thy favours sued;—
She hazards all, who will the least allow.

But hope not, courted idol of mankind,
On this proud eminence secure to stay;
Subduing and subdued, thou soon shalt find
Thy coldness soften, and thy pride give way.

Then, then, abandon each ambitious thought,
Conquest or rule thy heart shall feebly move,
In Nature's school, by her soft maxims taught,
That separate rights are lost in mutual love.

Frank Bidart

(b. 1939)

FOR THE TWENTIETH CENTURY

Bound, hungry to pluck again from the thousand
technologies of ecstacy

boundlessness, the world that at a drop of water
rises without boundaries,

I push the PLAY button:—

. . . *Callas, Laurel & Hardy, Szigeti*

you are alive again,—

the slow movement of K.218
once again no longer

bland, merely pretty, nearly
banal, as it is

in all but Szigeti's hands

•

Therefore you and I and Mozart
must thank the Twentieth Century, for

it made you pattern, form
whose infinite

repeatability within matter
defies matter—

Malibran. Henry Irving. The young
Joachim. They are lost, a mountain of

newspaper clippings, become words
not their own words. The art of the performer.

William Blake

(1757–1827)

THE TYGER

Tyger! Tyger! burning bright
In the forests of the night,
What immortal hand or eye
Could frame thy fearful symmetry?

In what distant deeps or skies
Burnt the fire of thine eyes?
On what wings dare he aspire?
What the hand, dare seize the fire?

And what shoulder, & what art,
Could twist the sinews of thy heart?
And when thy heart began to beat,
What dread hand? & what dread feet?

What the hammer? what the chain?
In what furnace was thy brain?
What the anvil? what dread grasp
Dare its deadly terrors clasp?

When the stars threw down their spears,
And water'd heaven with their tears,
Did he smile his work to see?
Did he who made the Lamb make thee?

Tyger! Tyger! burning bright
In the forests of the night,
What immortal hand or eye
Dare frame thy fearful symmetry?

Gwendolyn Brooks

(1917–2000)

BOY BREAKING GLASS
To Marc Crawford
from whom the commission

Whose broken window is a cry of art,
(success, that winks aware
as elegance, as a treasonable faith)
is raw: is sonic: is old-eyed première.
Our beautiful flaw and terrible ornament.
Our barbarous and metal little man.

"I shall create! If not a note, a hole.
If not an overture, a desecration."

Full of pepper and light
and Salt and night and cargoes.

"Don't go down the plank
if you see there's no extension.
Each to his grief, each to
his loneliness and fidgety revenge.

Nobody knew where I was and now I am no longer there."

The only sanity is a cup of tea.
The music is in minors.

Each one other
is having different weather.

"It was you, it was you who threw away my name!
And this is everything I have for me."

Who has not Congress, lobster, love, luau,
the Regency Room, the Statue of Liberty,
runs. A sloppy amalgamation.
A mistake.
A cliff.
A hymn, a snare, and an exceeding sun.

Charles Bukowski

(1920–1994)*

STARTLED INTO LIFE LIKE FIRE

in grievous deity my cat
walks around
he walks around and around
with
electric tail and
push-button
eyes

he is
alive and
plush and
final as a plum tree

neither of us understands
cathedrals or
the man outside
watering his
lawn

if I were all the man
that he is
cat—
if there were men
like this

* See *You Don't Know What Love Is* on page 437.

the world could
begin

he leaps up on the couch
and walks through
porticoes of my
admiration.

Thomas Campion

(1567–1620)

WHAT IF A DAY

What if a day, or a month, or a yeare
Crown thy delights with a thousand sweet contentings?
Cannot a chance of a night or an howre
Crosse thy desires with as many sad tormentings?
    Fortune, honor, beauty, youth
    Are but blossoms dying;
    Wanton pleasure, doating love,
    Are but shadowes flying.
    All our joyes are but toyes,
    Idle thoughts deceiving;
    None have power of an howre
    In their lives bereaving.

Earthes but a point to the world, and a man
Is but a point to the worlds compared centure:
Shall then a point of a point be so vaine
As to triumph in a seely points adventure?
    All is hassard that we have,
    There is nothing biding;
    Dayes of pleasure are like streames
    Through faire meadows gliding.
    Weale and woe, time doth goe,
    Time is never turning:
    Secret fates guide our states,
    Both in mirth and mourning.

Lucille Clifton

(b. 1936)

HOMAGE TO MY HIPS

these hips are big hips
they need space to
move around in.
they don't fit into little
petty places. these hips
are free hips.
they don't like to be held back.
these hips have never been enslaved,
they go where they want to go
they do what they want to do.
these hips are mighty hips.
these hips are magic hips.
i have known them
to put a spell on a man and
spin him like a top!

Samuel Taylor Coleridge
(1772–1834)

KUBLA KHAN

OR A VISION IN A DREAM. A FRAGMENT

In Xanadu did Kubla Khan
A stately pleasure dome decree:
Where Alph, the sacred river, ran
Through caverns measureless to man
    Down to a sunless sea.
So twice five miles of fertile ground
With walls and towers were girdled round:
And there were gardens bright with sinuous rills,
Where blossomed many an incense-bearing tree;
And here were forests ancient as the hills,
Enfolding sunny spots of greenery.

But oh! that deep romantic chasm which slanted
Down the green hill athwart a cedarn cover!
A savage place! as holy and enchanted
As e'er beneath a waning moon was haunted
By woman wailing for her demon lover!
And from this chasm, with ceaseless turmoil seething,
As if this earth in fast thick pants were breathing,
A mighty fountain momently was forced:
Amid whose swift half-intermitted burst
Huge fragments vaulted like rebounding hail,
Or chaffy grain beneath the thresher's flail:
And 'mid these dancing rocks at once and ever
It flung up momently the sacred river.

Five miles meandering with a mazy motion
Through wood and dale the sacred river ran,
Then reached the caverns measureless to man,
And sank in tumult to a lifeless ocean:
And 'mid this tumult Kubla heard from far
Ancestral voices prophesying war!

    The shadow of the dome of pleasure
    Floated midway on the waves;
    Where was heard the mingled measure
    From the fountain and the caves.
It was a miracle of rare device,
A sunny pleasure dome with caves of ice!

    A damsel with a dulcimer
    In a vision once I saw:
    It was an Abyssinian maid,
    And on her dulcimer she played,
    Singing of Mount Abora.
    Could I revive within me
    Her symphony and song,
    To such a deep delight 'twould win me,
That with music loud and long,
I would build that dome in air,
That sunny dome! those caves of ice!
And all who heard should see them there,
And all should cry, Beware! Beware!
His flashing eyes, his floating hair!
Weave a circle round him thrice,
And close your eyes with holy dread,
For he on honey-dew hath fed,
And drunk the milk of Paradise.

Billy Collins

(b. 1941)

Some Days

Some days I put the people in their places at the table,
bend their legs at the knees,
if they come with that feature,
and fix them into the tiny wooden chairs.

All afternoon they face one another,
the man in the brown suit,
the woman in the blue dress,
perfectly motionless, perfectly behaved.

But other days, I am the one
who is lifted up by the ribs,
then lowered into the dining room of a dollhouse
to sit with the others at the long table.

Very funny,
but how would you like it
if you never knew from one day to the next
if you were going to spend it

striding around like a vivid god,
your shoulders in the clouds,
or sitting down there amidst the wallpaper,
staring straight ahead with your little plastic face?

Alfred Corn

(b. 1943)

CAESAREA

A theater facing the sea,
Ranked seating like folds
In marble drapery
Or marching Roman legions.

Toppled columns, each drum
An epoch wrapped with the same
Stonecrop. The wild acanthus
Copies a capital

In green, supplying thorns
To a site as reckless as sand
Where visitors late in the day
Erase this morning's footprints.

What audience but ghosts
would still be here, captive
to Medea's rage, or Creon's—
Latin or Greek reverberant

In *personae* with tragic scowls,
Their stance hoisted by buskins
To the plane of pure idea. . . .
Yet a feat of perspective

Lifts the sea still higher:
Above the actors' heads

Waves break, the sun takes its bloodbath,
And a trireme beats shoreward,

Oars tensed aloft and streaming
Salt diamonds into the sea.

William Cowper

(1731–1800)

LINES WRITTEN DURING A PERIOD OF INSANITY

Hatred and vengeance, my eternal portion,
Scarce can endure delay of execution,
Wait, with impatient readiness, to seize my
                    Soul in a moment.

Damned below Judas: more abhorred than he was,
Who for a few pence sold his holy Master.
Twice betrayed Jesus me, the last delinquent,
                    Deems the profanest.

Man disavows, and Deity disowns me:
Hell might afford my miseries a shelter;
Therefore hell keeps her ever hungry mouths all
                    Bolted against me.

Hard lot! encompassed with a thousand dangers;
Weary, faint, trembling with a thousand terrors;
I'm called, if vanquished, to receive a sentence
                    Worse than Abiram's.

Him the vindictive rod of angry justice
Sent quick and howling to the center headlong;
I, fed with judgment, in a fleshly tomb, am
                    Buried above ground.

Hart Crane

(1899–1932)

To Brooklyn Bridge

How many dawns, chill from his rippling rest
The seagull's wings shall dip and pivot him,
Shedding white rings of tumult, building high
Over the chained bay waters Liberty—

Then, with inviolate curve, forsake our eyes
As apparitional as sails that cross
Some page of figures to be filed away;
—Till elevators drop us from our day . . .

I think of cinemas, panoramic sleights
With multitudes bent toward some flashing scene
Never disclosed, but hastened to again,
Foretold to other eyes on the same screen;

And Thee, across the harbor, silver-paced
As though the sun took step of thee, yet left
Some motion ever unspent in thy stride,—
Implicitly thy freedom staying thee!

Out of some subway scuttle, cell or loft
A bedlamite speeds to thy parapets,
Tilting there momently, shrill shirt ballooning,
A jest falls from the speechless caravan.

Down Wall, from girder into street noon leaks,
A rip-tooth of the sky's acetylene;
All afternoon the cloud-flown derricks turn . . .
Thy cables breathe the North Atlantic still.

And obscure as that heaven of the Jews,
Thy guerdon . . . Accolade thou dost bestow
Of anonymity time cannot raise:
Vibrant reprieve and pardon thou dost show.

O harp and altar, of the fury fused,
(How could mere toil align thy choiring strings!)
Terrific threshold of the prophet's pledge,
Prayer of pariah, and the lover's cry,—

Again the traffic lights that skim thy swift
Unfractioned idiom, immaculate sigh of stars,
Beading thy path—condense eternity:
And we have seen night lifted in thine arms.

Under thy shadow by the piers I waited;
Only in darkness is thy shadow clear.
The City's fiery parcels all undone,
Already snow submerges an iron year . . .

O Sleepless as the river under thee,
Vaulting the sea, the prairies' dreaming sod,
Unto us lowliest sometime sweep, descend
And of the curveship lend a myth to God.

Countee Cullen

(1903–1946)

Yet Do I Marvel

I doubt not God is good, well-meaning, kind,
And did he stoop to quibble could tell why
The little buried mole continues blind,
Why flesh that mirrors Him must some day die,
Make plain the reason tortured Tantalus
Is baited by the fickle fruit, declare
If merely brute caprice dooms Sisyphus
To struggle up a never-ending stair.
Inscrutable His ways are, and immune
To catechism by a mind too strewn
With petty cares to slightly understand
What awful brain compels His awful hand.
Yet do I marvel at this curious thing:
To make a poet black, and bid him sing!

E. E. Cummings

(1894–1962)

BUFFALO BILL'S

defunct
          who used to
          ride a watersmooth-silver
                              stallion
and break onetwothreefourfive pigeonsjustlikethat
                                        Jesus

he was a handsome man
                    and what i want to know is
how do you like your blueeyed boy
Mister Death

James Dickey

(1923–1997)

For the Last Wolverine

They will soon be down

To one, but he still will be
For a little while   still will be stopping

The flakes in the air with a look,
Surrounding himself with the silence
Of whitening snarls. Let him eat
The last red meal of the condemned

To extinction, tearing the guts

From an elk. Yet that is not enough
For me. I would have him eat

The heart, and, from it, have an idea
Stream into his gnawing head
That he no longer has a thing
To lose, and so can walk

Out into the open, in the full

Pale of the sub-Arctic sun
Where a single spruce tree is dying

Higher and higher. Let him climb it
With all his meanness and strength.

Lord, we have come to the end
Of this kind of vision of heaven,

As the sky breaks open

Its fans around him and shimmers
And into its northern gates he rises

Snarling   complete   in the joy of a weasel
With an elk's horned heart in his stomach
Looking straight into the eternal
Blue, where he hauls his kind. I would have it all

My way: at the top of that tree I place

The New World's last eagle
Hunched in mangy feathers   giving

Up on the theory of flight.
Dear God of the wildness of poetry, let them mate
To the death in the rotten branches,
Let the tree sway and burst into flame

And mingle them, crackling with feathers,

In crownfire. Let something come
Of it   something gigantic   legendary

Rise beyond reason over hills
Of ice   SCREAMING   that it cannot die,
That it has come back, this time
On wings, and will spare no earthly thing:

That it will hover, made purely of northern

Lights, at dusk   and fall
On men building roads: will perch

On the moose's horn like a falcon
Riding into battle   into holy war against
Screaming railroad crews: will pull
Whole traplines like fibres from the snow

In the long-jawed night of fur trappers.

But, small, filthy, unwinged,
You will soon be crouching

Alone, with maybe some dim racial notion
Of being the last, but none of how much
Your unnoticed going will mean:
How much the timid poem needs

The mindless explosion of your rage,

The glutton's internal fire   the elk's
Heart in the belly, sprouting wings,

The pact of the "blind swallowing
Thing," with himself, to eat
The world, and not to be driven off it
Until it is gone, even if it takes

Forever. I take you as you are

And make of you what I will,
Skunk-bear, carcajou, bloodthirsty

Non-survivor.
                    Lord, let me die   but not die
Out.

Stuart Dischell

(b. 1954)

Days of Me

When people say they miss me,
I think how much I miss me too,
Me, the old me, the great me,
Lover of three women in one day,
Modest me, the best me, friend
To waiters and bartenders, hearty
Laugher and name rememberer,
Proud me, handsome and hirsute
In soccer shoes and shorts
On the ball fields behind MIT,
Strong me in a weightbelt at the gym,
Mutual sweat dripper in and out
Of the sauna, furtive observer
Of the coeducated and scantily clad,
Speedy me, cyclist of rivers,
Goose and peregrine falcon
Counter, all season venturer,
Chatterer-up of corner cops,
Groundskeepers, mothers with strollers,
Outwitter of panhandlers and bill
Collectors, avoider of levies, excises,
Me in a taxi in the rain,
Pressing my luck all the way home.

That's me at the dice table, baby,
Betting come, little Joe, and yo,
Blowing the coals, laying thunder,

My foot on top a fifty dollar chip
Some drunk spilled on the floor,
Dishonest me, evener of scores,
Eager accepter of the extra change,
Hotel towel pilferer, coffee spoon
Lifter, fervent retailer of others'
Humor, blackhearted gossiper,
Poisoner at the well, dweller
In unsavory detail, delighted sayer
Of the vulgar, off course belier
Of the true me, empiric builder
Newly haircutted, stickerer-up
For pals, jam unpriser, medic
To the self-inflicted, attorney
To the self-indicted, petty accountant
And keeper of the double books,
Great divider of the universe
And all its forms of existence
Into its relationship to me,
Fellow trembler to the future,
Thin air gawker, apprehender
Of the frameless door.

Ernest Dowson

(1867–1900)

Non sum qualis eram bonae sub regno Cynarae

Last night, ah, yesternight, betwixt her lips and mine
There fell thy shadow, Cynara! thy breath was shed
Upon my soul between the kisses and the wine;
And I was desolate and sick of an old passion,
    Yea, I was desolate and bowed my head:
I have been faithful to thee, Cynara! in my fashion.

All night upon mine heart I felt her warm heart beat,
Night-long within mine arms in love and sleep she lay;
Surely the kisses of her bought red mouth were sweet;
But I was desolate and sick of an old passion,
    When I awoke and found the dawn was grey:
I have been faithful to thee, Cynara! in my fashion.

I have forgot much, Cynara! gone with the wind,
Flung roses, roses riotously with the throng,
Dancing, to put thy pale, lost lilies out of mind;
But I was desolate and sick of an old passion,
    Yea, all the time, because the dance was long:
I have been faithful to thee, Cynara! in my fashion.

I cried for madder music and for stronger wine,
But when the feast is finished and the lamps expire,
Then falls thy shadow, Cynara! the night is thine;
And I am desolate and sick of an old passion,
    Yea hungry for the lips of my desire:
I have been faithful to thee, Cynara! in my fashion.

Robert Duncan

(1919–1988)

My Mother Would Be a Falconress

My mother would be a falconress,
And I, her gay falcon treading her wrist,
would fly to bring back
from the blue of the sky to her, bleeding, a prize,
where I dream in my little hood with many bells
jangling when I'd turn my head.

My mother would be a falconress,
and she sends me as far as her will goes.
She lets me ride to the end of her curb
where I fall back in anguish.
I dread that she will cast me away,
for I fall, I mis-take, I fail in her mission.

She would bring down the little birds.
And I would bring down the little birds.
When will she let me bring down the little birds,
pierced from their flight with their necks broken,
their heads like flowers limp from the stem?

I tread my mother's wrist and would draw blood.
Behind the little hood my eyes are hooded.
I have gone back into my hooded silence,
talking to myself and dropping off to sleep.

For she has muffled my dreams in the hood she has made me,
sewn round with bells, jangling when I move.

She rides with her little falcon upon her wrist.
She uses a barb that brings me to cower.
She sends me abroad to try my wings
and I come back to her. I would bring down
the little birds to her
I may not tear into, I must bring back perfectly.

I tear at her wrist with my beak to draw blood,
and her eye holds me, anguisht, terrifying.
She draws a limit to my flight.
Never beyond my sight, she says.
She trains me to fetch and to limit myself in fetching.
She rewards me with meat for my dinner.
But I must never eat what she sends me to bring her.

Yet it would have been beautiful, if she would have carried me,
always, in a little hood with the bells ringing,
at her wrist, and her riding
to the great falcon hunt, and me
flying up to the curb of my heart from her heart
to bring down the skylark from the blue to her feet,
straining, and then released for the flight.

My mother would be a falconress,
and I her gerfalcon, raised at her will,
from her wrist sent flying, as if I were her own
pride, as if her pride
knew no limits, as if her mind
sought in me flight beyond the horizon.

Ah, but high, high in the air I flew.
And far, far beyond the curb of her will,
were the blue hills where the falcons nest.
And then I saw west to the dying sun—
it seemd my human soul went down in flames.

I tore at her wrist, at the hold she had for me,
until the blood ran hot and I heard her cry out,
far, far beyond the curb of her will   •

to horizons of stars beyond the ringing hills of the world where
    the falcons nest
I saw, and I tore at her wrist with my savage beak.
I flew, as if sight flew from the anguish in her eye beyond her
    sight,
sent from my striking loose, from the cruel strike at her wrist,
striking out from the blood to be free of her.

My mother would be a falconress,
and even now, years after this,
when the wounds I left her had surely heald,
and the woman is dead,

her fierce eyes closed, and if her heart
were broken, it is stilld   •

I would be a falcon and go free.
I tread her wrist and wear the hood,
talking to myself, and would draw blood.

Allen Ginsberg

(1926–1997)

AMERICA

America I've given you all and now I'm nothing.
America two dollars and twentyseven cents January 17, 1956.
I can't stand my own mind.
America when will we end the human war?
Go fuck yourself with your atom bomb.
I don't feel good don't bother me.
I won't write my poem till I'm in my right mind.
America when will you be angelic?
When will you take off your clothes?
When will you look at yourself through the grave?
When will you be worthy of your million Trotskyites?
America why are your libraries full of tears?
America when will you send your eggs to India?
I'm sick of your insane demands.
When can I go into the supermarket and buy what I need with
    my good looks?
America after all it is you and I who are perfect not the next
    world.
Your machinery is too much for me.
You made me want to be a saint.
There must be some other way to settle this argument.
Burroughs is in Tangiers I don't think he'll come back it's
    sinister.
Are you being sinister or is this some form of practical joke?
I'm trying to come to the point.
I refuse to give up my obsession.
America stop pushing I know what I'm doing.

America the plum blossoms are falling.

I haven't read the newspapers for months, everyday somebody goes on trial for murder.

America I feel sentimental about the Wobblies.

America I used to be a communist when I was a kid I'm not sorry.

I smoke marijuana every chance I get.

I sit in my house for days on end and stare at the roses in the closet.

When I go to Chinatown I get drunk and never get laid.

My mind is made up there's going to be trouble.

You should have seen me reading Marx.

My psychoanalyst thinks I'm perfectly right.

I won't say the Lord's Prayer.

I have mystical visions and cosmic vibrations.

America I still haven't told you what you did to Uncle Max after he came over from Russia.

I'm addressing you.

Are you going to let your emotional life be run by Time Magazine?

I'm obsessed by Time Magazine.

I read it every week.

Its cover stares at me every time I slink past the corner candystore.

I read it in the basement of the Berkeley Public Library.

It's always telling me about responsibility. Businessmen are serious. Movie producers are serious. Everybody's serious but me.

It occurs to me that I am America.

I am talking to myself again.

Asia is rising against me.

I haven't got a chinaman's chance.

I'd better consider my national resources.

My national resources consist of two joints of marijuana millions of genitals an unpublishable private literature that jetplanes 1400 miles an hour and twentyfive-thousand mental institutions.

I say nothing about my prisons nor the millions of under-
privileged who live in my flowerpots under the light of five
hundred suns.
I have abolished the whorehouses of France, Tangiers is the next
to go.
My ambition is to be President despite the fact that I'm a
Catholic.

America how can I write a holy litany in your silly mood?
I will continue like Henry Ford my strophes are as individual as
his automobiles more so they're all different sexes.
America I will sell you strophes $2500 apiece $500 down on
your old strophe
America free Tom Mooney
America save the Spanish Loyalists
America Sacco & Vanzetti must not die
America I am the Scottsboro boys.
America when I was seven momma took me to Communist
Cell meetings they sold us garbanzos a handful per ticket
a ticket costs a nickel and the speeches were free everybody
was angelic and sentimental about the workers it was all so
sincere you have no idea what a good thing the party was
in 1835 Scott Nearing was a grand old man a real mensch
Mother Bloor the Silk-strikers' Ewig-Weibliche made me cry
I once saw the Yiddish orator Israel Amter plain. Everybody
must have been a spy.
America you don't really want to go to war.
America it's them bad Russians.
Them Russians them Russians and them Chinamen. And them
Russians.
The Russia wants to eat us alive. The Russia's power mad. She
wants to take our cars from out our garages.
Her wants to grab Chicago. Her needs a Red *Reader's Digest*.
Her wants our auto plants in Siberia. Him big bureaucracy
running our fillingstations.
That no good. Ugh. Him make Indians learn read. Him need
big black niggers. Hah. Her make us all work sixteen hours
a day. Help.

America this is quite serious.

America this is the impression I get from looking in the television set.

America is this correct?

I'd better get right down to the job.

It's true I don't want to join the Army or turn lathes in precision parts factories, I'm nearsighted and psychopathic anyway.

America I'm putting my queer shoulder to the wheel.

Jorie Graham

(b. 1950)

PRAYER

Over a dock railing, I watch the minnows, thousands, swirl
themselves, each a minuscule muscle, but also, without the
way to *create* current, making of their unison (turning, re-
                                        infolding,
entering and exiting their own unison in unison) making of
    themselves a
visual current, one that cannot freight or sway by
minutest fractions the water's downdrafts and upswirls, the
dockside cycles of finally-arriving boat-wakes, there where
they hit deeper resistance, water that seems to burst into
itself (it has those layers), a real current though mostly
invisible sending into the visible (minnows) arrowing
                    motion that forces change—
this is freedom. This is the force of faith. Nobody gets
what they want. Never again are you the same. The longing
is to be pure. What you get is to be changed. More and more by
each glistening minute, through which infinity threads itself,
also oblivion, of course, the aftershocks of something
at sea. Here, hands full of sand, letting it sift through
in the wind, I look in and say take this, this is
what I have saved, take this, hurry. And if I listen
now? Listen, I was not saying anything. It was only
something I did. I could not choose words. I am free to go.
I cannot of course come back. Not to this. Never.
It is a ghost posed on my lips. Here: never.

George Herbert

(1593–1633)

CHURCH MONUMENTS

While that my soul repairs to her devotion,
Here I entomb my flesh, that it betimes
May take acquaintance of this heap of dust
To which the blast of death's incessant motion,
Fed with the exhalation of our crimes,
Drives all at last. Therefore I gladly trust

My body to this school, that it may learn
To spell his elements and find his birth
Written in dusty heraldry and lines
Which dissolution sure doth best discern,
Comparing dust with dust and earth with earth.
These laugh at jet and marble, put for signs

To sever the good fellowship of dust
And spoil the meeting. What shall point out them
When they shall bow and kneel and fall down flat
To kiss those heaps which now they have in trust?
Dear flesh, while I do pray, learn here thy stem
And true descent, that, when thou shalt grow fat

And wanton in thy cravings, thou mayest know
That flesh is but the glass which holds the dust
That measures all our time, which also shall
Be crumbled into dust. Mark here below
How tame these ashes are, how free from lust,
That thou mayest fit thyself against thy fall.

VIRTUE

Sweet day, so cool, so calm, so bright,
The bridal of the earth and sky:
The dew shall weep thy fall tonight;
           For thou must die.

Sweet rose, whose hue angry and brave
Bids the rash gazer wipe his eye:
Thy root is ever in its grave,
           And thou must die.

Sweet spring, full of sweet days and roses,
A box where sweets compacted lie;
My music shows ye have your closes,
           And all must die.

Only a sweet and virtuous soul,
Like seasoned timber, never gives;
But though the whole world turn to coal,
           Then chiefly lives.

Robert Herrick

(1591–1674)

AN ODE FOR HIM*

Ah Ben!
Say how, or when
Shall we thy guests
Meet at those lyric feats,
Made at the *Sun*,
The Dog, the triple Tun?
Where we such clusters had,
As made us nobly wild, not mad;
And yet each verse of thine
Out-did the meat, out-did the frolic wine.

My Ben
Or come agen,
Or send to us,
Thy wit's great over-plus;
But teach us yet
Wisely to husband it,
Lest we that talent spend
And having once brought to an end
That precious stock: the store
Of such a wit the world should have no more.

---

* Ben Jonson

CORINNA'S GOING A-MAYING

Get up! get up for shame! the blooming morn
Upon her wings presents the god unshorn.
    See how Aurora throws her fair
    Fresh-quilted colors through the air:
    Get up, sweet-slug-a-bed, and see
    The dew bespangling herb and tree.
Each flower has wept and bowèd toward the east
Above an hour since, yet you not dressed;
    Nay, not so much as out of bed?
    When all the birds have matins said,
    And sung their thankful hymns, 'tis sin,
    Nay, profanation to keep in,
Whenas a thousand virgins on this day
Spring, sooner than the lark, to fetch in May.

Rise, and put on your foliage, and be seen
To come forth, like the springtime, fresh and green,
    And sweet as Flora. Take no care
    For jewels for your gown or hair;
    Fear not; the leaves will strew
    Gems in abundance upon you;
Besides, the childhood of the day has kept,
Against you come, some orient pearls unwept;
    Come and receive them while the light
    Hangs on the dew-locks of the night,
    And Titan on the eastern hill
    Retires himself, or else stands still
Till you come forth. Wash, dress, be brief in praying:
Few beads are best when once we go a-Maying.

Come, my Corinna, come; and, coming mark
How each field turns a street, each street a park
    Made green, and trimmed with trees; see how
    Devotion gives each house a bough

  Or branch: each porch, each door, ere this,
   An ark, a tabernacle is,
Made up of whitethorn neatly interwove,
As if here were those cooler shades of love.
   Can such delights be in the street
   And open fields, and we not see 't?
   Come, we'll abroad; and let's obey
   The proclamation made for May,
And sin no more, as we have done, by staying;
But my Corinna, come, let's go a-Maying.

There's not a budding boy or girl this day
But is got up and gone to bring in May;
   A deal of youth, ere this, is come
   Back, and with whitethorn laden home.
   Some have dispatched their cakes and cream
   Before that we have left to dream;
And some have wept, and wooed, and plighted troth,
And chose their priest, ere we can cast off sloth.
   Many a green-gown has been given,
   Many a kiss, both odd and even,
   Many a glance, too, has been sent
   From out the eye, love's firmament;
Many a jest told of the keys betraying
This night, and locks picked; yet we're not a-Maying.

Come, let us go while we are in our prime,
And take the harmless folly of the time.
   We shall grow old apace, and die
   Before we know our liberty.
   Our life is short, and our days run
   As fast away as does the sun;
And, as a vapor or a drop of rain
Once lost, can ne'er be found again;

So when or you or I are made
A fable, song, or fleeting shade,
All love, all liking, all delight
Lies drowned with us in endless night.
Then while time serves, and we are but decaying,
Come, my Corinna, come, let's go a-Maying.

Gerard Manley Hopkins
(1844–1889)

GOD'S GRANDEUR

The world is charged with the grandeur of God.
    It will flame out, like shining from shook foil;
    It gathers to a greatness, like the ooze of oil
Crushed. Why do men then now not reck his rod?
Generations have trod, have trod, have trod;
    And all is seared with trade; bleared, smeared with toil;
    And wears man's smudge and shares man's smell: the soil
Is bare now, nor can foot feel, being shod.

And for all this, nature is never spent;
    There lives the dearest freshness deep down things;
And though the last lights off the black West went
    Oh, morning, at the brown brink eastwards, springs—
Because the Holy Ghost over the bent
    World broods with warm breast and with ah! bright wings.

PIED BEAUTY

Glory be to God for dappled things—
    For skies of couple-colour as a brinded cow;
      For rose-moles all in stipple upon trout that swim;
Fresh-firecoal chestnut-falls; finches' wings;
    Landscape plotted and pieced—fold, fallow, and plough;
      And áll trades, their gear and tackle and trim.

All things counter, original, spáre, strange;
   Whatever is fickle, frecklèd (who knows how?)
     With swíft, slów; sweet, sóur; adázzle, dím;
He fathers-forth whose beauty is pást change:
                 Práise hím.

Langston Hughes

(1902–1967)*

THE NEGRO SPEAKS OF RIVERS
To W. E. B. DuBois

I've known rivers:
I've known rivers ancient as the world and older than the flow
    of human blood in human veins.

My soul has grown deep like the rivers.

I bathed in the Euphrates when dawns were young.
I built my hut near the Congo and it lulled me to sleep.
I looked upon the Nile and raised the pyramids above it.
I heard the singing of the Mississippi when Abe Lincoln went
    down to New Orleans, and I've seen its muddy bosom turn
    all golden in the sunset.

I've known rivers:
Ancient, dusky rivers.

My soul has grown deep like the rivers.

* See *The Hustler Speaks of Places* on page 462.

Leigh Hunt

(1784–1859)

RONDEAU

Jenny kissed me when we met,
  Jumping from the chair she sat in;
Time, you thief, who love to get
  Sweets into your list, put that in;
Say I'm weary, say I'm sad,
  Say that health and wealth have missed me,
Say I'm growing old, but add,
  Jenny kissed me.

Samuel Johnson

(1709–1784)

On the Death of Dr. Robert Levet

Condemn'd to hope's delusive mine,
    As on we toil from day to day,
By sudden blasts, or slow decline,
    Our social comforts drop away.

Well tried through many a varying year,
    See LEVET to the grave descend;
Officious, innocent, sincere,
    Of ev'ry friendless name the friend.

Yet still he fills affection's eye,
    Obscurely wise, and coarsely kind;
Nor, letter'd arrogance, deny
    Thy praise to merit unrefin'd.

When fainting nature call'd for aid,
    And hov'ring death prepar'd the blow,
His vig'rous remedy display'd
    The power of art without the show.

In misery's darkest caverns known,
    His useful care was ever nigh,
Where hopeless anguish pour'd his groan,
    And lonely want retir'd to die.

No summons mock'd by chill delay,
    No petty gain disdain'd by pride,

The modest wants of ev'ry day
    The toil of ev'ry day supplied.

His virtues walk'd their narrow round,
    Nor made a pause, nor left a void;
And sure th' Eternal Master found
    The single talent well employ'd.

The busy day, the peaceful night,
    Unfelt, uncounted, glided by;
His frame was firm, his powers were bright,
    Tho' now his eightieth year was nigh.

Then with no throbbing fiery pain,
    No cold gradations of decay,
Death broke at once the vital chain,
    And free'd his soul the nearest way.

Ben Jonson

(1572–1637)

An Ode to Himself

Where dost thou careless lie
    Buried in ease and sloth?
Knowledge that sleeps doth die;
And this security,
    It is the common moth
That eats on wits and arts, and oft destroys them both.

Are all th' Aonian springs
    Dried up? Lies Thespia waste?
Doth Clarius' harp want strings,
That not a nymph now sings;
    Or droop they as disgraced,
To see their seats and bowers by chattering pies defaced?

If hence thy silence be,
    As 'tis too just a cause,
Let this thought quicken thee:
Minds that are great and free
    Should not on fortune pause;
'Tis crown enough to virtue still, her own applause.

What though the greedy fry
    Be taken with false baits
Of worded balladry,
And think it poesy?
    They die with their conceits,
And only piteous scorn upon their folly waits.

Then take in hand thy lyre,
    Strike in thy proper strain,
With Japhet's line, aspire
Sol's chariot for new fire
    To give the world again;
Who aided him will thee, the issue of Jove's brain.

And since our dainty age
    Cannot endure reproof,
Make not thyself a page
To that strumpet the stage,
    But sing high and aloof,
Safe from the wolve's black jaw, and the dull ass's hoof.

THE HOUR-GLASS

Do but consider this small dust
    Here running in the glass,
        By atoms moved;
Could you believe that this
    The body, ever, was
        Of one that loved?
And in his mistress' flame, playing like a fly,
    Turned to cinders by her eye?
    Yes; and in death, as life, unblessed,
        To have't expressed,
    Even ashes of lovers find no rest.

John Keats

(1795–1821)

ODE ON A GRECIAN URN

Thou still unravished bride of quietness,
    Thou foster-child of silence and slow time,
Sylvan historian, who canst thus express
    A flowery tale more sweetly than our rhyme:
What leaf-fringed legend haunts about thy shape
    Of deities or mortals, or of both,
        In Tempe or the dales of Arcady?
    What men or gods are these? What maidens loth?
What mad pursuit? What struggle to escape?
        What pipes and timbrels? What wild ecstasy?

Heard melodies are sweet, but those unheard
    Are sweeter; therefore, ye soft pipes, play on;
Not to the sensual ear, but, more endeared,
    Pipe to the spirit ditties of no tone:
Fair youth, beneath the trees, thou canst not leave
    Thy song, nor ever can those trees be bare;
        Bold Lover, never, never canst thou kiss,
Though winning near the goal—yet, do not grieve:
        She cannot fade, though thou hast not thy bliss,
    For ever wilt thou love, and she be fair!

Ah, happy, happy boughs! that cannot shed
    Your leaves, nor ever bid the Spring adieu;
And, happy melodist, unwearièd,
    For ever piping songs for ever new;
More happy love! more happy, happy love!

For ever warm and still to be enjoyed,
 For ever panting, and for ever young—
All breathing human passion far above,
 That leaves a heart high-sorrowful and cloyed,
  A burning forehead, and a parching tongue.

Who are these coming to the sacrifice?
 To what green altar, O mysterious priest,
Lead'st thou that heifer lowing at the skies,
 And all her silken flanks with garlands dressed?
What little town by river or sea shore,
 Or mountain-built with peaceful citadel,
  Is emptied of this folk, this pious morn?
And, little town, thy streets for evermore
 Will silent be; and not a soul to tell
  Why thou art desolate, can e'er return.

O Attic shape! Fair attitude! with brede
 Of marble men and maidens overwrought,
With forest branches and the trodden weed;
 Thou, silent form, dost tease us out of thought
As doth eternity: Cold Pastoral!
 When old age shall this generation waste,
  Thou shalt remain, in midst of other woe
  Than ours, a friend to man, to whom thou say'st,
"Beauty is truth, truth beauty,—that is all
  Ye know on earth, and all ye need to know."

ODE TO A NIGHTINGALE

My heart aches, and a drowsy numbness pains
 My sense, as though of hemlock I had drunk,
Or emptied some dull opiate to the drains
 One minute past, and Lethe-wards had sunk:
'Tis not through envy of thy happy lot,

But being too happy in thine happiness—
    That thou, light-wingèd Dryad of the trees,
        In some melodious plot
Of beechen green, and shadows numberless,
    Singest of summer in full-throated ease.

O, for a draught of vintage! that hath been
    Cooled a long age in the deep-delvèd earth,
Tasting of Flora and the country green,
    Dance, and Provençal song, and sunburnt mirth!
O for a beaker full of the warm South,
    Full of the true, the blushful Hippocrene,
        With beaded bubbles winking at the brim,
        And purple-stainèd mouth,
That I might drink, and leave the world unseen,
    And with thee fade away into the forest dim—

Fade far away, dissolve, and quite forget
    What thou among the leaves hast never known,
The weariness, the fever, and the fret
    Here, where men sit and hear each other groan;
Where palsy shakes a few, sad, last grey hairs,
    Where youth grows pale, and spectre-thin, and dies;
        Where but to think is to be full of sorrow
        And leaden-eyed despairs;
Where Beauty cannot keep her lustrous eyes,
    Or new Love pine at them beyond to-morrow.

Away! away! for I will fly to thee,
    Not charioted by Bacchus and his pards,
But on the viewless wings of Poesy,
    Though the dull brain perplexes and retards.
Already with thee! tender is the night,
    And haply the Queen-Moon is on her throne,
        Clustered around by all her starry Fays;
        But here there is no light,

Save what from heaven is with the breezes blown
     Through verdurous glooms and winding mossy ways.

I cannot see what flowers are at my feet,
     Nor what soft incense hangs upon the boughs,
But, in embalmèd darkness, guess each sweet
     Wherewith the seasonable month endows
The grass, the thicket, and the fruit-tree wild—
     White hawthorn, and the pastoral eglantine;
          Fast fading violets covered up in leaves;
               And mid-May's eldest child,
     The coming musk-rose, full of dewy wine,
          The murmurous haunt of flies on summer eves.

Darkling I listen; and, for many a time
     I have been half in love with easeful Death,
Called him soft names in many a musèd rhyme,
     To take into the air my quiet breath;
Now more than ever seems it rich to die,
     To cease upon the midnight with no pain,
          While thou art pouring forth thy soul abroad
               In such an ecstasy!
     Still wouldst thou sing, and I have ears in vain—
          To thy high requiem become a sod.

Thou wast not born for death, immortal Bird!
     No hungry generations tread thee down;
The voice I hear this passing night was heard
     In ancient days by emperor and clown:
Perhaps the self-same song that found a path
     Through the sad heart of Ruth, when, sick for home,
          She stood in tears amid the alien corn;
               The same that oft-times hath
     Charmed magic casements, opening on the foam
          Of perilous seas, in faery lands forlorn.

Forlorn! the very word is like a bell
    To toll me back from thee to my sole self!
Adieu! the fancy cannot cheat so well
    As she is famed to do, deceiving elf.
Adieu! adieu! thy plaintive anthem fades
    Past the near meadows, over the still stream,
        Up the hill-side; and now 'tis buried deep
        In the next valley-glades:
    Was it a vision, or a waking dream?
        Fled is that music—Do I wake or sleep?

To Autumn

1

Season of mists and mellow fruitfulness,
    Close bosom-friend of the maturing sun;
Conspiring with him how to load and bless
    With fruit the vines that round the thatch-eves run;
To bend with apples the moss'd cottage-trees,
    And fill all fruit with ripeness to the core;
        To swell the gourd, and plump the hazel shells
    With a sweet kernel; to set budding more,
And still more, later flowers for the bees,
Until they think warm days will never cease,
        For summer has o'er-brimm'd their clammy cells.

2

Who hath not seen thee oft amid thy store?
    Sometimes whoever seeks abroad may find
Thee sitting careless on a granary floor,
    Thy hair soft-lifted by the winnowing wind;
Or on a half-reap'd furrow sound asleep,
    Drows'd with the fume of poppies, while thy hook
        Spares the next swath and all its twined flowers:
And sometimes like a gleaner thou dost keep

Steady thy laden head across a brook;
Or by a cyder-press, with patient look,
    Thou watchest the last oozings hours by hours.

3
Where are the songs of spring? Ay, where are they?
    Think not of them, thou hast thy music too,—
While barred clouds bloom the soft-dying day,
    And touch the stubble-plains with rosy hue;
Then in a wailful choir the small gnats mourn
      Among the river sallows, borne aloft
        Or sinking as the light wind lives or dies;
And full-grown lambs loud bleat from hilly bourn;
    Hedge-crickets sing; and now with treble soft
    The red-breast whistles from a garden-croft;
      And gathering swallows twitter in the skies.

Kenneth Koch

(1925–2002)

To My Twenties

How lucky that I ran into you
When everything was possible
For my legs and arms, and with hope in my heart
And so happy to see any woman—
O woman! O my twentieth year!
Basking in you, you
Oasis from both growing and decay
Fantastic unheard of nine- or ten-year oasis
A palm tree, hey! And then another
And another—and water!
I'm still very impressed by you. Whither,
Midst falling decades, have you gone? Oh in what lucky fellow,
Unsure of himself, upset, and unemployable
For the moment in any case, do you live now?
From my window I drop a nickel
By mistake. With
You I race down to get it
But I find there on
The street instead, a good friend,
X——N——, who says to me
Kenneth do you have a minute?
And I say yes! I am in my twenties!
I have plenty of time! In you I marry,
In you I first go to France; I make my best friends
In you, and a few enemies. I
Write a lot and am living all the time
And thinking about living. I loved to frequent you

After my teens and before my thirties.
You three together in a bar
I always preferred you because you were midmost
Most lustrous apparently strongest
Although now that I look back on you
What part have you played?
You never, ever, were stingy.
What you gave me you gave whole
But as for telling
Me how best to use it
You weren't a genius at that.
Twenties, my soul
Is yours for the asking
You know that, if you ever come back.

Walter Savage Landor

(1775–1864)

On Seeing a Hair of Lucretia Borgia

Borgia, thou once wert almost too august
And high for adoration; now thou 'rt dust.
All that remains of thee these plaits unfold,
Calm hair, meandering in pellucid gold.

Past Ruin'd Ilion Helen Lives

Past ruin'd Ilion Helen lives,
    Alcestis rises from the shades;
Verse calls them forth; 'tis verse that gives
    Immortal youth to mortal maids.

Soon shall Oblivion's deepening veil
    Hide all the peopled hills you see,
The gay, the proud, while lovers hail
    These many summers you and me.

D. H. Lawrence

(1885–1930)

PIANO

Softly, in the dusk, a woman is singing to me;
Taking me back down the vista of years, till I see
A child sitting under the piano, in the boom of the tingling
    strings
And pressing the small, poised feet of a mother who smiles as
    she sings.

In spite of myself, the insidious mastery of song
Betrays me back, till the heart of me weeps to belong
To the old Sunday evenings at home, with winter outside
And hymns in the cosy parlour, the tinkling piano our guide.

So now it is vain for the singer to burst into clamour
With the great black piano appassionato. The glamour
Of childish days is upon me, my manhood is cast
Down in the flood of remembrance, I weep like a child for the
    past.

Denise Levertov

(1923–1997)

WHERE IS THE ANGEL?

Where is the angel for me to wrestle?
No driving snow in the glass bubble,
but mild September.

Outside, the stark shadows
menace, and fling their huge arms about
unheard. I breathe

a lepid air, the blur
of asters, of brown fern and gold-dust
seems to murmur,

and that's what I hear, only that.
Such clear walls of curved glass:
I see the violent gesticulations

and feel—no, not nothing. But in this
gentle haze, nothing commensurate.
It is pleasant in here. History

mouths, volume turned off. A band of iron
like they put round a split tree,
circles my heart, In here

it is pleasant, but when I open
my mouth to speak, I too
am soundless. Where is the angel

to wrestle with me and wound
not my thigh but my throat,
so curses and blessings flow storming out

and the glass shatters, and the iron sunders?

Robert Lowell

(1917–1977)

Skunk Hour

For Elizabeth Bishop

Nautilus Island's hermit
heiress still lives through winter in her Spartan cottage;
her sheep still graze above the sea.
Her son's a bishop. Her farmer
is first selectman in our village;
she's in her dotage.

Thirsting for
the hierarchic privacy
of Queen Victoria's century,
she buys up all
the eyesores facing her shore,
and lets them fall.

The season's ill—
we've lost our summer millionaire,
who seemed to leap from an L. L. Bean
catalogue. His nine-knot yawl
was auctioned off to lobstermen.
A red fox stain covers Blue Hill.

And now our fairy
decorator brightens his shop for fall;
his fishnet's filled with orange cork,
orange, his cobbler's bench and awl;

there is no money in his work,
he'd rather marry.

One dark night,
my Tudor Ford climbed the hill's skull;
I watched for love-cars. Lights turned down,
they lay together, hull to hull,
where the graveyard shelves on the town. . . .
My mind's not right.

A car radio bleats,
"Love, O careless Love. . . ." I hear
my ill-spirit sob in each blood cell,
as if my hand were at its throat. . . .
I myself am hell;
nobody's here—

only skunks, that search
in the moonlight for a bite to eat.
They march on their soles up Main Street:
white stripes, moonstruck eyes' red fire
under the chalk-dry and spar spire
of the Trinitarian Church.

I stand on top
of our back steps and breathe the rich air—
a mother skunk with her column of kittens swills the garbage
    pail.
She jabs her wedge-head in a cup
of sour cream, drops her ostrich tail,
and will not scare.

Gail Mazur

(b. 1937)

In Houston

I'd dislocated my life, so I went to the zoo.
It was December but it wasn't December. Pansies
just planted were blooming in well-groomed beds.
Lovers embraced under the sky's Sunday blue.
Children rode around and around on pastel trains.
I read the labels stuck on every cage the way
people at museums do, art being less interesting
than information. Each fenced-in plot had a map,
laminated with a stain to tell where in the world
the animals had been taken from. Rhinos waited
for rain in the rhino-colored dirt, too grief-struck
to move their wrinkles, their horns too weak
to ever be hacked off by poachers for aphrodisiacs.
Five white ducks agitated the chalky waters
of a duck pond with invisible orange feet
while a little girl in pink ruffles
tossed pork rinds at their disconsolate backs.

This wasn't my life! I'd meant to look
with the wise tough eye of exile, I wanted
not to anthropomorphize, not to equate, for instance,
the lemur's displacement with my displacement.
The arched aviary flashed with extravagance,
plumage so exuberant, so implausible, it seemed
cartoonish, and the birdsongs unintelligible,
babble, all their various languages unraveling—

no bird can get its song sung right, separated from
models of its own species.

For weeks I hadn't written a sentence,
for two days I hadn't spoken to an animate thing.
I couldn't relate to a giraffe—
I couldn't look one in the face.
I'd have said, if anyone had asked,
I'd been mugged by the Gulf climate.
In a great barren space, I watched a pair
of elephants swaying together, a rhythm
too familiar to be mistaken, too exclusive.
My eyes sweated to see the bull, his masterful trunk
swinging, enter their barn of concrete blocks,
to watch his obedient wife follow. I missed
the bitter tinny Boston smell of first snow,
the huddling in a cold bus tunnel.

At the House of Nocturnal Mammals,
I stepped into a furtive world of bats,
averted my eyes at the gloomy dioramas,
passed glassed-in booths of lurking rodents—
had I known I'd find what I came for at last?
How did we get here, dear sloth, my soul, my sister?
Clinging to a tree-limb with your three-toed feet,
your eyes closed tight, you calm my idleness,
my immigrant isolation. But a tiny tamarin monkey
who shares your ersatz rainforest runs at you,
teasing, until you move one slow, dripping,
hairy arm, then the other, the other, the other,
pulling your tear-soaked body, its too-few
vertebrae, its inferior allotment of muscles
along the dead branch, going almost nowhere
slowly as is humanly possible, nudged
by the bright orange primate taunting, nipping,
itching at you all the time, like ambition.

W. S. Merwin

(b. 1927)

THE DRUNK IN THE FURNACE

For a good decade
The furnace stood in the naked gully, fireless
And vacant as any hat. Then when it was
No more to them than a hulking black fossil
To erode unnoticed with the rest of the junk-hill
By the poisonous creek, and rapidly to be added
     To their ignorance.

They were afterwards astonished
To confirm, one morning, a twist of smoke like a pale
Resurrection, staggering out of its chewed hole,
And to remark then other tokens that someone,
Cozily bolted behind the eye-holed iron
Door of the drafty burner, had there established
     His bad castle.

Where he gets his spirits
It's a mystery. But the stuff keeps him musical:
Hammer-and-anviling with poker and bottle
To his jugged bellowings, till the last groaning clang
As he collapses onto the rioting
Springs of a litter of car-seats ranged on the grates,
     To sleep like an iron pig.

In their tar-paper church
On a text about stoke-holes that are sated never

Their Reverend lingers. They nod and hate trespassers.
When the furnace wakes, though, all afternoon
Their witless offspring flock like piped rats to its siren
Crescendo, and agape on the crumbling ridge
  Stand in a row and learn.

Paul Muldoon

(b. 1951)

MOY SAND AND GRAVEL

To come out of the Olympic Cinema and be taken aback
by how, in the time it took a dolly to travel
along its little track
to the point where two movie stars' heads
had come together smackety-smack
and their kiss filled the whole screen,

those two great towers directly across the road
at Moy Sand and Gravel
had already washed, at least once, what had flowed
or been dredged from the Blackwater's bed
and were washing it again, load by load,
as if washing might make it clean.

Lorine Niedecker

(1903–1970)

POET'S WORK

Grandfather
   advised me:
      Learn a trade

I learned
   to sit at desk
      and condense

No layoff
   from this
      condensery

Frank O'Hara

(1926–1966)

NAPHTHA

Ah Jean Dubuffet
when you think of him
doing his military service in the Eiffel Tower
as a meteorologist
in 1922
you know how wonderful the 20th Century
can be
and the gaited Iroquois on the girders
fierce and unflinching-footed
nude as they should be
slightly empty
like a Sonia Delaunay
there is a parable of speed
somewhere behind the Indians' eyes
they invented the century with their horses
and their fragile backs
which are dark

we owe a debt to the Iroquois
and to Duke Ellington
for playing in the buildings when they are built
we don't do much ourselves
but fuck and think
of the haunting Métro
and the one who didn't show up there
while we were waiting to become part of our century
just as you can't make a hat out of steel

and still wear it
who wears hats anyway
it is our tribe's custom
to beguile

how are you feeling in ancient September
I am feeling like a truck on a wet highway
how can you
you were made in the image of god
I was not
I was made in the image of a sissy truck-driver
and Jean Dubuffet painting his cows
"with a likeness burst in the memory"
apart from love (don't say it)
I am ashamed of my century
for being so entertaining
but I have to smile

George Oppen

(1908–1984)

PSALM

VERITAS SEQUITUR . . .

In the small beauty of the forest
The wild deer bedding down—
That they are there!

      Their eyes
Effortless, the soft lips
Nuzzle and the alien small teeth
Tear at the grass

      The roots of it
Dangle from their mouths
Scattering earth in the strange woods.
They who are there.

      Their paths
Nibbled thru the fields, the leaves that shade them
Hang in the distances
Of sun

      The small nouns
Crying faith
In this in which the wild deer
Startle, and stare out.

Elise Partridge

(b. 1960)

CHEMO SIDE EFFECTS: MEMORY

Where is the word I want?

Groping
in the thicket,
about to pinch the
dangling
berry, my fingerpads
close on
air.

I can hear it
scrabbling like a squirrel
on the oak's far side.

Word, please send over this black stretch of ocean
your singular flare,
blaze
your topaz in the mind's blank.

I could always pull the gift
from the lucky-dip barrel,
scoop the right jewel
from my dragon's trove. . . .

Now I flail,
the wrong item creaks up
on the mental dumbwaiter.

No use—
it's turning
out of sight,
a bicycle down a
Venetian alley—
I clatter after, only to find
gondolas bobbing in sunny silence,
a pigeon mumbling something
I just can't catch.

George Peele
(1556–1596)

Bethsabe's Song

Hot sun, cool fire, tempered with sweet air,
Black shade, fair nurse, shadow my white hair;
Shine, sun; burn, fire; breathe, air, and ease me;
Black shade, fair nurse, shroud me and please me:
Shadow, my sweet nurse, keep me from burning,
Make not my glad cause cause of mourning.
      Let not my beauty's fire
      Inflame unstaid desire,
      Nor pierce any bright eye
      That wandereth lightly.

Sylvia Plath
(1932–1963)

NICK AND THE CANDLESTICK

I am a miner. The light burns blue.
Waxy stalactites
Drip and thicken, tears

The earthen womb
Exudes from its dead boredom.
Black bat airs

Wrap me, raggy shawls,
Cold homicides.
They weld to me like plums.

Old cave of calcium
Icicles, old echoer.
Even the newts are white,

Those holy Joes.
And the fish, the fish——
Christ! They are panes of ice,

A vice of knives,
A piranha
Religion, drinking

It's first communion out of my live toes.
The candle
Gulps and recovers its small altitude,

Its yellows hearten.
O love, how did you get here?
O embryo

Remembering, even in sleep,
Your crossed position.
The blood blooms clean

In you, ruby.
The pain
You wake to is not yours.

Love, love,
I have hung our cave with roses.
With soft rugs——

The last of Victoriana.
Let the stars
Plummet to their dark address,

Let the mercuric
Atoms that cripple drip
Into the terrible well,

You are the one
Solid the spaces lean on, envious.
You are the baby in the barn.

Sir Walter Raleigh

(1554–1618)

On the Cards and Dice

Before the sixth day of the next new year,
Strange wonders in this kingdom shall appear.
Four kings shall be assembled in this isle,
Where they shall keep great tumult for a while.
Many men then shall have an end of crosses,
And many likewise shall sustain great losses.
Many that now full joyful are and glad,
Shall at that time be sorrowful and sad.
Full many a Christian's heart shall quake for fear,
The dreadful sound of trump when he shall hear.
Dead bones shall then be tumbled up and down,
In every city and in every town.
By day or night this tumult shall not cease,
Until an herald shall proclaim a peace,
An herald strange, the like was never born
Whose very beard is flesh, and mouth is horn.

Adrienne Rich

(b. 1929)

DIVING INTO THE WRECK

First having read the book of myths,
and loaded the camera,
and checked the edge of the knife-blade,
I put on
the body-armor of black rubber
the absurd flippers
the grave and awkward mask.
I am having to do this
not like Cousteau with his
assiduous team
aboard the sun-flooded schooner
but here alone.

There is a ladder.
The ladder is always there
hanging innocently
close to the side of the schooner.
We know what it is for,
we who have used it.
Otherwise
it's a piece of maritime floss
some sundry equipment.

I go down.
Rung after rung and still
the oxygen immerses me
the blue light

the clear atoms
of our human air.
I go down.
My flippers cripple me,
I crawl like an insect down the ladder
and there is no one
to tell me when the ocean
will begin.

First the air is blue and then
it is bluer and then green and then
black I am blacking out and yet
my mask is powerful
it pumps my blood with power
the sea is another story
the sea is not a question of power
I have to learn alone
to turn my body without force
in the deep element.

And now: it is easy to forget
what I came for
among so many who have always
lived here
swaying their crenellated fans
between the reefs
and besides
you breathe differently down here.

I came to explore the wreck.
The words are purposes.
The words are maps.
I came to see the damage that was done
and the treasures that prevail.
I stroke the beam of my lamp
slowly along the flank
of something more permanent
than fish or weed

the thing I came for:
the wreck and not the story of the wreck
the thing itself and not the myth
the drowned face always staring
toward the sun
the evidence of damage
worn by salt and sway into this threadbare beauty
the ribs of the disaster
curving their assertion
among the tentative haunters.

This is the place.
And I am here, the mermaid whose dark hair
streams black, the merman in his armored body
We circle silently
about the wreck
we dive into the hold.
I am she: I am he — ⟶ paradox

whose drowned face sleeps with open eyes
whose breasts still bear the stress
whose silver, copper, vermeil cargo lies
obscurely inside barrels
half-wedged and left to rot
we are the half-destroyed instruments
that once held to a course
the water-eaten log
the fouled compass

We are, I am, you are
by cowardice or courage
the one who find our way
back to this scene
carrying a knife, a camera
a book of myths
in which
our names do not appear.

Rainer Maria Rilke

translated by M. D. Herter Norton

(1875–1926)

ARCHAIC TORSO OF APOLLO

We did not know his legendary head,
in which the eyeballs ripened. But
his torso still glows like a candelabrum
in which his gaze, only turned low,

holds and gleams. Else could not the curve
of the breast blind you, nor in the slight turn
of the loins could a smile be running
to that middle, which carried procreation.

Else would this stone be standing maimed and short
under the shoulders' translucent plunge
nor flimmering like the fell of beasts of prey

nor breaking out of all its contours
like a star: for there is no place
that does not see you. You must change your life.

Philip Schultz

(b. 1945)

For My Father

SAMUEL SCHULTZ, 1903–1963

Spring we went into the heat of lilacs
& his black eyes got big as onions & his fat lower lip
hung like a bumper & he'd rub his chin's hard fur on my cheek
& tell stories: he first saw America from his father's arms
& his father said here he could have anything if he wanted it
with all his life & he boiled soap in his back yard & sold it door
    to door
& invented clothespins shaped like fingers & cigarette lighters
that played *Stars & Stripes* when the lid snapped open.

Mornings he lugged candy into factories
& his vending machines turned peanuts into pennies
my mother counted on the kitchen table & nights he came
    home
tripping on his laces & fell asleep over dinner & one night
he carried me outside & said only God knew what God had up
    His sleeve
& a man only knew what he wanted & he wanted a big white
    house
with a porch so high he could see all the way back to Russia
& the black moon turned on the axis of his eye & his breath
filled the red summer air with the whisky of first light.

The morning his heart stopped I borrowed money to bury him
& his eyes still look at me out of mirrors & I hear him kicking

the coalburner to life & can taste the peanut salt on his hands
& his advice on lifting heavy boxes helps with the books I lug
town to town
& I still count thunder's distance in heartbeats as he taught me
& one day
I watched the sun's great rose open over the ocean as I swayed
on the bow
of the Staten Island Ferry & I was his father's age when he
arrived
with one borrowed suit & such appetite for invention & the
bridges
were mountains & the buildings gold & the sky lifted back-
ward
like a dancer & her red hair fanning the horizon & my eyes
burning
in a thousand windows & the whole Atlantic breaking at my
feet.

James Shirley

(1596–1666)

THE GLORIES OF OUR BLOOD AND STATE

The glories of our blood and state
Are shadows, not substantial things;
There is no armor against fate;
Death lays his icy hand on kings.
 Scepter and crown
 Must tumble down
And in the dust be equal made
With the poor crooked scythe and spade.

Some men with swords may reap the field
And plant fresh laurels where they kill,
But their strong nerves at last must yield;
They tame but one another still.
 Early or late
 They stoop to fate
And must give up their murmuring breath,
When they, pale captives, creep to death.

The garlands wither on your brow,
Then boast no more your mighty deeds;
Upon death's purple altar now
See where the victor-victim bleeds.
 Your heads must come
 To the cold tomb;
Only the actions of the just
Smell sweet and blossom in their dust.

Tom Sleigh

(b. 1953)

LAMENTATION ON UR

FROM A SUMERIAN SPELL, 2000 B.C.

Like molten bronze and iron shed blood
     pools. Our country's dead
melt into the earth
     as grease melts in the sun, men whose
helmets now lie scattered, men annihilated

by the double-bladed axe. Heavy, beyond
     help, they lie still as a gazelle
exhausted in a trap,
     muzzle in the dust. In home
after home, empty doorways frame the absence

of mothers and fathers who vanished
     in the flames remorselessly
spreading claiming even
     frightened children who lay quiet
in their mother's arms, now borne into

oblivion, like swimmers swept out to sea
     by the surging current.
May the great barred gate
     of blackest night again swing shut
on silent hinges. Destroyed in its turn,

may this disaster too be torn out of mind.

Gerald Stern

(b. 1925)

BEHAVING LIKE A JEW

When I got there the dead opossum looked like
an enormous baby sleeping on the road.
It took me only a few seconds — just
seeing him there — with the hole in his back
and the wind blowing through his hair
to get back again into my animal sorrow.
I am sick of the country, the bloodstained
bumpers, the stiff hairs sticking out of the grilles,
the slimy highways, the heavy birds
refusing to move;
I am sick of the spirit of Lindbergh over everything,
that joy in death, that philosophical
understanding of carnage, that
concentration on the species.
— I am going to be unappeased at the opossum's death.
I am going to behave like a Jew
and touch his face, and stare into his eyes,
and pull him off the road.
I am not going to stand in a wet ditch
with the Toyotas and the Chevies passing over me
at sixty miles an hour
and praise the beauty and the balance
and lose myself in the immortal lifestream
when my hands are still a little shaky
from his stiffness and his bulk
and my eyes are still weak and misty
from his round belly and his curved fingers
and his black whiskers and his little dancing feet.

Wallace Stevens

(1879–1955)

MADAME LA FLEURIE

Weight him down, O side-stars, with the great weightings of
    the end.
Seal him there. He looked in a glass of the earth and thought
    he lived in it.
Now, he brings all that he saw into the earth, to the waiting
    parent.
His crisp knowledge is devoured by her, beneath a dew.

Weight him, weight, weight him with the sleepiness of the
    moon.
It was only a glass because he looked in it. It was nothing he
    could be told.
It was a language he spoke, because he must, yet did not know.
It was a page he had found in the handbook of heartbreak.

The black fugatos are strumming the blacknesses of black . . .
The thick strings stutter the finial gutturals.
He does not lie there remembering the blue-jay, say the jay.
His grief is that his mother should feed on him, himself and
    what he saw,
In that distant chamber, a bearded queen, wicked in her dead
    light.

THE SNOW MAN

One must have a mind of winter
To regard the frost and the boughs
Of the pine-trees crusted with snow;

And have been cold a long time
To behold the junipers shagged with ice,
The spruces rough in the distant glitter

Of the January sun; and not to think
Of any misery in the sound of the wind,
In the sound of a few leaves,

Which is the sound of the land
Full of the same wind
That is blowing in the same bare place

For the listener, who listens in the snow,
And, nothing himself, beholds
Nothing that is not there and the nothing that is.

Robert Louis Stevenson

(1850–1894)

THE LAND OF COUNTERPANE

When I was sick and lay a-bed,
I had two pillows at my head,
And all my toys beside me lay
To keep me happy all the day.

And sometimes for an hour or so
I watched my leaden soldiers go,
With different uniforms and drills,
Among the bed-clothes, through the hills;

And sometimes sent my ships in fleets
All up and down among the sheets;
Or brought my trees and houses out,
And planted cities all about.

I was the giant great and still
That sits upon the pillow-hill,
And sees before him, dale and plain,
The pleasant land of counterpane.

Jane Taylor

(1783–1824)

THE STAR

Twinkle, twinkle, little star,
How I wonder what you are!
Up above the world so high,
Like a diamond in the sky.

When the blazing sun is gone,
When he nothing shines upon,
Then you show your little light,
Twinkle, twinkle, all the night.

Then the traveller in the dark,
Thanks you for your tiny spark!
He could not see which way to go,
If you did not twinkle so.

In the dark blue sky you keep,
And often through my curtains peep,
For you never shut your eye,
Till the sun is in the sky.

As your bright and tiny spark
Lights the traveler in the dark,
Though I know not what you are,
Twinkle, twinkle, little star.

Walt Whitman

(1819–1892)

ITALIAN MUSIC IN DAKOTA

["THE SEVENTEENTH—
THE FINEST REGIMENTAL BAND I EVER HEARD."]

Through the soft evening air enwinding all,
Rocks, woods, fort, cannon, pacing sentries, endless wilds,
In dulcet streams, in flutes' and cornets' notes,
Electric, pensive, turbulent, artificial
(Yet strangely fitting even here, meanings unknown before,
Subtler than ever, more harmony, as if born here, related here,
Not to the city's fresco'd rooms, not to the audience of the
    opera house,
Sounds, echoes, wandering strains, as really here at home,
Sonnambula's innocent love, trios with *Norma's* anguish,
And thy ecstatic chorus *Poliuto*);
Ray'd in the limpid yellow slanting sundown,
Music, Italian music in Dakota.
While Nature, sovereign of this gnarl'd realm,
Lurking in hidden barbaric grim recesses,
Acknowledging rapport however far remov'd
(As some old root or soil of earth its last-born flower or fruit),
Listens well pleas'd.

William Carlos Williams

(1883–1963)

THE TURTLE

For My Grandson

Not because of his eyes,
      the eyes of a bird,
            but because he is beaked,
birdlike, to do an injury,
      has the turtle attracted you.
            He is your only pet.
When we are together
      you talk of nothing else
            ascribing all sorts
of murderous motives
      to his least action.
            You ask me
to write a poem,
      should I have poems to write,
            about a turtle.

The turtle lives in the mud
      but is not mud-like,
            you can tell it by his eyes
which are clear.
      When he shall escape
            his present confinement
he will stride about the world
      destroying all
            with his sharp beak.

Whatever opposes him
           in the streets of the city
                      shall go down.
Cars will be overturned.
           And upon his back
                  shall ride,
to his conquests,
          my Lord,
                  you!

You shall be master!
          In the beginning
                  there was a great tortoise
who supported the world.
          Upon him
              all ultimately
rests.
          Without him
              nothing will stand.
He is all wise
          and can outrun the hare.
              In the night
his eyes carry him
          to unknown places.
              He is your friend.

William Wordsworth
(1770–1850)

LINES

COMPOSED A FEW MILES ABOVE TINTERN ABBEY ON
REVISITING THE BANKS OF THE WYE DURING A TOUR,
JULY 13, 1798.

Five years have past; five summers, with the length
Of five long winters! and again I hear
These waters, rolling from their mountain-springs
With a soft inland murmur.—Once again
Do I behold these steep and lofty cliffs,
That on a wild secluded scene impress
Thoughts of more deep seclusion; and connect
The landscape with the quiet of the sky.
The day is come when I again repose
Here, under this dark sycamore, and view
These plots of cottage-ground, these orchard-tufts,
Which at this season, with their unripe fruits,
Are clad in one green hue, and lose themselves
'Mid groves and copses. Once again I see
These hedge-rows, hardly hedge-rows, little lines
Of sportive wood run wild: these pastoral farms,
Green to the very door; and wreaths of smoke
Sent up, in silence, from among the trees!
With some uncertain notice, as might seem
Of vagrant dwellers in the houseless woods,
Or of some Hermit's cave, where by his fire
The Hermit sits alone.

                              These beauteous forms,
Through a long absence, have not been to me
As is a landscape to a blind man's eye:
But oft, in lonely rooms, and 'mid the din
Of towns and cities, I have owed to them
In hours of weariness, sensations sweet,
Felt in the blood, and felt along the heart;
And passing even into my purer mind,
With tranquil restoration:—feelings too
Of unremembered pleasure: such, perhaps,
As have no slight or trivial influence
On that best portion of a good man's life,
His little, nameless, unremembered, acts
Of kindness and of love. Nor less, I trust,
To them I may have owed another gift,
Of aspect more sublime; that blessed mood,
In which the burthen of the mystery,
In which the heavy and the weary weight
Of all this unintelligible world,
Is lightened:—that serene and blessed mood,
In which the affections gently lead us on,—
Until, the breath of this corporeal frame
And even the motion of our human blood
Almost suspended, we are laid asleep
In body, and become a living soul:
While with an eye made quiet by the power
Of harmony, and the deep power of joy,
We see into the life of things.
                              If this
Be but a vain belief, yet, oh! how oft—
In darkness and amid the many shapes
Of joyless daylight; when the fretful stir
Unprofitable, and the fever of the world,
Have hung upon the beatings of my heart—
How oft, in spirit, have I turned to thee,
O sylvan Wye! thou wanderer thro' the woods,
How often has my spirit turned to thee!

And now, with gleams of half-extinguished thought,
With many recognitions dim and faint,
And somewhat of a sad perplexity,
The picture of the mind revives again:
While here I stand, not only with the sense
Of present pleasure, but with pleasing thoughts
That in this moment there is life and food
For future years. And so I dare to hope,
Though changed, no doubt, from what I was when first
I came among these hills; when like a roe
I bounded o'er the mountains, by the sides
Of the deep rivers, and the lonely streams,
Wherever nature led: more like a man
Flying from something that he dreads, than one
Who sought the thing he loved. For nature then
(The coarser pleasures of my boyish days,
And their glad animal movements all gone by)
To me was all in all.—I cannot paint
What then I was. The sounding cataract
Haunted me like a passion: the tall rock,
The mountain, and the deep and gloomy wood,
Their colours and their forms, were then to me
An appetite; a feeling and a love,
That had no need of a remoter charm,
By thought supplied, nor any interest
Unborrowed from the eye.—That time is past,
And all its aching joys are now no more,
And all its dizzy raptures. Not for this
Faint I, nor mourn nor murmur; other gifts
Have followed; for such loss, I would believe,
Abundant recompence. For I have learned
To look on nature, not as in the hour
Of thoughtless youth; but hearing oftentimes
The still, sad music of humanity,
Nor harsh nor grating, though of ample power
To chasten and subdue. And I have felt
A presence that disturbs me with the joy

Of elevated thoughts; a sense sublime
Of something far more deeply interfused,
Whose dwelling is the light of setting suns,
And the round ocean and the living air,
And the blue sky, and in the mind of man;
A motion and a spirit, that impels
All thinking things, all objects of all thought,
And rolls through all things. Therefore am I still
A lover of the meadows and the woods,
And mountains; and of all that we behold
From this green earth; of all the mighty world
Of eye, and ear,—both what they half create,
And what perceive; well pleased to recognise
In nature and the language of the sense,
The anchor of my purest thoughts, the nurse,
The guide, the guardian of my heart, and soul
Of all my moral being.
                                 Nor perchance,
If I were not thus taught, should I the more
Suffer my genial spirits to decay:
For thou art with me here upon the banks
Of this fair river; thou my dearest Friend,
My dear, dear Friend; and in thy voice I catch
The language of my former heart, and read
My former pleasures in the shooting lights
Of thy wild eyes. Oh! yet a little while
May I behold in thee what I was once,
My dear, dear Sister! and this prayer I make,
Knowing that Nature never did betray
The heart that loved her; 'tis her privilege,
Through all the years of this our life, to lead
From joy to joy: for she can so inform
The mind that is within us, so impress
With quietness and beauty, and so feed
With lofty thoughts, that neither evil tongues,
Rash judgements, nor the sneers of selfish men,

Nor greetings where no kindness is, nor all
The dreary intercourse of daily life,
Shall e'er prevail against us, or disturb
Our cheerful faith, that all which we behold
Is full of blessings. Therefore let the moon
Shine on thee in thy solitary walk;
And let the misty mountain-winds be free
To blow against thee: and, in after years,
When these wild ecstasies shall be matured
Into a sober pleasure; when thy mind
Shall be a mansion for all lovely forms,
Thy memory be as a dwelling-place
For all sweet sounds and harmonies; oh then,
If solitude, or fear, or pain, or grief,
Should be thy portion, with what healing thoughts
Of tender joy wilt thou remember me,
And these my exhortations! Nor, perchance—
If I should be where I no more can hear
Thy voice nor catch from thy wild eyes these gleams
Of past existence—wilt thou then forget
That on the banks of this delightful stream
We stood together; and that I, so long
A worshipper of Nature, hither came
Unwearied in that service: rather say
With warmer love—oh! with far deeper zeal
Of holier love. Nor wilt thou then forget,
That after many wanderings, many years
Of absence, these steep woods and lofty cliffs,
And this green pastoral landscape, were to me
More dear, both for themselves and for thy sake!

Composed upon Westminster Bridge, September 3, 1802

Earth has not any thing to shew more fair:
Dull would he be of soul who could pass by
A sight so touching in its majesty:
This City now doth like a garment wear
The beauty of the morning; silent, bare,
Ships, towers, domes, theatres, and temples lie
Open unto the fields, and to the sky;
All bright and glittering in the smokeless air.
Never did sun more beautifully steep
In his first splendor valley, rock, or hill;
Ne'er saw I, never felt, a calm so deep!
The river glideth at his own sweet will:
Dear God! the very houses seem asleep;
And all that mighty heart is lying still!

William Butler Yeats

(1865–1939)*

THE LAKE ISLE OF INNISFREE

I will arise and go now, and go to Innisfree,
And a small cabin build there, of clay and wattles made:
Nine bean-rows will I have there, a hive for the honey-bee,
And live alone in the bee-loud glade.

And I shall have some peace there, for peace comes dropping
    slow,
Dropping from the veils of the morning to where the cricket
    sings;
There midnight's all a glimmer, and noon a purple glow,
And evening full of the linnet's wings.

I will arise and go now, for always night and day
I hear lake water lapping with low sounds by the shore;
While I stand on the roadway, or on the pavements grey,
I hear it in the deep heart's core.

* See *The Lake Isle* on page 463.

VII

PARODIES, RIPOSTES, JOKES, AND INSULTS

THAT I DO not like you; that life is boring; that nice people are often less interesting than drunks, drug-takers, and "perverts unnerved"—these sentiments expressed by the first poems in this section may not fit a stereotypical notion of what is poetic. Nor does comedy itself. However, insults and irreverence have an important place in the poetry of Greek and Latin antiquity: a model followed by poets writing in English.

I don't mean "light verse" or limericks. Marianne Moore, in her charmingly titled "To Be Liked by You Would Be a Calamity" (p. 460), shows how the comedy of ordinary dislike can be a serious subject: evoking all the musicality, emotional nuance, and discovery of poetry:

TO BE LIKED BY YOU WOULD BE A CALAMITY

"Attack is more piquant than concord," but when
    You tell me frankly that you would like to feel
        My flesh beneath your feet,
            I'm all abroad; I can but put my weapon up, and
                Bow you out.
Gesticulation—it is half the language.
    Let unsheathed gesticulation be the steel
        Your courtesy must meet,

> Since in your hearing words are mute, which to my senses
> Are a shout.

Moore is true to the pettiness that infects her like a virus, and to the profound mystery of that contagion: the "piquant" animosity that is a subject of great comedy, as in the work of Molière, Swift, and Gogol. The intricate, in its way oblique, movement of what she says corresponds to the declaration that her opponent is as though deaf to language. To "put my weapon up" is to resist the infection in a way, while also striking a last blow in the squabble.

Parody involves a quite different kind of contagion: the impression of a distinctive style, akin to the irritable pleasure of a catchy tune. Parody does not necessarily entail dislike or insult. On the contrary, truly good parody is a tribute, acknowledging the power, along with the distortion, of its original. Often, the parodist is a generation or more younger than the writer parodied. Kenneth Koch's poem (p. 452) salutes the magnetism of William Carlos Williams while laughing at a certain preening element in that magnetism. Ezra Pound acknowledges influences on his own, rather misty early work in his cadences parodying (p. 463) a misty quality in the early poetry of William Butler Yeats. Henry Reed's parody (p. 465) of T. S. Eliot evoked this appreciation from Eliot:

> Most parodies of one's own work strike one as very poor. In fact
> one is apt to think one could parody oneself much better. (As
> a matter of fact some critics have said that I have done so.) But
> there is one which deserves the success it has had, Henry Reed's
> Chard Whitlow.

The deft, complicated joke in Eliot's parenthesis suggests resemblances between the spirit of the poet and that of the comedian: vocal, daring, gracefully teasing the obvious, delighting in contradictions and ambiguities, upending the world, or tilting it, with a stroke of imagination or a trick of rhythm.

Reed's brilliant parody makes its subject not merely a specific work but Eliot's entire work and its moral personality. Wallace Stevens, with his ability to intensify his figures of sound, can combine melancholy and absurdity, jingle and philosophy (p. 476):

THE PLEASURES OF MERELY CIRCULATING

The garden flew round with the angel,
The angel flew round with the clouds,
And the clouds flew round and the clouds flew round
And the clouds flew round with the clouds.

Is there any secret in skulls,
The cattle skulls in the woods?
Do the drummers in black hoods
Rumble anything out of their drums?

Mrs. Anderson's Swedish baby
Might well have been German or Spanish,
Yet that things go round and again go round
Has rather a classical sound.

Philosophical questions about meaning—the significance of death in the middle stanza, the apparent arbitrariness of life in the final one—are made the more piercing, not diminished, by the echoes of nursery rhyme. Poetry here formalizes and makes precise the human voice's ability to say something urgent or profound, while also giving to what is said the backspin of doubt or reservation—or laughter.

Erin Belieu

(b. 1965)

On Being Fired Again

I've known the pleasures of being
fired at least eleven times—

most notably by Larry who found my snood
unsuitable, another time by Jack,
whom I was sleeping with. Poor attitude,
tardiness, a contagious lack
of team spirit; I have been unmotivated

squirting perfume onto little cards,
while stocking salad bars, when stripping
covers from romance novels, their heroines
slaving on the chain gang of obsessive love—

and always the same hard candy
of shame dissolving in my throat;

handing in my apron, returning the cash-
register key. And yet, how fine it feels,
the perversity of freedom which never signs
a rent check or explains anything to one's family.

I've arrived again, taking one more last
walk through another door, thinking "*I* am
what is wrong with America," while outside
in the emptied, post-rushhour street,

the sun slouches in a tulip tree and the sound
of a neighborhood pool floats up on the heat.

John Berryman
(1914–1972)

DREAM SONG 14

Life, friends, is boring. We must not say so.
After all, the sky flashes, the great sea yearns,
we ourselves flash and yearn,
and moreover my mother told me as a boy
(repeatingly) "Ever to confess you're bored
means you have no

Inner Resources." I conclude now I have no
inner resources, because I am heavy bored.
Peoples bore me,
literature bores me, especially great literature,
Henry bores me, with his plights & gripes
as bad as achilles,

who loves people and valiant art, which bores me.
And the tranquil hills, & gin, look like a drag
and somehow a dog
has taken itself & its tail considerably away
into mountains or sea or sky, leaving
behind: me, wag.

Louise Bogan

(1897–1970)

SEVERAL VOICES OUT OF A CLOUD

Come, drunks and drug-takers; come, perverts unnerved!
Receive the laurel, given, though late, on merit; to whom
    and wherever deserved.

Parochial punks, trimmers, nice people, joiners true-blue,
Get the hell out of the way of the laurel. It is deathless
    And it isn't for you.

Thomas Brown

(1663–1704)

Doctor Fell

I do not like thee, Doctor Fell;
The reason why I cannot tell;
But this I know, and know full well,
I do not like thee, Doctor Fell!

Roy Campbell

(1901–1957)

ON SOME SOUTH AFRICAN NOVELISTS

You praise the firm restraint with which they write—
I'm with you there, of course:
They use the snaffle and the curb all right,
But where's the bloody horse?

Raymond Carver

(1938–1988)*

You Don't Know What Love Is

AN EVENING WITH CHARLES BUKOWSKI

You don't know what love is Bukowski said
I'm 51 years old look at me
I'm in love with this young broad
I got it bad but she's hung up too
so it's all right man that's the way it should be
I get in their blood and they can't get me out
They try everything to get away from me
but they all come back in the end
They all come back to me except
the one I planted
I cried over that one
but I cried easy in those days
Don't let me get onto the hard stuff man
I get mean then
I could sit here and drink beer
with you hippies all night
I could drink ten quarts of this beer
and nothing it's like water
But let me get onto the hard stuff
and I'll start throwing people out windows
I've done it
But you don't know what love is
You don't know because you've never

* See *startled into life like fire* on page 334.

been in love it's that simple
I got this young broad see she's beautiful
She calls me Bukowski
Bukowski she says in this little voice
and I say What
But you don't know what love is
I'm telling you what it is
but you aren't listening
There isn't one of you in this room
would recognize love if it stepped up
and buggered you in the ass
I used to think poetry readings were a copout
Look I'm 51 years old and I've been around
I *know* they're a copout
but I said to myself Bukowski
starving is even more of a copout
So there you are and nothing is like it should be
That fellow what's his name Galway Kinnell
I saw his picture in a magazine
He has a handsome mug on him
but he's a *teacher*
Christ can you imagine
But then you're teachers too
here I am insulting you already
No I haven't heard of him
or him either
They're all termites
Maybe it's ego I don't read much anymore
but these people who build
reputation on five or six books
termites
Bukowski she says
Why do you listen to classical music all day
Can't you hear her saying that
Bukowski why do you listen to classical music all day
That surprises you doesn't it
You wouldn't think a crude bastard like me

would listen to classical music all day
Brahms Rachmaninoff Bartok Telemann
Shit I couldn't write up here
Too quiet up here too many trees
I like the city that's the place for me
I put on my classical music each morning
and sit down in front of my typewriter
I light a cigar and I smoke it like this see
and I say Bukowski you're a lucky man
Bukowski you've gone through it all
and you're a lucky man
and the blue smoke drifts across the table
and I look out the window onto Delongpre Avenue
and I see people walking up and down the sidewalk
and I puff on the cigar like this
and then I lay the cigar in the ashtray like this
and take a deep breath
and I begin to write
Bukowski this is the life I say
it's good to be poor it's good to have hemorrhoids
it's good to be in love
But you don't know what it's like
You don't know what it's like to be in love
If you could see her you'd know what I mean
She thought I'd come up here and get laid
She just knew it
She told me she knew it
Shit I'm 51 years old and she's 25
and we're in love and she's jealous
Jesus it's beautiful
She said she'd claw my eyes out if I came up here and got laid
Now that's love for you
What do any of you know about it
Let me tell you something
I've met men in jail who had more style
than the people who hang around colleges
and go to poetry readings

They're bloodsuckers who come to see
if the poet's socks are dirty
or if he smells under the arms
Believe me I won't disappoint em
But I want you to remember this
there's only one poet in this room tonight
only one poet in this town tonight
maybe only one real poet in this country tonight
and that's me
What do any of you know about life
What do any of you know about anything
Which of you here has been fired from a job
or else has beaten up your broad
or else has been beaten up by your broad
I was fired from Sears and Roebuck five times
They'd fire me then hire me back again
I was a stockboy for them when I was 35
and then got canned for stealing cookies
I know what it's like I've been there
I'm 51 years old and I'm in love
This little broad she says
Bukowski
and I say What and she says
I think you're full of shit
and I say baby you understand me
She's the only broad in the world
man or woman
I'd take that from
But you don't know what love is
They all come back to me in the end too
everyone of em came back
except that one I told you about
the one I planted
We were together seven years
We used to drink a lot
I see a couple of typers in this room but
I don't see any poets

I'm not surprised
You have to have been in love to write poetry
and you don't know what it is to be in love
that's your trouble
Give me some of that stuff
That's right no ice good
That's good that's just fine
So let's get this show on the road
I know what I said but I'll have just one
That tastes good
Okay then let's go let's get this over with
only afterwards don't anyone stand close
to an open window

Gregory Corso

(1930–2001)

MARRIAGE

Should I get married? Should I be good?
Astound the girl next door with my velvet suit and faustus hood?
Don't take her to movies but to cemeteries
tell all about werewolf bathtubs and forked clarinets
then desire her and kiss her and all the preliminaries
and she going just so far and I understanding why
not getting angry saying You must feel! It's beautiful to feel!
Instead take her in my arms lean against an old crooked
    tombstone
and woo her the entire night the constellations in the sky—

When she introduces me to her parents
back straightened, hair finally combed, strangled by a tie,
should I sit knees together on their 3rd degree sofa
and not ask Where's the bathroom?
How else to feel other than I am,
often thinking Flash Gordon soap—
O how terrible it must be for a young man
seated before a family and the family thinking
We never saw him before! He wants our Mary Lou!
After tea and homemade cookies they ask What do you do for a
    living?

Should I tell them? Would they like me then?
Say All right get married, we're losing a daughter
but we're gaining a son—
And should I then ask Where's the bathroom?

O God, and the wedding! All her family and her friends
and only a handful of mine all scroungy and bearded
just wait to get at the drinks and food—
And the priest! he looking at me as if I masturbated
asking me Do you take this woman for your lawful wedded
    wife?
And I trembling what to say say Pie Glue!
I kiss the bride all those corny men slapping me on the back
She's all yours, boy! Ha-ha-ha!
And in their eyes you could see some obscene honeymoon going
    on—
Then all that absurd rice and clanky cans and shoes
Niagara Falls! Hordes of us! Husbands! Wives! Flowers!
    Chocolates!
All streaming into cozy hotels
All going to do the same thing tonight
The indifferent clerk he knowing what was going to happen
The lobby zombies they knowing what
The whistling elevator man he knowing
The winking bellboy knowing
Everybody knowing! I'd be almost inclined not to do anything!
Stay up all night! Stare that hotel clerk in the eye!
Screaming: I deny honeymoon! I deny honeymoon!
running rampant into those almost climactic suites
yelling Radio belly! Cat shovel!
O I'd live in Niagara forever! in a dark cave beneath the Falls
I'd sit there the Mad Honeymooner
devising ways to break marriages, a scourge of bigamy
a saint of divorce—

But I should get married I should be good
How nice it'd be to come home to her
and sit by the fireplace and she in the kitchen
aproned young and lovely wanting my baby
and so happy about me she burns the roast beef
and comes crying to me and I get up from my big papa chair
saying Christmas teeth! Radiant brains! Apple deaf!

God what a husband I'd make! Yes, I should get married!
So much to do! like sneaking into Mr Jones' house late at night
and cover his golf clubs with 1920 Norwegian books
Like hanging a picture of Rimbaud on the lawnmower
like pasting Tannu Tuva postage stamps all over the picket
    fence
like when Mrs Kindhead comes to collect for the Community
    Chest
grab her and tell her There are unfavorable omens in the sky!
And when the mayor comes to get my vote tell him
When are you going to stop people killing whales!
And when the milkman comes leave him a note in the bottle
Penguin dust, bring me penguin dust, I want penguin dust—

Yet if I should get married and it's Connecticut and snow
and she gives birth to a child and I am sleepless, worn,
up for nights, head bowed against a quiet window, the past
    behind me,
finding myself in the most common of situations a trembling
    man
knowledged with responsibility not twig-smear nor Roman coin
    soup—
O what would that be like!
Surely I'd give it for a nipple a rubber Tacitus
For a rattle a bag of broken Bach records
Tack Della Francesca all over its crib
Sew the Greek alphabet on its bib
And build for its playpen a roofless Parthenon

No, I doubt I'd be that kind of father
Not rural not snow no quiet window
but hot smelly tight New York City
seven flights up, roaches and rats in the walls
a fat Reichian wife screeching over potatoes Get a job!
And five nose running brats in love with Batman
And the neighbors all toothless and dry haired
like those hag masses of the 18th century

all wanting to come in and watch TV
The landlord wants his rent
Grocery store Blue Cross Gas & Electric Knights of Columbus
Impossible to lie back and dream Telephone snow, ghost
    parking—
No! I should not get married I should never get married!
But—imagine If I were married to a beautiful sophisticated
    woman
tall and pale wearing an elegant black dress and long black
    gloves
holding a cigarette holder in one hand and a highball in the
    other
and we lived high up in a penthouse with a huge window
from which we could see all of New York and ever farther on
    clearer days
No, can't imagine myself married to that pleasant prison
    dream—

O but what about love? I forget love
not that I am incapable of love
it's just that I see love as odd as wearing shoes—
I never wanted to marry a girl who was like my mother
And Ingrid Bergman was always impossible
And there's maybe a girl now but she's already married
And I don't like men and—
but there's got to be somebody!
Because what if I'm 60 years old and not married,
all alone in a furnished room with pee stains on my underwear
and everybody else is married! All the universe married but me!

Ah, yet well I know that were a woman possible as I am possible
then marriage would be possible—
Like SHE in her lonely alien gaud waiting her Egyptian lover
so I wait—bereft of 2,000 years and the bath of life.

J. V. Cunningham

(1911–1985)

Epigram 42

Soft found a way to damn me undefended:
I was forgiven who had not offended.

Epigram 60

Here lies New Critic who would fox us
With his poetic paradoxes.
Though he lies here rigid and quiet,
If he could speak he would deny it.

Epigram 62

You ask me how Contempt who claims to sleep
With every woman that has ever been
Can still maintain that women are skin deep?
They never let him any deeper in.

Alan Dugan

(1923–2003)

How We Heard the Name

The river brought down
dead horses, dead men
and military debris,
indicative of war
or official acts upstream,
but it went by, it all
goes by, that is the thing
about the river. Then
a soldier on a log
went by. He seemed drunk
and we asked him Why
had he and this junk
come down to us so
from the past upstream.
"Friends," he said, "the great
Battle of Granicus
has just been won
by all of the Greeks except
the Lacedaemonians and
myself: this is a joke
between me and a man
named Alexander, whom
all of you ba-bas
will hear of as a god."

T. S. Eliot

(1888–1965)*

How Unpleasant to Meet Mr. Eliot

How unpleasant to meet Mr. Eliot!
With his features of clerical cut,
And his brow so grim
And his mouth so prim
And his conversation, so nicely
Restricted to What Precisely
And If and Perhaps and But.
How unpleasant to meet Mr. Eliot!
With a bobtail cur
In a coat of fur
And a porpentine cat
And a wopsical hat:
How unpleasant to meet Mr. Eliot!
             (Whether his mouth be open or shut).

* See *How Pleasant to Know Mr. Lear* on page 454.

David Gewanter

(b. 1954)

ZERO-ACCOUNT
for my sister

Your "x," withdrawn, vengeful,
undertakes the spousal

rip-off. Quivering passion,
once negated, murders love—

Kindness? "Justice"
is how greed frames
every divorce:

cupid's backstabbing
alphabet.

Barnabe Googe

(1540–1594)

OF MONEY

Give money me, take friendship whoso list,
For friends are gone come once adversity,
When money yet remaineth safe in chest,
That quickly can thee bring from misery;
Fair face show friends when riches do abound;
Come time of proof, farewell, they must away;
Believe me well, they are not to be found
If God but send thee once a lowering day.
Gold never starts aside, but in distress,
Finds ways enough to ease thine heaviness.

Seamus Heaney

(b. 1939)

An Afterwards

She would plunge all poets in the ninth circle
And fix them, tooth in skull, tonguing for brain;
For backbiting in life she'd make their hell
A rabid egotistical daisy-chain.

Unyielding, spurred, ambitious, unblunted,
Lockjawed, mantrapped, each a fastened badger
Jockeying for position, hasped and mounted
Like Ugolino on Archbishop Roger.

And when she'd make her circuit of the ice,
Aided and abetted by Virgil's wife,
I would cry out, "My sweet, who wears the bays
In our green land above, whose is the life

Most dedicated and exemplary?"
And she: "I have closed my widowed ears
To the sulphurous news of poets and poetry.
Why could you not have, oftener, in our years

Unclenched, and come down laughing from your room
And walked the twilight with me and your children—
Like that one evening of elder bloom
And hay, when the wild roses were fading?"

And (as some maker gaffs me in the neck)
"You weren't the worst. You aspired to a kind,
Indifferent, faults-on-both-sides tact.
You left us first, and then those books, behind."

Kenneth Koch

(1925–2002)*

Variations on a Theme by William Carlos Williams

1

I chopped down the house that you had been saving to live in
    next summer.
I am sorry, but it was morning, and I had nothing to do
and its wooden beams were so inviting.

2

We laughed at the hollyhocks together
and then sprayed them with lye.
Forgive me. I simply do not know what I am doing.

3

I gave away the money that you had been saving to live on for
    next ten years.
The man who asked for it was shabby
and the firm March wind on the porch was so juicy and cold.

4

Last evening we went dancing and I broke your leg.
Forgive me. I was clumsy, and
I wanted you here in the wards, where I am a doctor.

* See *This Is Just to Say* on page 311.

Philip Larkin

(1922–1985)

THIS BE THE VERSE

They fuck you up, your mum and dad.
  They may not mean to, but they do.
They fill you with the faults they had
  And add some extra, just for you.

But they were fucked up in their turn
  By fools in old-style hats and coats,
Who half the time were soppy-stern
  And half at one another's throats.

Man hands on misery to man.
  It deepens like a coastal shelf.
Get out as early as you can.
  And don't have any kids yourself.

Edward Lear

(1812–1888)*

How Pleasant to Know Mr. Lear

"How pleasant to know Mr. Lear!"
    Who has written such volumes of stuff!
Some think him ill-tempered and queer,
    But a few think him pleasant enough.

His mind is concrete and fastidious,
    His nose is remarkably big;
His visage is more or less hideous,
    His beard it resembles a wig.

He has ears, and two eyes, and ten fingers,
    Leastways if you reckon two thumbs;
Long ago he was one of the singers,
    But now he is one of the dumbs.

He sits in a beautiful parlor,
    With hundreds of books on the wall;
He drinks a great deal of Marsala,
    But never gets tipsy at all.

He has many friends, lay men and clerical,
    Old Foss is the name of his cat;
His body is perfectly spherical,
    He weareth a runcible hat.

---

* See *How Unpleasant to Meet Mr. Eliot* on page 448.

When he walks in waterproof white,
    The children run after him so!
Calling out, "He's come out in his night-
    Gown, that crazy old Englishman, oh!"

He weeps by the side of the ocean,
    He weeps on the top of the hill;
He purchases pancakes and lotion,
    And chocolate shrimps from the mill.

He reads, but he cannot speak, Spanish,
    He cannot abide ginger beer:
Ere the days of his pilgrimage vanish,
    How pleasant to know Mr. Lear!

Edna St. Vincent Millay

(1892–1950)

I, Being Born a Woman and Distressed

I, being born a woman and distressed
By all the needs and notions of my kind,
Am urged by your propinquity to find
Your person fair, and feel a certain zest
To bear your body's weight upon my breast:
So subtly is the fume of life designed,
To clarify the pulse and cloud the mind,
And leave me once again undone, possessed.
Think not for this, however, the poor treason
Of my stout blood against my staggering brain,
I shall remember you with love, or season
My scorn with pity,—let me make it plain:
I find this frenzy insufficient reason
For conversation when we meet again.

Lady Mary Wortley Montagu

(1689–1762)*

THE REASONS THAT INDUCED DR. SWIFT TO WRITE A POEM CALLED THE LADY'S DRESSING ROOM

The Doctor in a clean starched band,
His golden snuff box in his hand,
With care his diamond ring displays
And artful shows its various rays,
While grave he stalks down ——— Street,
His dearest Betty ——— to meet.
    Long had he waited for this hour,
Nor gained admittance to the bower,
Had joked and punned, and swore and writ,
Tried all his gallantry and wit,
Had told her oft what part he bore
In Oxford's schemes in days of yore,
But bawdy, politics, nor satyr
Could move this dull hard-hearted creature.
Jenny her maid could taste a rhyme
And grieved to see him lose his time,
Had kindly whispered in his ear,
"For twice two pound you enter here;
My lady vows without that sum
It is in vain you write or come."
    The destined offering now he brought
And in a paradise of thought
With a low bow approached the dame

* See *The Lady's Dressing Room* on page 478.

Who smiling heard him preach his flame.
His gold she takes (such proofs as these
Convince most unbelieving shes)
And in her trunk rose up to lock it
(Too wise to trust it in her pocket)
And then, returned with blushing grace,
Expects the Doctor's warm embrace.

But now this is the proper place
Where morals stare me in the face
And for the sake of fine expression
I'm forced to make a small digression.
Alas for wretched humankind,
With learning mad, with wisdom blind!
The ox thinks he's for saddle fit
(As long ago friend Horace writ)
And men their talents still mistaking,
The stutterer fancies his is speaking.
With admiration oft we see
Hard features heightened by toupee,
The beau affects the politician,
Wit is the citizen's ambition,
Poor Pope philosophy displays on
With so much rhyme and little reason,
And though he argues ne'er so long
That all is right, his head is wrong.

None strive to know their proper merit
But strain for wisdom, beauty, spirit,
And lose the praise that is their due
While they've the impossible in view.
So have I seen the injudicious heir
To add one window the whole house impair.

Instinct the hound does better teach
Who never undertook to preach;
The frighted hare from dogs does run
But not attempts to bear a gun.
Here many noble thoughts occur
But I prolixity abhor,

And will pursue the instructive tale
To show the wise in some things fail.
    The reverend lover with surprise
Peeps in her bubbies, and her eyes,
And kisses both, and tries—and tries.
The evening in this hellish play,
Beside his guineas thrown away,
Provoked the priest to that degree
He swore, "The fault is not in me.
Your damned close stool so near my nose,
Your dirty smock, and stinking toes,
Would make a Hercules as tame
As any beau that you can name."
    The nymph grown furious roared, "By God!
The blame lies all in sixty odd,"
And scornful pointing to the door
Cried, "Fumbler, see my face no more."
"With all my heart I'll go away,
But nothing done, I'll nothing pay.
Give back the money."—"How," cried she,
"Would you palm such a cheat on me!
For poor four pound to roar and bellow,
Why sure you want some new Prunella?"
"I'll be revenged, you saucy quean"
(Replies the disappointed Dean),
"I'll so describe your dressing room
The very Irish shall not come."
She answered short, "I'm glad you'll write,
You'll furnish paper when I shite."

Marianne Moore

(1887–1972)

To Be Liked by You Would Be a Calamity

"Attack is more piquant than concord," but when
.   You tell me frankly that you would like to feel
My flesh beneath your feet,
I'm all abroad; I can but put my weapon up, and
Bow you out.
Gesticulation—it is half the language.
Let unsheathed gesticulation be the steel
Your courtesy must meet,
Since in your hearing words are mute, which to my senses
Are a shout.

Katherine Philips

(1631–1664)

A MARRIED STATE

A married state affords but little ease
The best of husbands are so hard to please.
This in wives' careful faces you may spell
Though they dissemble their misfortunes well.
A virgin state is crowned with much content;
It's always happy as it's innocent.
No blustering husbands to create your fears;
No pangs of childbirth to extort your tears;
No children's cries for to offend your ears;
Few worldly crosses to distract your prayers:
Thus are you freed from all the cares that do
Attend on matrimony and a husband too.
Therefore Madam, be advised by me
Turn, turn apostate to love's levity,
Suppress wild nature if she dare rebel.
There's no such thing as leading apes in hell.

Carl Phillips

(b. 1959)*

THE HUSTLER SPEAKS OF PLACES

(AFTER LANGSTON HUGHES)

I've known places:
I've known places weary as the flesh when it's had some, as
    rivers at last done with flowing.

My soul has been changed in places.

I mouthed a man dry in the Ritz-Carlton men's room.
I built a life upon a man's chest and, briefly, found peace.
I watched a man sleeping; I raised a prayer over his brow.
I heard the stinging, in bars, of lashes coming down on a man's
    bare ass, until it tore to the red that is sunset.

I've known places:
shaven, uncut places.

My soul has been changed in places.

* See *The Negro Speaks of Rivers* on page 370.

Ezra Pound

(1885–1972)*

THE LAKE ISLE

O God, O Venus, O Mercury, patron of thieves,
Give me in due time, I beseech you, a little tobacco-shop,
With the little bright boxes
       piled up neatly upon the shelves
And the loose fragrant Cavendish
       and the shag,
And the bright Virginia
       loose under the bright glass cases,
And a pair of scales not too greasy,
And the whores dropping in for a word or two in passing,
For a flip word, and to tidy their hair a bit.

O God, O Venus, O Mercury, patron of thieves,
Lend me a little tobacco-shop,
       or install me in any profession
Save this damn'd profession of writing,
       where one needs one's brains all the time.

* See *The Lake Isle of Innisfree* on page 427.

Sir Walter Raleigh

(1554–1618)

Epitaph on the Earl of Leicester

Here lies the noble Warrior that never blunted sword;
Here lies the noble Courtier that never kept his word;
Here lies his Excellency that governed all the state;
Here lies the Lord of Leicester that all the world did hate.

Henry Reed
(1914–1986)

CHARD WHITLOW

(MR. ELIOT'S SUNDAY EVENING POSTSCRIPT)

As we get older we do not get any younger.
Seasons return, and to-day I am fifty-five,
And this time last year I was fifty-four,
And this time next year I shall be sixty-two.
And I cannot say I should care (to speak for myself)
To see my time over again—if you can call it time,
Fidgeting uneasily under a draughty stair,
Or counting sleepless nights in the crowded Tube.

There are certain precautions—though none of them very
      reliable—
Against the blast from bombs, or the flying splinter,
But not against the blast from Heaven, *vento dei venti*,
The wind within a wind, unable to speak for wind;
And the frigid burnings of purgatory will not be touched
By any emollient.
                    I think you will find this put,
Far better than I could ever hope to express it,
In the words of Kharma: "It is, we believe,
Idle to hope that the simple stirrup-pump
Can extinguish hell."

            Oh, listeners,
And you especially who have switched off the wireless,

And sit in Stoke or Basingstoke, listening appreciatively to the
   silence
(Which is also the silence of hell), pray not for yourselves but
   your souls.

And pray for me also under the draughty stair.
As we get older we do not get any younger.

And pray for Kharma under the holy mountain.

Theodore Roethke

(1908–1963)

ACADEMIC

The stethoscope tells what everyone fears:
You're likely to go on living for years,
With a nurse-maid waddle and a shop-girl simper,
And the style of your prose growing limper and limper.

Lloyd Schwartz
(b. 1941)

WHO'S ON FIRST?

"You can be so inconsiderate."

"You are too sensitive."

"Then why don't you take my feelings into consideration?"

"If you weren't so sensitive it wouldn't matter."

•

"You seem to really care about me only when you want me to do something for you."

"You do too much for people."

•

"I thought you were going home because you were too tired to go with me to a bar."

"I was. But Norman didn't want to come here alone."

•

"I'm awfully tired. Do you mind taking the subway home?"

(*Silence.*)

"You could stay over . . ."

(*Silence.*)

"I'll take you home."

(*Silence.*)

•

"Why do we have sex only when you want to?"

"Because you want to have sex all the time."

•

"Relationships work when two people equally desire to give to
each other."

"Relationships rarely work."

•

"Do you love me?"

"Of course—; but I resent it."

•

"Why aren't you more affectionate?"

"I am."

•

"Couldn't we ever speak to each other without irony?"

"Sure."

•

"I love you, you know."

"Yes . . . but why?"

•

"Do you resent my advice?"

"Yes. Especially because you're usually right."

•

"Why do you like these paintings?"

"What isn't there is more important
than what is."

•

"Your taste sometimes seems strange to me."

"I'm a Philistine."

"A real Philistine would never admit it."

"I suppose you're right."

•

"Aren't you interested in what I care about?"

"Yes. But not now."

•

"We should be more open with each other."

"Yes."

"Shall we talk things over?"

"What is there to say?"

•

"Are you ever going to cut down on your smoking?"

"It's all right—
I don't inhale."

●

"Sometimes I get very annoyed with you."

"The world is annoying."

●

"Your cynicism is too easy."

"Words interfere with the expression
of complex realities."

●

"Do you enjoy suffering?"

"You can't work if you don't suffer."
"But we suffer anyway."
"I know."

●

"Do you think we ever learn anything?"

"I've learned to do without."

●

"You're always so negative."

"I feel death all the time."
"Are you afraid of anything?"

"Not working."

●

"What shall we do for dinner?"

"It doesn't matter—whatever you'd like."

●

"Why don't you care more?"

"I do."

Alan Shapiro

(b. 1952)

OLD JOKE

Radiant child of Leto, farworking Lord Apollo,
with lyre in hand and golden plectrum, you sang to the gods
on Mount Olympus almost as soon as you were born.

You sang, and the Muses sang in answer, and together
your voices so delighted all your deathless elders
that their perfect happiness was made more perfect still.

What was it, though, that overwhelmed them, that suffused,
astonished, even the endless ether? Was it the freshest,
most wonderful stops of breath, the flawless intervals

and scales whose harmonies were mimicking in sound
the beauty of the gods themselves, or what you joined
to that, what you were singing of, our balked desires,

the miseries we suffer at your indifferent hands,
devastation and bereavement, old age and death?
Farworking, radiant child, what do you know about us?

Here is my father, half blind, and palsied, at the toilet,
he's shouting at his penis, Piss, you! Piss! Piss!
but the penis (like the heavenly host to mortal prayers)

is deaf and dumb; here, too, my mother with her bad knee,
on the eve of surgery, hobbling by the bathroom,
pausing, saying, who are you talking to in there?

and he replies, no one you would know, sweetheart.
Supernal one, in your untested mastery,
your easy excellence, with nothing to overcome,

and needing nothing but the most calamitous
and abject stories to prove how powerful you are,
how truly free, watch them as they laugh so briefly,

godlike, better than gods, if only for a moment
in which what goes wrong is converted to a rightness,
if only because now she's hobbling back to bed

where she won't sleep, if only because he pees at last,
missing the bowl, and has to get down on his knees
to wipe it up. You don't know anything about us.

Stevie Smith

(1902–1971)

THOUGHTS ABOUT THE PERSON FROM PORLOCK

Coleridge received the Person from Porlock
And ever after called him a curse,
Then why did he hurry to let him in?
He could have hid in the house.

It was not right of Coleridge in fact it was wrong
(But often we all do wrong)
As the truth is I think he was already stuck
With Kubla Khan.

He was weeping and wailing: I am finished, finished,
I shall never write another word of it,
When along comes the Person from Porlock
And takes the blame for it.

It was not right, it was wrong,
But often we all do wrong.

∾

May we inquire the name of the Person from Porlock?
Why, Porson, didn't you know?
He lived at the bottom of Porlock Hill
So had a long way to go,

He wasn't much in the social sense
Though his grandmother was a Warlock,

One of the Rutlandshire ones I fancy
And nothing to do with Porlock,

And he lived at the bottom of the hill as I said
And had a cat named Flo,
And had a cat named Flo.

I long for the Person from Porlock
To bring my thoughts to an end,
I am becoming impatient to see him
I think of him as a friend,

Often I look out of the window
Often I run to the gate
I think, He will come this evening,
I think it is rather late.

I am hungry to be interrupted
For ever and ever amen
O Person from Porlock come quickly
And bring my thoughts to an end.

∾

I felicitate the people who have a Person from Porlock
To break up everything and throw it away
Because then there will be nothing to keep them
And they need not stay.

∾

Why do they grumble so much?
He comes like a benison
They should be glad he has not forgotten them
They might have had to go on.

∾

These thoughts are depressing I know. They are depressing,
I wish I was more cheerful, it is more pleasant,

Also it is a duty, we should smile as well as submitting
To the purpose of One Above who is experimenting
With various mixtures of human character which goes best,
All is interesting for him it is exciting, but not for us.
There I go again. Smile, smile, and get some work to do
Then you will be practically unconscious without positively
    having to go.

Wallace Stevens

(1879–1955)

The Pleasures of Merely Circulating

The garden flew round with the angel,
The angel flew round with the clouds,
And the clouds flew round and the clouds flew round
And the clouds flew round with the clouds.

Is there any secret in skulls,
The cattle skulls in the woods?
Do the drummers in black hoods
Rumble anything out of their drums?

Mrs. Anderson's Swedish baby
Might well have been German or Spanish,
Yet that things go round and again go round
Has rather a classical sound.

Mark Strand

(b. 1934)

EATING POETRY

Ink runs from the corners of my mouth.
There is no happiness like mine.
I have been eating poetry.

The librarian does not believe what she sees.
Her eyes are sad
and she walks with her hands in her dress.

The poems are gone.
The light is dim.
The dogs are on the basement stairs and coming up.

Their eyeballs roll,
their blond legs burn like brush.
The poor librarian begins to stamp her feet and weep.

She does not understand.
When I get on my knees and lick her hand,
she screams.

I am a new man.
I snarl at her and bark.
I romp with joy in the bookish dark.

Jonathan Swift

(1667–1745)*

THE LADY'S DRESSING ROOM

Five hours (and who can do it less in?)
By haughty Celia spent in dressing,
The goddess from her chamber issues,
Arrayed in lace, brocade, and tissues.
Strephon, who found the room was void,
And Betty otherwise employed,
Stole in, and took a strict survey
Of all the litter as it lay;
Whereof, to make the matter clear,
An inventory follows here.

And first a dirty smock appeared,
Beneath the armpits well besmeared.
Strephon, the rogue, displayed it wide,
And turned it round on every side.
In such a case few words are best,
And Strephon bids us guess the rest;
But swears how damnably the men lie,
In calling Celia sweet and cleanly.

Now listen while he next produces
The various combs for various uses,
Filled up with dirt so closely fixed,
No brush could force a way betwixt;
A paste of composition rare,
Sweat, dandruff, powder, lead, and hair;

---

* See *The Reasons That Induced Dr. Swift to Write a Poem Called the Lady's Dressing Room* on page 457.

A forehead cloth with oil upon't
To smooth the wrinkles on her front;
Here alum flower to stop the steams
Exhaled from sour unsavory streams;
There night-gloves made of Tripsy's hide,
Bequeathed by Tripsy when she died,
With puppy water, beauty's help,
Distilled from Tripsy's darling whelp;
Here gallipots and vials placed,
Some filled with washes, some with paste,
Some with pomatum, paints, and slops,
And ointments good for scabby chops.
Hard by a filthy basin stands,
Fouled with the scouring of her hands;
The basin takes whatever comes,
The scraping of her teeth and gums,
A nasty compound of all hues,
For here she spits, and here she spews.
    But oh! it turned poor Strephon's bowels,
When he beheld and smelt the towels,
Begummed, bemattered, and beslimed,
With dirt, and sweat, and earwax grimed.
No object Strephon's eye escapes;
Here petticoats in frowzy heaps,
Nor be the handkerchiefs forgot,
All varnished o'er with snuff and snot.
The stockings why should I expose,
Stained with the marks of stinking toes,
Or greasy coifs and pinners reeking,
Which Celia slept at least a week in?
A pair of tweezers next he found
To pluck her brows in arches round,
Or hairs that sink the forehead low,
Or on her chin like bristles grow.
    The virtues we must not let pass
Of Celia's magnifying glass.
When frighted Strephon cast his eye on't,

It showed the visage of a giant—
A glass that can to sight disclose
The smallest worm in Celia's nose,
And faithfully direct her nail
To squeeze it out from head to tail;
For catch it nicely by the head,
It must come out alive or dead.

    Why Strephon will you tell the rest?
And must you needs describe the chest?
That careless wench! no creature warn her
To move it out from yonder corner,
But leave it standing full in sight,
For you to exercise your spite,
In vain the workman showed his wit
With rings and hinges counterfeit
To make it seem in this disguise
A cabinet to vulgar eyes;
For Strephon ventured to look in,
Resolved to go through thick and thin;
He lifts the lid, there needs no more,
He smelt it all the time before.

    As from within Pandora's box,
When Epimetheus oped the locks,
A sudden universal crew
Of human evils upward flew,
He still was comforted to find
That Hope at last remained behind;
So Strephon, lifting up the lid
To view what in the chest was hid,
The vapors flew from out the vent,
But Strephon cautious never meant
The bottom of the pan to grope,
And foul his hands in search of Hope.
Oh never may such vile machine
Be once in Celia's chamber seen!
Oh may she better learn to keep
"Those secrets of the hoary deep"!

As mutton cutlets, prime of meat,
Which though with art you salt and beat,
As laws of cookery require,
And roast them at the clearest fire,
If from adown the hopeful chops
The fat upon a cinder drops,
To stinking smoke it turns the flame,
Poisoning the flesh from whence it came,
And thence exhales a greasy stench,
For which you curse the careless wench;
So things which must not be expressed,
When plumped into the reeking chest,
Send up an excremental smell
To taint the parts from which they fell,
The petticoats and gown perfume,
And waft a stink round every room.

    Thus finishing his grand survey,
The swain disgusted slunk away,
Repeating in his amorous fits,
"Oh! Celia, Celia, Celia shits!"

    But Vengeance, goddess never sleeping,
Soon punished Strephon for his peeping.
His foul imagination links
Each dame he sees with all her stinks,
And, if unsavory odors fly,
Conceives a lady standing by.
All women his description fits,
And both ideas jump like wits,
By vicious fancy coupled fast,
And still appearing in contrast.

    I pity wretched Strephon, blind
To all the charms of womankind.
Should I the queen of love refuse
Because she rose from stinking ooze?
To him that looks behind the scene,
Statira's but some pocky quean.
When Celia in her glory shows,

If Strephon would but stop his nose,
Who now so impiously blasphemes
Her ointments, daubs, and paints, and creams,
Her washes, slops, and every clout
With which she makes so foul a rout,
He soon would learn to think like me,
And bless his ravished eyes to see
Such order from confusion sprung,
Such gaudy tulips raised from dung.

Mark Twain

(1835–1910)

ODE TO STEPHEN DOWLING BOTS, DEC'D.

And did young Stephen sicken,
    And did young Stephen die?
And did the sad hearts thicken,
    And did the mourners cry?

No; such was not the fate of
    Young Stephen Dowling Bots;
Though sad hearts round him thickened,
    'Twas not from sickness' shots.

No whooping-cough did rack his frame,
    Nor measles drear, with spots;
Not these impaired the sacred name
    Of Stephen Dowling Bots.

Despised love struck not with woe
    That head of curly knots,
Nor stomach troubles laid him low,
    Young Stephen Dowling Bots.

O no. Then list with tearful eye,
    Whilst I his fate do tell.
His soul did from this cold world fly,
    By falling down a well.

They got him out and emptied him;
    Alas it was too late;
His spirit was gone for to sport aloft
    In the realms of the good and great.

John Wilmot

(1647–1680)

GRECIAN KINDNESS

A SONG

1

The utmost Grace the *Greeks* could shew,
    When to the *Trojans* they grew kind,
Was with their Arms to let 'em go,
    And leave their lingring Wives behind.
They beat the Men, and burnt the Town,
Then all the Baggage was their own.

2

There the kind Deity of Wine
    Kiss'd the soft wanton God of Love;
This clapp'd his Wings, that press'd his Vine,
    And their best Pow'rs united move.
While each brave *Greek* embrac'd his Punk,
Lull'd her asleep, and then grew drunk.

UPON NOTHING

Nothing thou Elder Brother even to Shade
Thou hadst a being ere the world was made
And (well fixt) art alone of ending not afraid.

Ere Time and Place were, Time and Place were not
When Primitive Nothing, somthing straight begott
Then all proceeded from the great united what—

Somthing, the Generall Attribute of all
Severed from thee its sole Originall
Into thy boundless selfe must undistinguisht fall.

Yet Somthing did thy mighty power command
And from thy fruitfull Emptinesses hand
Snatcht, Men, Beasts, birds, fire, water, Ayre, and land.

Matter, the Wickedst offspring of thy Race
By forme assisted flew from thy Embrace
And Rebell-Light obscured thy Reverend dusky face.

With forme and Matter, Time and Place did joyne
Body thy foe with these did Leagues combine
To spoyle thy Peaceful Realme and Ruine all thy Line.

But Turncote-time assists the foe in vayne
And brib'd by thee destroyes their short liv'd Reign
And to thy hungry wombe drives back thy slaves again.

Though Misteries are barr'd from Laick Eyes
And the Divine alone with warrant pries
Into thy Bosome, where thy truth in private lyes

Yet this of thee the wise may truly say
Thou from the virtuous Nothing doest delay
And to be part of thee the wicked wisely pray.

Great Negative how vainly would the wise
Enquire, define, distinguish, teach, devise,
Didst Thou not stand to point their blind Phylosophies.

Is or is not, the two great Ends of Fate
And true or false the Subject of debate
That pérfect or destroy the vast designes of State—

When they have wrackt the Politicians Brest
Within thy Bosome most Securely rest
And when reduc't to thee are least unsafe and best.

But (Nothing) why does Somthing still permitt
That Sacred Monarchs should at Councell sitt
With persons highly thought, at best for nothing fitt,

Whilst weighty Somthing modestly abstaynes
From Princes Coffers and from Statesmens braines
And nothing there like Stately nothing reignes?

Nothing who dwell'st with fooles in grave disguise
For whom they Reverend Shapes and formes devise
Lawn-sleeves and Furrs and Gowns, when they like thee looke
    wise:

French Truth, Dutch Prowess, Brittish policy
Hibernian Learning, Scotch Civility
Spaniards Dispatch, Danes witt, are Mainly seen in thee;

The Great mans Gratitude to his best freind
Kings promises, Whores vowes towards thee they bend
Flow Swiftly into thee, and in thee ever end.

C. D. Wright

(b. 1949)

PERSONALS

Some nights I sleep with my dress on. My teeth
are small and even. I don't get headaches.
Since 1971 or before, I have hunted a bench
where I could eat my pimento cheese in peace.
If this were Tennessee and across that river, Arkansas,
I'd meet you in West Memphis tonight. We could
have a big time. Danger, shoulder soft.
Do not lie or lean on me. I am still trying to find a job
for which a simple machine isn't better suited.
I've seen people die of money. Look at Admiral Benbow. I wish
like certain fishes, we came equipped with light organs.
Which reminds me of a little known fact:
if we were going the speed of light, this dome
would be shrinking while we were gaining weight.
Isn't the road crooked and steep.
In this humidity, I make repairs by night. I'm not one
among millions who saw Monroe's face
in the moon. I go blank looking at that face.
If I could afford it I'd live in hotels. I won awards
in spelling and the Australian crawl. Long long ago.
Grandmother married a man named Ivan. The men called him
Eve. Stranger, to tell the truth, in dog years I am up there.

William Butler Yeats

(1865–1939)

THE SCHOLARS

Bald heads forgetful of their sins,
Old, learned, respectable bald heads
Edit and annotate the lines
That young men, tossing on their beds,
Rhymed out in love's despair
To flatter beauty's ignorant ear.

All shuffle there; all cough in ink;
All wear the carpet with their shoes;
All think what other people think;
All know the man their neighbour knows.
Lord, what would they say
Did their Catullus walk that way?

PERMISSIONS
ACKNOWLEDGMENTS

by New Directions Publishing Corp. Reprinted by permission of New Directions Publishing Corp.

Hart Crane: "To Brooklyn Bridge," from *The Complete Poems of Hart Crane* by Hart Crane, edited by Marc Simon. Copyright 1933, 1958, 1966 by Liveright Publishing Corporation. Copyright © 1986 by Marc Simon. Used by permission of Liveright Publishing Corporation.

Robert Creeley: "If You" from *The Collected Poems of Robert Creeley, 1945–1975* by Robert Creeley. Reproduced with permission of The University of California Press via Copyright Clearance Center.

Countee Cullen: "Yet Do I Marvel," published in *Color* © 1925 Harper & Bros., N.Y. Renewed 1952 Ida M. Cullen.

E. E. Cummings: "Buffalo Bill's." Copyright © 1923, 1951, 1991 by the Trustees for the E. E. Cummings Trust. Copyright © 1976 by George James Firmage, from *Complete Poems: 1904–1962* by E. E. Cummings, edited by George J. Firmage. Used by permission of Liveright Publishing Corporation.

J. V. Cunningham: "Epigrams 42, 60, and 62" (originally published as "Epigrams 28, 5, and 7") and "For My Contemporaries" from *The Poems of J. V. Cunningham*, edited with an introduction and commentary by Timothy Steele. Reprinted with the permission of Swallow Press / Ohio University Press, Athens, Ohio (www.ohio swallow.com).

James Dickey: "For the Last Wolverine" from *Falling, Mat Day, And Other Poems*, © 1981 by James Dickey and reprinted by permission of Wesleyan University Press.

Stuart Dischell: "Days of Me" from *Dig Safe* by Stuart Dischell, copyright © 2003 by Stuart Dischell. Used by permission of Penguin, a division of Penguin Group (USA) Inc.

Stephen Dobyns: "Tomatoes" from *Velocities* by Stephen Dobyns, copyright © 1994 by Stephen Dobyns. Used by permission of Penguin, a division of Penguin Group (USA) Inc.

Rita Dove: "Gospel" from *Thomas and Beulah*, Carnegie Mellon University Press, © 1986 by Rita Dove. Reprinted by permission of the author.

Alan Dugan: "How We Heard the Name" and "Love Song: I and Thou" from *Poems Seven: New and Complete Poetry*. Copyright © 2001 by Alan Dugan. Reprinted with the permission of Seven Stories Press, www.sevenstories.com.

Robert Duncan: "My Mother Would Be a Falconress" from *Bending the Bow* by Robert Duncan. Copyright © 1968 by Robert Duncan. Reprinted by permission of New Directions Publishing Corp.

T. S. Eliot: "How Unpleasant to Meet Mr. Eliot" and "The Love Song of J. Alfred Prufrock" from *Collected Poems, 1909–1962* by T. S. Eliot. Used with permission by Faber and Faber Ltd, The Estate of T. S. Eliot. Excerpt from "Five-finger exercises" in *Collected Poems, 1909–1962* by T. S. Eliot, copyright 1936 by Houghton Mifflin Harcourt Publishing Company and renewed 1964 by T. S. Eliot, reprinted by permission of the publisher.

David Ferry: "Gilgamesh, I: The Story" from *Gilgamesh: A New Rendering in English Verse* by David Ferry. Copyright © 1992 by David Ferry. Reprinted by permission of Farrar, Straus and Giroux, LLC.

Robert Frost: "Dust of Snow," "Home Burial," "Putting in the Seed," and "To Earthward" from *The Poetry of Robert Frost*, edited by Edward Connery Lathem. Copyright 1923, 1969 by Henry Holt and Company. Copyright 1944, 1951 by Robert Frost. Reprinted by permission of Henry Holt and Company, LLC.

David Gewanter: "Zero-Account" from *The Sleep of Reason* by David Gewanter. Published by permission of the author.

Jack Gilbert: "Measuring the Tyger" from *The Great Fires Poems 1982–1992* by Jack Gilbert, copyright © 1994 by Jack Gilbert. Used by permission of Alfred A. Knopf, a division of Random House, Inc.

Allen Ginsberg: "America" from *Collected Poems 1947–1980* by Allen Ginsberg. Copyright © 1956, 1959 by Allen Ginsberg. Reprinted by permission of HarperCollins Publishers. "A Supermarket in California" from *Collected Poems 1947–1980* by Allen Ginsberg. Copyright ©1955 by Allen Ginsberg. Reprinted by permission of HarperCollins Publishers.

Louise Glück: "Mock Orange" from *The First Four Books of Poems* by Louise Glück. Copyright 1968, 1971, 1972, 1973, 1974, 1975, 1976, 1977, 1978, 1979, 1980, 1985, 1995 by Louise Glück. Reprinted by permission of HarperCollins Publishers. "Tributaries" by Louise Glück. Reprinted by permission of the author.

Jorie Graham: "Prayer" from *Never* by Jorie Graham. Copyright 2002 by Jorie Graham. Reprinted by permission of HarperCollins Publishers.

Thom Gunn: "Tamer and Hawk" and "Yoko" from *Collected Poems* by Thom Gunn. Copyright © 1994 by Thom Gunn. Reprinted by permission of Farrar, Straus and Giroux, LLC.

Robert Hass: "A Story About the Body" from *Human Wishes* by Robert Hass. Copyright © 1989 by Robert Hass. "Then Time" from *Time and Material: Poems 1997–2005* by Robert Hass. Copyright 2007 by Robert Hass. Reprinted by permission of HarperCollins Publishers.

Robert Hayden: "Frederick Douglass." Copyright © 1966 by Robert Hayden. "Those Winter Sundays." Copyright © 1966 by Robert Hayden, from *Collected Poems of Rob-*

Stevie Smith: "Not Waving but Drowning" and "Thoughts about the Person from Porlock" from *Collected Poems of Stevie Smith*, copyright © 1972 by Stevie Smith. Reprinted by permission of New Directions Publishing Corp.

Gerald Stern: "Behaving Like a Jew," by Gerald Stern. Permission granted by the author.

Wallace Stevens: "Final Soliloquy of the Interior Paramour," "Madame La Fleurie," "The Pleasures of Merely Circulating," and "The Snow Man" from *The Collected Poems of Wallace Stevens* by Wallace Stevens, copyright 1954 by Wallace Stevens and renewed by Holly Stevens. Used by permission of Alfred A. Knopf, a division of Random House, Inc.

Mark Strand: "Eating Poetry" from *Selected Poems* by Mark Strand, copyright © 1979, 1980 by Mark Strand. "Old Man Leaves Party" from *Blizzard of One* by Mark Strand, copyright © 1998 by Mark Strand. Used by permission of Alfred A. Knopf, a division of Random House, Inc.

May Swenson: "Question." Reprinted with permission of The Literary Estate of May Swenson.

James Tate: "The Lost Pilot" from *The Lost Pilot* by James Tate. Copyright © 1978 by James Tate. Reprinted by permission of HarperCollins Publishers.

Ellen Voigt: "The Hen" from *Claiming Kin*, © 1969 by Ellen Bryant Voigt and reprinted by permission of Wesleyan University Press.

Charles Harper Webb: "Liver," © 1999. Reprinted by permission of The University of Wisconsin Press.

C. K. Williams: "The Dog" and "The Singing" from *Collected Poems* by C. K. Williams. Copyright © 2006 by C. K. Williams. Reprinted by permission of Farrar, Straus and Giroux, LLC.

William Carlos Williams: "Dedication for a Plot of Ground," "Fine Work with Pitch and Copper," "Love Song," "Poem ('As the cat')," "This Is Just to Say," and "To Waken an Old Lady" from *The Collected Poems Volume I, 1909–1939*, copyright © 1938 by New Directions Publishing Corp. " Sappho" and "The Turtle" from *The Collected Poems Volume II, 1939–1962*, copyright © 1962 by William Carlos Williams. Reprinted by permission of New Directions Publishing Corp.

Anne Winters: "Night Wash" from *The Key to the City*. Permission granted by the author.

Yvor Winters: "Sir Gawaine and the Green Knight" from *The Selected Poems of Yvor Winters*. Reprinted with the permission of Swallow Press / Ohio University Press, Athens, Ohio (www.ohioswallow.com).

INDEX

CD Track Listing:

PoemsOutLoud.net

Poems read aloud by Robert Pinsky
Recorded by Frank Antonelli at Boston University, August 2008